THE *Promise* OF IMMORTALITY

THE

Promise

OF IMMORTALITY

THE TRUE TEACHING OF THE BIBLE AND THE BHAGAVAD GITA

J. DONALD WALTERS
(SWAMI KRIYANANDA)

Cover and book design by C. A. Starner Schuppe
Cover photo by J. Donald Walters

ISBN: 1-56589-150-3

Printed in Canada

1   3   5   7   9   10   8   6   4   2

Crystal

Clarity

Crystal Clarity Publishers
14618 Tyler-Foote Road
Nevada City, CA 95959-8599

Phone: 800-424-1055 or 530-478-7600
Fax: 530-478-7610
E-mail: clarity@crystalclarity.com
Website: www.crystalclarity.com

Library of Congress Cataloging-in-Publication Data

Walters, J. Donald.
   The promise of immortality: the true teaching of the Bible and the
Bhagavad Gita / J. Donald Walters (Swami Kriyananda).
      p. cm.
   Includes bibliographical references and index.
   ISBN 1-56589-150-3 (cloth)
   1. Immortality. 2. Future life.   I. Title.
BL530 .W35 2001
294.5'2--dc21
                                                          2001042500

CONTENTS

Part IV
The Soul's Ascent

INTRODUCTION

One of the most urgent needs in the world today is for the major religions to be presented from a perspective of the truths they have in common, and not of the teachings which, their proponents insist, make them unique. Much energy has been directed through books and sermons toward demonstrating the superiority of one religion over all others: of Christianity, because it holds that Jesus Christ is the world's Savior; of Islam, because it offers Mohammed to the faithful as the prophet of Allah; of Buddhism, because only those who follow the way of the Buddha can win release from the cycle of death and rebirth. These claims are mutually exclusive, and have discouraged many conscientious people from considering religion as even central to the needs of humanity. Indeed, so many people scoff at religion nowadays that civilization is beginning to resemble a ship that, on the point of crashing against the rocks (in civilization's case, of global disaster), has lost its rudder.

There is, however, another aspect to religion: not divisive, but unitive. Indeed, there are numerous points on which all religions are agreed: the issue, for example, of what constitutes right action. No religion considers it a virtue to lie, or steal, or harm others. All religions, moreover, preach some variant of the Golden Rule: "Do unto others as you would have them do unto you." Virtue is recommended in other areas besides religion, of course, if only as being socially desirable. In none of these areas, however, is guidance given for developing virtue, and in none of them is primary attention given to *uplifting* human consciousness.

For these reasons, religion deserves recognition as the very cornerstone of civilization. Without it, society would sink into a morass of cynicism, selfishness, matter-worship, and violence. Far from being "the opiate of the people," as Karl Marx claimed, religion gives mankind the ultimate cure for its age-old addiction to "opiates" of all kinds: alcohol, drugs, money, sense-pleasure.

How sad it is, then, that religion has become one of the most neglected, not to say belittled, of human concerns! Such disdain would not exist had religion not undergone virtual mummification by the skilled application of unprovable dogmas, and been enclosed in the coffin of wooden sectarianism. Dogmas are not to blame for this evil, for they are simply definitions of beliefs. *Dogmatism,* however, is another matter altogether. Its narrow emphasis stifles intelligence. Sectarianism moreover, which quickly follows, alienates people from one another, stifles their sympathies, and encourages meanness of spirit with the presumed sanction of scripture.

Yet religion has the potential to unite all humanity in the highest ideals. When religion is lived rightly, it expands people's sympathies and encourages them to embrace all, however different their customs and beliefs.

Nowadays, as the peoples of different cultures come into increasing contact with one another, those who identify truth with principles rather than with limited forms and definitions find it less than edifying to be told that one religion alone is true, and all others false. Blindly dogmatic statements have caused many to back off from religion altogether and to seek substitutes for religion in the sciences, or in politics, or in ecology.

For human nature needs some ideal toward which it can aspire. The search for perfection on earth proves, however, in the end, illusory. "Votaries" at those shrines find themselves left at last merely with arid hearts.

The chief purpose of religion is the upliftment of human consciousness. This inner transformation manifests spontaneously as virtue, for it makes people naturally kind, humble, and compassionate. Without inner upliftment, however, virtue itself becomes little but a pose practiced at convenience—or else ignored, equally at convenience.

It is urgently necessary in our time to promote understanding among the world's religions. Religious leaders need to treat one another as colleagues, not as rival vendors in an outdoor market where people hawk their wares while shouting accusations of unfair competition at one another. Only by mutual appreciation for each other's spiritual sincerity can people be inspired to pull themselves out of the morass of irreligion. Whether Jesus be the only Savior, or Mohammed, or Buddha, one may safely assume that those great teachers will be better pleased with even the so-called "heathen" if he is kind and considerate of others, and if he loves truth and God, than they will with their own followers who, though shouting dogmatic slogans, are cruel and demonstrate a willingness to deceive others in dealing with them.

Jesus Christ said, *"Why say ye Lord, Lord, and do not the things that I say?"* And when his disciples reprimanded a certain man for casting out devils in his name, Jesus reprimanded them, in turn, saying, *"Forbid him not . . . for he that is not against us is with us."* (Mark 9:39,40)

Unity in spiritual matters is, for all these reasons, urgently needed today.

It was in furtherance of this ideal that a historic event occurred near the end of the Nineteenth Century, in the Indian Himalaya. A great spiritual master, Mahavatar Babaji, requested a spiritual "grandson" of his named Swami Sri Yukteswar—a disciple of his own foremost disciple—to write a book with the aim of explaining certain passages in the Bible and the Bhagavad Gita, to demonstrate the essential unanimity of teaching in those scriptures. The purpose of this commission was to further people's understanding of the universality of truth.

Swami Sri Yukteswar wrote his book in 1894, calling it *Kaivalya Darsanam,* or, in English, *The Holy Science.* The English edition is subtitled, *"An Exposition of Final Truth"* (which is the literal translation of its Bengali title). *The Holy Science* is still in print; it is published by Self-Realization Fellowship in Los Angeles, California. The book contains fewer than a hundred pages: a small volume, considering its extraordinary depth. Indeed, much of what it contains is not easy to grasp by the average reader, who has to have new ideas spelled out for him so as to bridge the gap between them and his own usual understanding of things. It should be added, however, that *The Holy Science* was not such a bridge. It did, however, play a seminal role in the development of Babaji's plan, which was to bring East and West together in a spirit of understanding and cooperation.

Sri Yukteswar passed on that ideal to his foremost disciple, Paramhansa Yogananda, who is widely known today through his spiritual classic, *Autobiography of a Yogi*. The training this young disciple received was aimed at the dissemination of ancient insights in Western countries, and from the West on throughout the modern world.

Yogananda's mission was not to Indianize the West, as a number of teachers from India have tried to do, but to uplift it spiritually within the context of its own culture. He reminded Jews and Christians alike of their deep roots in ancient meditative practices.

Meditation, Paramhansa Yogananda explained, exerts a positive influence on every aspect of one's life. By inner calmness and concentration, one can be successful in anything he attempts. Modern men and women, adopting his teachings, soon found themselves more deeply aware of God's guidance in their lives. They found also that they became better businessmen, musicians, carpenters, home-makers, scientists. Above all, they became happier, more fulfilled human beings. In the higher teachings of yoga they discovered a science that was rooted in provable truths, and not the vague mysticism that so often passes among Westerners for "Eastern wisdom."

Yogananda sought practical ways of instilling the truth of his teachings in society at all levels. To fulfill this aim it would, he realized, be necessary for the entire social structure to be transformed. His vision therefore expanded beyond present horizons to include schools, spiritual communities, a "Yoga Institute," an annual congress of religions to which he planned to invite "delegates from all lands." He suggested guidelines for businessmen based on a spirit of service rather than on a desire for personal gain. He created businesses to support his projected communities, and saw them also as models to demonstrate the validity of the guidelines he proposed for businesses everywhere. He wrote music; sponsored concerts; proposed architecture as a means of giving outward definition to spiritual concepts. He even expressed creativity in several inventions, to show that creative expression is a valid aspect of the spiritual life and is not inimical to it.

It was not possible, of course, for all of his projects to bear fruit during his lifetime, extraordinarily productive though his life was. His vision went far into the future. The ideas he expressed, and the numerous ventures he proposed (some of which he actually attempted), were seeds of energy that he planted for future germination. As he himself put it, "I am sowing these ideas in the ether, in the spirit of God."

One of his early ventures in America was to found a school for children based on the principles he'd already developed in a school for boys in Ranchi, India. America, however, was not ripe for this project, and he was obliged to abandon it for the time being. Nevertheless, he often spoke of the importance of education to the spread of his ideals. Indeed, as the child grows, so does the adult proclaim himself. First, however, as Yogananda confided to me personally, the parents would need to be converted to the truths he taught. Only then would they send their children to his schools.

Another of his efforts was the creation of small, non-monastic communities where spiritually minded men and women would share harmoniously in the quest for God, inspire one another, and offer examples to others of how people can guide their lives by high ideals. This concept harked back to the early communitarian experiments in America.

He was successful in founding several monasteries of the more traditional kind. Americans, however, were not yet ready to embrace his communitarian project. On countless occasions, nevertheless, having seen the great strain people endure under the stresses of modern life, Yogananda urged all who could do so to live dedicated lives together, when the time proved right, in simple, rustic surroundings.

Always, his central teaching was spiritual upliftment. For he emphasized that no earthly Eden can ever satisfy the soul's hunger for divine fulfillment. He therefore emphasized the importance above all of meditation and inner communion. To this end he taught meditation techniques, especially those central to the ancient science of *yoga*.

In furtherance of his spiritual mission, Yogananda continued the task given by Babaji to Sri Yukteswar, to show the underlying oneness of the Holy Bible and the Bhagavad Gita. "I was sent to the West," Yogananda explained, "to emphasize *original* Christianity as taught by Jesus Christ, and *original* yoga as taught by Krishna." A visitor once said in my presence, "You've

13

called yours a 'Church of All Religions.' Why, then, do you confine yourself to explaining only Christianity and the teachings of Hinduism? Why not other religions as well?" The Master replied simply, "Because that was the wish of Babaji."

Pondering his reply, I've come to realize that a detailed study of the world's religions would provoke only intellectual interest, but would not inspire people to develop spiritual love and intuitive understanding. It may be also that Hinduism and Christianity are the two religions best suited by tradition to the practice of inner communion with God. Yogananda tried, at the same time, to show that the quest for divine truth is the essence of *all* religions.

In pursuance of this purpose, he wrote separate commentaries on the Bhagavad Gita and the Holy Bible. In his Bible commentaries he concentrated primarily on the teachings of Jesus Christ, though quoting extensively also from the Old Testament. He wrote commentaries in addition on the Books of Genesis and Revelation. The reason for treating the Bible and the Bhagavad Gita separately was that the first need was for an in-depth explanation of each scripture. Side-by-side comparisons of the two scriptures would have to come later.

The present book is an attempt to address that further need, though far from exhaustively. Originally this book was intended for week-by-week study over the course of one year. The more deeply I delved into the subject, however, the more evident it became to me that these scriptures, even taking them one passage at a time, are so deep that a whole lifetime would not suffice to plumb their depths. Thus, my hope is that this relatively little book (long of course, however, by modern standards) will provide not only food for the intellect, but inspiration for the soul.

Paramhansa Yogananda told me when I was twenty-three, "Your job will be writing and lecturing." Other tasks have evolved indirectly out of that commission, for anything I wrote needed the validation of first-hand experience. In 1968 I founded a community, which I named Ananda Village, in fulfillment of his communitarian ideal. Shortly thereafter I also founded a school, where the children of community members, and others also, might be instructed in the principles developed by Yogananda in India. Later, with this experience for a basis, I wrote a book, *Education for Life,* to elaborate on his educational ideas and on our application of them.

When my guru told me that my job was writing, I expressed surprise. "Sir," I exclaimed, "haven't you already written all that needs to be said?"

The narrowness of my vision astonished him, in turn. "Don't say that!" he replied. "*Much* more is needed."

This book is one of many endeavors to carry out that commission. (I've written over seventy books so far, and composed over 400 works of music.) An earlier version of the present book was written for Sunday morning services at Ananda. The present work represents a considerable expansion of that earlier one.

I have done my best in these pages to refrain from offering any opinion of my own. Instead, it has been my aim to present in depth the teachings I received from my guru—through his written works, his public lectures, his informal talks with a few of us disciples, and his lengthy discussions with me personally. This book does, however, contain insights of my own—not, be it noted, my opinions—gained over a lifetime as his disciple. For it is the duty of the disciple to do more than repeat his guru's words. Yogananda himself said that disciples cannot but filter their gurus' teachings according to their own spiritual understanding.

In *Autobiography of a Yogi* Paramhansa Yogananda wrote concerning the life of Lahiri Mahasaya (the guru of Sri Yukteswar) that the great guru often said to his disciples: "I will guide your thoughts, that the right interpretation be uttered." The account continued, "In this way, many of Lahiri Mahasaya's perceptions came to be recorded, with voluminous commentaries, by various students."* For many years now, I have prayed sincerely to my own guru, "May everything I say express only your insight."

In all my books I have done my best to attune myself to his consciousness. The present book was, in the above sense, written *through* me, rather than *by* me. Many of the insights it contains had never occurred to me before. Often, indeed, thrilled by their clarity and simplicity, I have found myself exclaiming, "How true! And how beautiful!"

Everything in this book is consistent, moreover, with Paramhansa Yogananda's actual words and writings. It is, I therefore repeat, not really my book. My own contribution has been to marshal thoughts that he

---

* Page 40 of the first edition reprint, available from Crystal Clarity Publishers.

expressed from time to time on these subjects, and to bring selected passages from the two scriptures together in such a way as to show that they parallel one another. My goal has been, in my own small way, to continue the commission originally given by Babaji to Swami Sri Yukteswar, which Sri Yukteswar then passed on to Paramhansa Yogananda, and which it will be others' responsibility in future generations to continue sharing with the world.

I have not limited myself to my guru's specific writings on these subjects (the reader may go to his books for that), but have drawn from and assembled countless memories of things he said, wrote elsewhere, and did that might give a fuller dimension to his published writings.

Such, indeed, is the duty of the sincere disciple: to present his guru's teachings in such a way as to show them, as much as possible, in all their subtlety and variety. Thus, may they reach an ever-wider and more enlightened audience.

PART I

The Eternal Christ

CHAPTER ONE

The Eternal "Word": Key to Manifested Existence

The greatness of a scripture depends on the extent to which it addresses the grand issues with authority. The Holy Bible begins with the words: *"In the beginning God created the heaven and the earth."* In the New Testament, the Gospel of St. John begins similarly: *"In the beginning was the Word, and the Word was with God, and the Word was God. The same was in the beginning with God. All things were made by him; and without him was not any thing made that was made."* (John 1:1–3)

The grand issues concern the What, the How, and the Why of existence: *What* is reality? *How* did it come into being? *How* do we, or *How* should we, relate to it? And *Why* is awareness of our relationship important?

The Bhagavad Gita addresses these issues also, though in a different sequence. It begins with the question, *Why?*, addressing the human predicament before going on to the broader questions: *What* is the true nature of things? and, *How* did everything come into being? And then again it asks: *What* relationship have we to that reality? Chapter Seven states: *"I make and unmake this universe. Apart from Me, O Arjuna, nothing exists. Like the beads of a necklace, all things are strung upon the thread of My consciousness; they are sustained by Me."*

God, the Infinite Spirit, is the sole reality. Creation is only a manifestation of His consciousness. The essence of our being is spiritual, not physical; in our souls we are a part of Him. Christian saints have sometimes used the term "spiritual marriage" to describe the soul's union with God. The Indian scriptures express the same concept, though in different words; they call it, "Self-realization." To know one's own reality to its depths is, they say, to know God.

The emphasis in the greatest scriptures is on this supreme attainment. They describe the cosmic verities not merely to satisfy people's curiosity, but to help them understand that union with God is their destiny. Indeed, those writings would not even *be* scripture, were not their fundamental teaching based on the insight that, underlying everything, is *consciousness.*

Herein lies the essential difference between scripture and science. Both fields are dedicated to knowing the truth. Astronomy, for example, explains facts of the universe endlessly. In its explanations, however, it doesn't suggest a causative awareness. Science as a whole is dedicated to satisfying our curiosity about things. It helps us also in practical ways to live more comfortable lives. The knowledge and the material improvements it provides leave us adrift, however, in our need for practical *understanding* and wisdom. Though astronomers postulate *how* the universe was made, and *what* keeps it functioning; and though physicists ask *What* is the nature of matter? and *How* does that nature differ from its appearances? all the sciences ignore the most important question of all: *What* does it all mean? Science provides no answer. Indeed, apart from telling us that we must all do our best to survive, it robs people of their sense of meaning, and leaves them drifting like sailboats stripped of their sails. If science addressed those issues authoritatively, it too would be scripture. But of course it does not, and cannot, and is therefore committed to avoiding them altogether. To scientists, such matters cannot be investigated rationally, and are therefore useless even to think about; issues like these are outside their purview. An unwritten "Law of Science" is, to paraphrase the German philosopher Georg Hegel*: "All that is real is scientific. And all that is scientific is real." Thus, whereas most scientists would not actually say it, their prevalent attitude is that there is no deep meaning in anything.

Modern education is science-based. Its teaching, formerly perhaps agnostic, is now fairly committed to atheism. Simple agnosticism might be fair enough, considering that most people don't really *know* whether life has a higher purpose, and can only hope such a purpose exists. But education today denies that there is any such thing as ultimate verity. Young people, whose natural need is to believe in at least *something,* find their need discarded sneeringly and left in broken fragments about their feet—like the psychology professor who began his first class in every course by announcing, "If anyone here thinks he has a soul, I request him please to park it outside the room before he enters." Is it any

---

* Hegel wrote, "All that is real is rational. And all that is rational is real."

wonder that so many young people become cynical, violent, and destructive? St. James said, "Faith without works is dead." Equally true would it be to say, "Works without faith are stillborn"!

Scripture differs from science in that it is not intellectual, rational, or speculative. Speculation is for philosophers, whose nomenclature derives from a combination of two Greek words: *philos,* love; and *sophia,* wisdom. Scripture transcends mere fondness for wisdom: It is the very expression of wisdom. True scripture is the fruit not of theorizing, but of direct inner experience achieved in deep communion with God. The message of scripture is not "dictated" from Above, as if trumpeted from clouds to a few solitary, and—some people might say—superstitious scribes. True scripture is, indeed, the noblest work of mankind. It is written by human beings out of their own deep spiritual insight.

The remarkable thing is that all who have achieved such insight have declared the same truths. No spiritual master has ever contradicted another, though most masters have not known more than a handful of others. Unlike modern scientists, in other words, those masters don't owe their unanimity on fundamental issues to the "cross-pollination" of ideas.

It is interesting to note that physicists are beginning also, in increasing numbers, to speculate that the universe may actually be an idea in the mind of a cosmic creator. Their speculations, while intellectually stimulating, still give virtually no thought to the part human beings play in the cosmic drama, and offer no suggestion for our spiritual transformation. As Paramhansa

Yogananda put it, "Science can only study the activity of the atom; it cannot, like the person of intuitive insight, become one in consciousness with the atom."

Scriptural utterances on the grand issues have a concrete, not an abstract, purpose. They explain the part human beings play on the great stage of time and space. They show us the direction in which to channel our energies so as ultimately to achieve enlightenment.

The grand issues are central to the teachings of the Holy Bible and the Bhagavad Gita. Were they not, these would not be great scriptures. They might still, of course, in the case of the Bible, be revealing as history, which is the claim many modern scholars make for them. Those hoary records of biblical events, however, are not scriptural in the true sense—unless, indeed, they also represent great truths. Even Jesus Christ would not fit this high criterion had he lived merely a wonderful life on earth, shaken a few people with revolutionary ideas, died tragically on the cross, and thereafter inspired a devoted following. His greatness lay in the fact that, by his clarity, spiritual authority, and personal example he made eternal truths real and immediate for mankind.

Love is not great because Jesus loved. Jesus, rather, was great because he demonstrated so perfectly the quality of love. Humility is not great because Jesus was humble. Jesus, rather, was great because of the perfection of his humility. Jesus, again, was not great because he performed miracles: He was great because, in humility, he gave the credit for everything he did to a Higher Power—a power to which, he assured people, all human beings have access. It is a mistake, indeed, to narrow our understanding of humility by defining it as "Christian."

Many Bible stories give no hint of being deep spiritual allegories. Without deeper meaning, they don't belong in the same classification of greatness as the Bible's truly profound teachings. To give equal credence to everything "the Good Book" says is to trivialize the very meaning of the word, scripture. Some of those stories may, despite their questionable spiritual merit, be history, since archaeologists, by careful study of them, have made a number of important discoveries. Moreover, even if those stories *are* historical, they may still be deep allegories, the meaning of which has yet to be discerned. Perhaps their meaning will be clarified someday, by people with the interest and the wisdom to probe deeply enough.

For in fact it is quite usual for scriptural stories to be allegorical. Famous examples include the parables of Jesus. The context in which the Bhagavad Gita appears is another case in point. This scripture is a brief episode in the longest epic in the world, the *Mahabharata*. This epic contains numerous stories that are every bit as strange as any to be found in the Bible. The only, or at least the most striking, difference between those two works is that underlying the *Mahabharata* is one continuous story, whereas the Bible is fragmented. The *Mahabharata* is at the same time a profound spiritual allegory. This fact was brought to light by Lahiri Mahasaya, a disciple, as we mentioned in the Introduction, of Babaji and the spiritual "grandfather," or "grand" guru, of Paramhansa Yogananda.

Lahiri Mahasaya showed that the *Mahabharata* is a

sweeping account of the soul's descent into matter, and of the challenges it faces in retracing the way back to its source in Spirit. Taken as a whole, this epic, too, deserves to be considered a great scripture. So also does the Holy Bible, for the deep truths it teaches.

The Book of Genesis was explained by Paramhansa Yogananda. He showed it to be full of cosmic truths, relevant also to the human condition. Other portions of the Old Testament he cited as well, showing their deep meaning. Dr. M. W. Lewis, a prominent disciple of Yogananda's as well as a profound student of the Bible, discovered other passages in the Old Testament that contain deep, indeed deeply *yogic,* meaning. For the rest of the Old Testament, and for some of the New— notably the Letters—such an in-depth study still remains to be made.

The Bhagavad Gita—the "Gita," as Hindus lovingly refer to it—recounts a conversation between Krishna (representing God, or man's highest Self) and Arjuna (representing the devotee, or aspirant toward divine union). Krishna, in brief but extraordinarily profound dissertations, explains cosmic truths, then relates them to human needs. The succinctness of his exposition is perhaps unique in all scripture. The New Testament by contrast presents its teaching more discursively through the life of Jesus Christ and his disciples, including in its account many deep teachings. Jesus frequently spoke in parables, which he may have explained later on to his disciples but which the Bible leaves, for the most part, as Jesus told them publicly.

Of the four Gospels, St. John's is the most explicit about cosmic verities and man's inner, spiritual life.

His Gospel begins with the grand issues. St. Matthew, on the other hand, begins with the genealogy of Jesus; St. Mark, with an account of John the Baptist and his heralding of Jesus Christ's mission on earth; St. Luke, with an account of the birth of Jesus and the miracles that presaged that event. St. John completes the picture by presenting us from the start with the *spiritual significance* of Christ's birth: of his descent to earth from Infinity, and of his manifestation as a human being for the redemption of mankind.

The Bhagavad Gita, having little or no story to relate (that story is told in the *Mahabharata*), begins by describing the predicament faced by Arjuna, hero of the epic, as he and Krishna pass between two armies that are ranged against one another, ready for battle. Kurukshetra, the name of the battlefield, symbolizes human life, and the human body. On one side of this field are marshalled the forces of Good, whose warriors represent, so Lahiri Mahasaya explained, different spiritual qualities that are revealed in the Sanskrit roots of their names. On the other side are marshalled the forces of delusion, or Evil. On that side, the warriors— their names, again, having Sanskrit roots—represent human weaknesses.

Arjuna poses questions to Krishna that are personally meaningful to all devotees. His first concerns a universal dilemma: "Is it right for me to fight my human tendencies? They are part of my own self, after all! They define me as I am. By destroying them, unspiritual though they are, would I not be killing a part of my own self? Of what use to me, then, would victory itself be, if, by achieving it, I diminish myself?"

The decision to seek God seems, to the ego, a direct threat to its just and natural hegemony. Human beings fear to renounce their lower nature, thinking that, by doing so, they would deprive themselves of everything that is right and natural: their habits and desires; the personalities they have long nurtured, so lovingly; even their consciousness of themselves as individuals. It is difficult for the ego to understand that, by renouncing its personal attributes, the result to it will be not loss, but infinite gain! It is, indeed, the very fact that we cling to the ego that causes all our suffering.

Jesus Christ stated this truth cryptically in these words: *"Whosoever will save his life shall lose it: and whosoever will lose his life for my sake shall find it."* (Matthew 16:25)

Krishna responds to Arjuna's lament by describing the true nature of fulfillment. "Nothing is lost by realizing the Self," he reassures his friend and disciple. "The same energy you have been devoting to your unspiritual qualities will simply be remanifested in higher ones. No 'killing,' and no suppression, are involved. Rather, your nature will simply be transformed, and you will know all the happiness and fulfillment you have ever craved."

Such, in its entirety, is the "story" of the Bhagavad Gita. It forms the background for the profound teachings that follow.

In St. John's Gospel, more than in the other three, the emphasis is on the inner, spiritual life. John describes Christ from the beginning as the universal Divinity, an infinite consciousness distinct from its expression in Jesus as a human being. Indeed,

Yogananda declared that both *Christ* and *Krishna* have the same etymological root. Both men, in their human bodies, manifested Infinite Consciousness. Christ, and not Jesus, is the Son of God. Jesus the man lived for a few years in a little country. He himself, often, when referring to his humanity, used the expression, "the son of man." But when speaking of himself in his infinite reality, he referred to himself as the son of God. Of that state he was able to say in all truth, *"I and my Father are one"*; and again, *"Where two or three are gathered together in my name, there am I in the midst of them."*

The first sentences of John are particularly profound. What do those words mean, "In the beginning was the Word"? To what "Word" was he referring?

The expression is symbolic. When human beings communicate with one another, they express their thoughts through the medium of speech. Their words, as sound-vibrations, give expression to their ideas. The Word of God, similarly, is a *vibratory manifestation* of divine consciousness. That manifestation is the basic reality of the universe.

The Book of Genesis makes a statement similar in nature: *"And God said, Let there be light: and there was light."* (Genesis 1:3) Vibration produces sound; it also produces light.

What is vibration? It is repetitive movement in opposite directions from a state of potential rest at the center. As the tines of a tuning fork produce sound when they are struck, so, when a portion of Infinite Consciousness is set in motion, what results is vibration: the "Word," the "Light."

It would be absurd to imagine God as actually

30

saying, "Let there be light!" He had no body, no vocal cords, tongue, and lips with which to utter words! In all creation, nothing exists except vibration. Even the rocks are insubstantial: Science has found that matter is only a particular vibration of energy. Were vibration to cease, matter would revert back to its essence, Spirit.

The Cosmic Vibration is inaudible to the human ear, but can be heard inwardly by the "ear" of intuition. People sometimes get a hint of it in places where there is complete silence. They may hear a soft hum, or a gentle murmur like the whisper of wind in the trees. The sound emerges from no discernible point in space, but seems rather to come from everywhere. Often, it is most easily audible in the right ear. Patanjali, a great master in ancient India, compared this sound to "oil flowing smoothly out of a barrel." What is heard in quiet surroundings is not so much a spiritually uplifting experience as simply a whisper—like that of a waterfall from afar—of the mighty thunder of AUM perceived in deep meditation. To attune oneself to that sound, one must commune with it in the inner silence. Deep communion with AUM makes one conscious of the underlying reality of everything in existence, God.

God manifests directly through the Cosmic Sound. The "Word," in its primordial manifestation, may be compared to the swells heaving on an ocean's surface. When ripples develop on those swells, our awareness of an underlying calmness is slightly distorted; the calmness becomes less noticeable. As ripples grow and become waves, that deeper calmness becomes increasingly overlooked in the mounting excitement. In a gale, the focus of our minds may be entirely on saving our own lives!

And yet, considering the ocean as a whole, nothing is really happening. The over-all ocean level remains unchanged.

The Divine Spirit, like those ocean deeps, remains unaffected by the superficial vibrations of creation. The Book of Genesis states, *"The earth was without form, and void: and darkness was upon the face of the deep."* God as Spirit is vibrationless, beyond form, absolute. Shankaracharya, a well-known master during ancient times in India, described the calm state of Spirit as *satchidanandam* ("existence-consciousness-bliss"), a definition that was amplified by Paramhansa Yogananda as: "ever-existing, ever-conscious, ever-new bliss."

The Book of Genesis says, *"The Spirit of God moved upon the face of the waters."* Movement is vibration, the "Word" of God. The scriptures describe this sound variously. The Book of Revelation calls it the "Amen." In the *Veda's* it is called "AUM." To the Zoroastrians it was *"Ahunavar."* In Islam it is known as *"Amin."*

St. John's Gospel states that the "Word" of God not only proceeds from God: It *is* God. To return to our analogy: broad ocean swells suggest to the mind an underlying calmness. As small ripples of thought appear in our minds, however, they distract our attention from that calmness, which remains ever present in our depths of awareness. In meditation we can commune directly with the Cosmic Vibration as sound or light, or in one of its other aspects such as love, joy, or wisdom. At such times, the soul knows that it is in

touch with God. In restlessness, however, our awareness of calmness diminishes. With increasing restlessness, all awareness of our deeper reality is lost.

When consciousness is calm, it is also benign, open
to the needs and ideas of others, and loving to all. The
more, however, our thoughts and emotions are disturbed and agitated, the more we find ourselves in the
grip of emotions—sometimes passionate, sometimes
even violent. In the upheaval of intense emotion, God,
though never absent, is banished from human awareness altogether. Hatred, anger, and similar negative
emotions seize us as their own. Such emotions are not,
in themselves, evil: They simply warp our perception of
reality and cause us to lose touch with that which all of
us most desire in life: true peace, true love, true happiness. Therein lies the evil of those emotions: They
obstruct attunement to our own deeper nature. The
Bhagavad Gita poses the question rhetorically: *"To one
who is without peace, how is happiness possible?"*

Without vibration, the universe would cease to
exist. That which existed, WAS already; nor could anything have come into being except that which was.
"And without him," St. John says, *"was not any thing
made that was made."* The Divine Vibration itself is not
responsible for the behavior of the waves. Once the creative impulse has been set into motion, it assumes a
motive power of its own. Indeed, the "organization" of
the universe might justifiably be termed the ultimate
in decentralization! Divine vision, Paramhansa
Yogananda said, is "center everywhere, circumference
nowhere."

The ocean analogy fails to clarify a fundamental

truth, however. For an ocean is not conscious, as the "Word of God" is conscious. An ocean's waves cannot agitate themselves; they are whipped up by outside forces, which also lack any specific will of their own to whip up the waves. The "ripples" of cosmic vibration, however, are self-aware, and self-generating. The universal influence to which they respond—the "wind," let us say—is also conscious, for nothing exists, anywhere, except gradations of consciousness. The individual ripples, growing to become waves as their strength of movement increases, owe that movement to the "wind" only to the extent that they cooperate with it consciously.

Thus, there are *two* conscious activities: the "wind," or power of *maya,* or delusion, itself; and the "ripples" of individual vibration. Cosmic delusion is first set into motion by the Spirit. This pristine power is the "Word," or *AUM.* After that manifestation, every ripple has free will to cooperate with the outward-impelling "wind" of *maya,* or with the inward pull toward divine union with God.

The "Word" itself is not responsible for evil, but only for setting vibration into motion; it is responsible for the initial "wind" of creativity. That motion is, itself, benign. Had only ripples continued to exist, the universe would have remained harmonious, serene, and beautiful. All beings would have lived in harmony with God's will. Of their own free will, however, they chose to excite themselves by responding to the wind of *maya,* allowing it to whip them to greater and greater excitement. Evil is the conscious impulse toward increasing motion and "outwardness."

Imagine a conscious wave setting itself in rebellion against its own inherent reality, which is the calm ocean beneath it. Seeking its fulfillment in restlessness, it increases in size, affirming with ever greater fervor its own individuality.

Evil is individualized in the case of human beings, but it is also a universal, conscious force which suggests to them, like the wind to the waves: "Grow taller! Be proud! Be different from all others!" What makes that force evil is that it draws the mind away from that which all human beings truly want from life: happiness, above all, and peace of mind.

Evil has a magnetic attraction. Its roots grow, not in the individual mind, but in infinite consciousness. That universal impulse toward movement opposes the inward-drawing, magnetic attraction of divine love, reminding us ever silently that outward restlessness is not our true nature. Temptation draws us because it resonates with our subconscious tendency toward material involvement. In resonating with the subconscious, however, it increases its hold on us.

Fortunately, the attractive power of delusion affects us only to the extent that we open ourselves to it. By opening ourselves to its influence, we become agitated in spirit, proud, and increasingly self-absorbed. *"From him who has not,"* Jesus said, *"shall be taken away even that which he has."*

The Bhagavad Gita also speaks of creation as a manifestation of God's consciousness. In sleep, we dream. Similarly, the Infinite Consciousness, dreamlike, vibrates its thoughts of creation into the great void. Nothing in creation is real, except as dreams are real. All is a mere seeming. The chief difference between God's dream and our own is that His is clear, for it is superconscious, whereas our own are vague, because they are subconscious. The cosmic dream has a certain coherence, moreover, that is lacking in sub-consciousness.

Electrons—the "building blocks" of matter—are what create the dream-material universe, in accordance with the "blueprint" of what Yogananda called the Divine Architect. The divine presence resides deep beneath the surface of restless minds, dwelling forever at their center, and, indeed, at the center of every atom. The divine consciousness runs unnoticed through everything, like the thread passing through the beads of a necklace.

We find this truth hinted at in one of the primary commandments of Jesus: *"Love thy neighbor as thy self."* Your neighbor *is,* in the highest sense, your very Self. For infinite consciousness is our deepest reality.

Modern physicists are beginning to discover the existence of subtle interactive ties in natural phenomena. An electron's movement is simultaneously matched by movement elsewhere, in another electron, even though the two are distant from each other. Every thought we think has a subtle influence on our environment. Sensitive people, often, are aware that "thoughts" permeate an environment, and that a room full of people may contain a subtle mental "atmosphere."

Since all life is one, the more sensitive we become to it, the more we find ourselves sustained by it, as sound is amplified by the sounding board of a musical instrument.

A proud ego resembles in this sense a piano wire stretched tight but without the resonance of a piano underneath it. The more we isolate ourselves in ego-consciousness, the less power we have to accomplish anything worthwhile or meaningful in life. Successful people are attuned to a greater reality than their own. Unsuccessful people lack such attunement. People fail not so much because they lack strength, or talent, or intelligence, as because they are not attuned to life's natural rhythms. It is these which produce the flow of abundance.

Is it not clear, then, why all the scriptures tell us to be kind, humble, and serviceful to others? Such attitudes are necessary if only because, by the openness and receptivity they engender in us, they help us to become more aware of all life. Nietzsche's diatribes against humility were motivated by the delusion that every human being is an island unto himself. In fact, even islands are united by the landmass underneath them. True humility, therefore, is not self-abasement: It is self-honesty.

As we treat others, so—invariably—do we treat ourselves. For the energy we project to them is generated first in ourselves. Our thoughts and energy create a vortex, which draws to us whatever vibrations out of the great ocean of consciousness resound in sympathy with our own. "Thoughts," Yogananda wrote in *Autobiography of a Yogi,* "are universally and not individually rooted." Whatever vibrations we attract, and then project outward to others, have their first and greatest impact on ourselves: adversely, if our thoughts are unkind; beneficially, if they are generous.

The more aware we become of life's underlying oneness, the closer we come to knowing God. Ultimately we arrive at that truth which was pronounced in the ancient *Vedas*: *"Thou art that!"* Jesus said it also: *"Do not your scriptures say, Ye are gods?"*

Our task, ordained for us by Divine Will itself, is to harmonize ourselves on deeper and deeper levels with our own inner divinity. As Jesus said, "The kingdom of God is within you." To deepen our awareness, we must banish the delusion of ego which encourages desires and attachments. These in turn whip up the restless waves of likes and dislikes in the mind, and the emotion-driven currents of action and reaction.

The cosmic "Word" is no mere poetic abstraction. And the divine consciousness, permeating everything like the string that passes through a pearl necklace, is nearer to us than our most secret thoughts.

The Lord calls to us unceasingly, urging us to seek Him, the Changeless Spirit, beneath all the storms of life. Inner communion with Him is the highest teaching in every scripture. It is the truth that great masters have taken birth to declare to us who, struggling in delusion though we are, seek the way to enlightenment.

CHAPTER TWO

What Is the Source of Life?

Matter is energy. Energy, when perceived by the inner or spiritual eye, is seen as light; by the inner ear, is heard as sound. Cosmic light and sound are vibrations of Divine Consciousness. Both are the "Word" of God. From that vibration came the thoughts and energy-forms which manifested the universe. Life itself may be defined as *conscious energy*. As the Gospel of St. John states: *"In him was life; and the life was the light of men."* (1:4)

Human beings think of life as an outcome of the right combination of chemicals, or of the union of male and female cells: in any case the product of outer causes, rather than being itself the primordial cause. They think of things in terms of appearances; they look *at* life from the outside in, rather than *with* life, from their own living center. They seek understanding superficially, and never seem to realize the need for refining their own awareness.

The Bible in this passage emphasizes life as a cause, not an effect. It states that it is life which creates the body, not the body which creates life. Life, St. John states in frank opposition to most people's view of things, is pre-existent in eternity. It is not brought into being by the body's creation. Life is the indwelling spirit without which everything would be unconscious, unbreathing, and inert.

Life, always, is a radiation *outward* from a core of conscious vibration. The things made by man can only suggest, by shape and movement, the existence of an indwelling consciousness. Both life and consciousness, however, await manifestation at the heart of every atom, and await fulfillment in the spiritual development of human beings. The "light" of understanding is not the knowledge that dawns in the mind as information is absorbed from without. In fact, understanding is already innate in all of us: not as the result of education, but rather as the ability to *recognize and relate intelligently to* whatever information we receive.

Understanding, above all of spiritual truths, must be sought within ourselves. Only to the extent that we awaken inner awareness of them can we manifest our understanding outwardly. Churches and temples cannot give us wisdom. Understanding is self-discovered. As Jesus Christ put it, the real temple is the body.* Here alone, in stillness of heart and mind, can God be truly worshiped. We cannot draw Him to us by loud shouting, or by searching for Him in the sky. He hides at the wellspring of every thought. He inspires us to remember Him—increasingly so, as we invite Him to do so.

Divine consciousness is, as we read in the above verse, the true "light of men." It is this Inner Presence which gives us awareness. Divine consciousness gives us cognizance of our very egos. Inwardness is, in this

---

* "'Destroy this temple, and in three days I will raise it up.' . . . But he spake of the temple of his body." (John 2:19,21)

sense, a direction, not a static condition. It is a process of tracing every thought and feeling back to its source. This inward journey is the secret key to spiritual development. The more conscious we are of the light within, the more aware we become of the reality of life itself. This was what Jesus meant when he said elsewhere, *"I am come that they may have life, and have it more abundantly."* (John 10:10) True life is much more than existence, however aware and self-directed, though it is that also. True life is *intense* awareness of our existence. When expressed outwardly, it manifests as enthusiasm, whereas a merely aware existence manifests only as apathy, half-hearted reactions, or indifference. When experienced in the inner Self, life reveals itself as divine joy and bliss. What indeed is existence itself, if we, though existing, are not also glowingly alive? Merely to *be* is spiritual death! Jesus made this point forcefully in his reply to a prospective disciple who had asked his permission, before following him, to go and bury his father: *"Follow me,"* said the Master, *"and let the dead bury their dead!"* (Matthew 8:22)

Divine consciousness is the true life which enlightens human minds. That consciousness is only dimly manifested in people of little spiritual awareness. Nevertheless, God's presence is in them also, for it is everywhere. Theologians err in their claim that only human beings have souls. Everything—even things that, to human perception, seem inanimate—has a soul, at least in the inchoate sense of being a dim manifestation of divine consciousness. The Lord Himself, through Cosmic Vibration, the "Word," resides at the heart of everything.

The divine presence is not, however, manifested *equally* in all things. Just as human beings are more vitally aware than are the rocks, so great saints, who are spiritually awake in cosmic consciousness, manifest awareness more dynamically than ordinary human beings, who are spiritually asleep, dreaming themselves to be limited by their individual egos. Indeed, it is no exaggeration to say that the difference in awareness between an enlightened master and the unenlightened crush of humanity is as great as that which exists between ordinary human beings and the rocks!

The Bhagavad Gita states, in Chapter Seven:

"I am the fluidity of water. I am the silver light of the moon and the golden light of the sun. I am the AUM chanted in all the Vedas: *the Cosmic Sound moving, as if soundlessly, through the ether. I am the manliness of men. I am the good sweet smell of the moist earth. I am the luminescence of fire; the sustaining life of all living creatures. I am self-offering in those who would expand their little lives into cosmic life. O Arjuna, know Me as the eternal seed of all creatures. In the perceptive, I am their perception. In the great, I am their greatness. In the glorious, it is I who am their glory."*

Wise is he who is able to perceive God as the hidden Doer behind His multifarious roles in creation. Wise are we also, then, if we give God the credit for anything we do well, and attribute any failure simply to a deficiency in our attunement with Him. To blame ourselves, or to hurl accusations at others, is futile. Ignorance, and wisdom: Both are simply the tying and untying of the knots of cosmic delusion.

Wise are we, too, if we can sense in all things the

hidden divine power: if we can see in human laughter God's inward smile, and in human sorrow the tenderness of His compassion, or kindly reproach.

The world is God's dream. Our allotted task is to wake from our own dreams within the cosmic dream, and to live in obedience to the Dreamer's plan for us.

Everything should be loved for God's sake—nothing, for its own sake. This was the message conveyed by St. Francis of Assisi in his wonderful "Canticle of the Creatures," a hymn of thanksgiving to God for His love in creating "brother Sun and sister Moon." Francis's canticle was written not, as many believe, in praise of God's creation itself, but in joyous love for its all-beneficent Creator. Had it been written merely in praise of Nature, it would have been, from the point of view of divine adoration, idolatrous. For while it is good to find inspiration in Nature's beauty, it is best if that beauty inspires us to love God all the more fervently.

To deny to creation, however, the reciprocity of love that we receive through it from God, and all the while to tell ourselves austerely that we are reserving our love for God alone, would more than likely harden us in our egoism. For we honor God when we love all things in His name. We honor Him every time we find divine inspiration in a sunset; energy and joy in a burst of sunlight through the trees; heavenly music in the songs of birds; and inner freedom in every gust of wind. Everything becomes more wonderful when we perceive life's inner secret: that at the heart of everything is Love Itself.

It helps also to look beyond things that only inspire

us aesthetically. For God sends messages in many forms.

Consider the rocks: Are they not, in their massiveness and immobility, divine lessons in steadfastness? Consider the bees: Don't they teach us, wordlessly, to sip only sweetness from life, and to turn aside from all anger and bitterness? Consider the clouds: Isn't their message one of aloofness from petty, daily preoccupations, and of impartial service to all, as they themselves render when they send nourishing rain?

These are not imaginary projections merely, for the divine consciousness manifests itself through our very thoughts—the more so, the more we lift our consciousness up to God. Few people are naturally disposed to seek truth inwardly. For the rest especially, sources of inspiration can provide a faltering first step toward the inner light. It is God Himself, finally, who inspires us to seek Him inwardly.

God is perceived directly by the soul in the sound of AUM, and in the calm inner Light. Thus have great saints communed with the "Word." As is stated in Ezekiel, 43:1,2: *"Afterward he brought me to the gate, even the gate that looketh toward the east: And, behold, the glory of the God of Israel came from the way of the east: and His voice was like a noise of many waters: and the earth shined with his glory."*

By offering up to God every experience we receive from life, and by communing deeply in ourselves with the "Word," we shall reclaim at last our eternal heritage in Him.

CHAPTER THREE

Why Is the Light "Incomprehensible" to Darkness?

"And the light shineth in darkness, and the darkness comprehended it not." (John 1:5)

This obscure verse suggests several apparent impossibilities: one, that darkness can comprehend anything at all; two, that, although able to comprehend, it cannot see; three, that light can shine in darkness without transforming it into light; and four, that darkness can even be expected to see and comprehend, rather than *be* seen and *be* comprehended: that it is a conscious agent rather than an object merely perceived.

How can the divine light, "shining in darkness," make no impression on it? Earthly light is visible in darkness, certainly: sometimes blindingly so. We may not understand its nature or its source, but we cannot fail to perceive the simple fact of its existence. Here, however, darkness itself is described as doing the perceiving, and, even so, as incapable of perceiving something that should be supremely obvious to it.

What the Bible is describing here is consciousness itself. It is comparing the light of truth to the darkness of ignorance.

As a telescope can bring distant galaxies into view, so our ability to see the inner light depends on the power and clarity of our own mental "telescope." And as a television set makes us aware of sounds and images that surround us always, but that are imperceptible to our senses, so our ability to perceive the inner light depends on how well we "tune in" to it. For the light, too, is with us always. Clear perception comes in calmness, when our thoughts and feelings are focused on the inner "universe." The mirror of a telescope must be kept free of dust, and a television set must have a good antenna, placed properly to protect it from static interference. Human consciousness, similarly, must be cleansed of the "dust" of material desires, and protected from the "static" of mental restlessness. Otherwise, the calm inner light will remain both invisible and incomprehensible to it.

The single most prevalent theme in all spiritual literature is the contrast between light and darkness. The Bible doesn't refer to it here as a struggle, but rather describes the darkness as a simple lack of awareness: not two opposing realities, in other words, but one reality, light, opposed by a lack of light: ignorance, incapable of even imagining that superconscious awareness to which it owes its very existence.

The darkness is Satanic delusion. It is a conscious, not a passive, urge, a deliberate will to seek ever-greater darkness. Its power lies in that very determination. It can exert control over us only to the extent that we accept it, and blind ourselves to the light of truth. "Sin" means error, simply: the error of a wrong understanding.

The light of wisdom shines calmly in the midst of ignorance. Dark ignorance, however, is incapable of imagining anything more luminous than itself. When confronted by wisdom, it wraps itself more closely than ever in its cloak of delusion. Nobility of character it views as merely ignoble. Generosity it sneers at as being selfishly motivated. Kindness it considers a mere shield for its own scheming intentions. Compassion it dismisses as hypocritical, while it boasts self-right-eously, "Well, at least I'm sincere about my selfish-ness!" Darkened minds betray their lack of comprehension by resenting any suggestion that they are not already living in light.

The Bible explains in terms of degrees of compre-hension the eternal struggle between demonic dark-ness, rooted in ignorance, and divine light. Darkness, though blind, is aware of *something* menacing it. Hatred, for example, though incapable of comprehend-ing love, senses in love a power that might deprive hatred of all meaning. Ignoble motives cannot tolerate pure and noble motives. Instead, they imagine their very survival depends on opposing them. Spiritual ignorance doesn't realize that light is the only life there is, and darkness, the only death.

If ignorance could rise out of its darkness into light, it would find life also. Alas, it identifies itself with that darkness, unaware that darkness is the source of all its misery. The darkened mind imagines, foolishly, that the farther back it huddles in its darkened cave, the more secure it will be. Darkness is a pseudo-light, a reflection from outside the cave on the rocks within, but it seems to those who are attached to it a very source of light.

In Shakespeare's play "Othello," Iago's hatred is motivated by antipathy to Othello's inherent nobility. Jealousy was Othello's "tragic weakness." Iago, playing upon it, persuades him that his happiness is threatened by his very generosity, which Iago describes as "naive."

This is the response, always, of darkness to light. The darkness cannot comprehend the light, but it intuits it vaguely as an intrusion on its familiar shadows. It seeks justification by claiming, "Ignorance is bliss!" It equates lack of spiritual awareness with the false "freedom" of irresponsibility. Not interested in greater awareness, it looks upon that as merely a "burden" of greater responsibility.

The darkness described here is spiritual. Sometimes this darkness seeks social respectability, perhaps by joining some church congregation, but its interest, if so, lies in appearances. It considers spirituality itself quite unnecessary: an affront to propriety. For it enjoys the snug feeling of ego-consciousness. Limitless self-expansion, if offered for its serious contemplation, makes it recoil as if from an abyss. Even the simple religious counsel "Love all," awakens the instinctive response: "What about *me?*"

The "menace" it fears is the one thing in existence, however, that can *never* do it harm! Light offers that fulfillment which people seek mistakenly in dark materialism.

Harmonious chords and beautiful melodies are no threat to cacophony. They simply rearrange the notes and make them pleasing to the ear. It is of course true that in beautiful music cacophony ceases to exist. Those who identify themselves with cacophony have an active dislike of harmony. There is, however, a relationship between harmony and discord, for both use essentially the same notes. Darkness, similarly, senses vaguely its affinity with the light, for both have in common the fact of consciousness. Darkness, however, resents any challenge to its present state of awareness, and considers any new outlook as foreign to itself, commenting on it, "I am quite satisfied with things as they are now, thank you!"

St. John's reference in this passage is to the darkness of ignorance. Those who close their eyes to higher awareness cling stubbornly to their bedlam of desires and emotions. Only when they tire of this raging conflict do they dream of escape from pandemonium, and long for inner peace. The inner light dawns in time upon their consciousness. By steadily deeper attunement with that light, they attain the realization of God.

It is fitting that "comprehended," in this verse of the Gospel, be put in the past tense, as opposed to the present-tense verb, "shineth," for our lack of comprehension lasts only until our darkness has been dispelled by the light.

A beautiful passage in the Bhagavad Gita, in the poetic translation of Sir Edwin Arnold, puts it this way:

If there should rise suddenly within the skies
Sunburst of a thousand suns
Flooding earth with beams undeemed-of,
Then might be that Holy One's
Majesty and radiance dreamed-of!

Brighter God's light is than that of countless suns combined into one. Infinitely more majestic and powerful it is than the greatest earthly glory.

Unenlightened human beings, in their rejection of truth, enclose themselves in shrouds of darkness. They don't see that the divine light is with them always, and offers the simplest possible solution to all their problems. Instead, they think to escape their misery by sinking to ever-more sunless deeps. They hope to dissolve their bewilderment in a vortex of increasing confusion. Finally, bruised and battered by suffering, they seek rest in God.

They cannot imagine Him, at first, as anything but a larger-than-life image of themselves, subject to all the emotions that afflict them also: anger, pride, jealousy, and the whole Pandora's box of human weaknesses.

Nor is an anthropomorphic image so absurd, though their concept of an all-too-human God shows little spiritual sophistication. For it is difficult for anyone to imagine a conscious, infinite Being capable of manifesting the vast universe with its countless billions of galaxies, each one containing hundreds of billions of suns like our own. Add to this immensity the seemingly contradictory, because softening, quality of love, and describe that love as caring for each of us separately and individually, and we have a concept that is vast beyond all the powers of human imagination. We can only shelve this concept for a time, while we visualize infinity reduced to dimensions comprehensible to our human brains. Rare indeed is that seeker of Truth who feels no need to visualize God in some human aspect: the Divine Mother, Heavenly Father, or Eternal Friend.

The experience of cosmic consciousness was described by Paramhansa Yogananda as "beyond imagination of expectancy." The mind must prepare itself for that experience. Fear of the light, born of egoic darkness, is something most people feel so long as they retain any hint of ego-consciousness. To know God is, every great scripture declares, the true goal of life. Our problem lies not in that goal's distance, but in its very closeness to us. We, ourselves, are that goal! Ultimate Truth embraces everything in existence. It is ineffable bliss. To each of us it calls, "Reclaim your birthright in Infinity!"

Ours is the choice. As long as we choose to live in delusion, we shall never behold the light of Truth. As long as we choose to live selfishly, we can never know the light of pure love, untainted by any selfishness. As long as we are cruel or aggressive to others, we are doomed to experience suffering if only in our awareness that we lack joy.

Yet divine joy surrounds us! God's light shines at the very heart of our spiritual darkness. It whispers to us in the inner silence, "Claim Me for thy own!"

The blissful Lord is never indifferent to us, nor to our needs. He is compassionate to us in our grief, but He awaits us in the light. For there alone lies salvation from suffering. To receive Him, we must seek Him within, in deep inner communion.

The dark corners we conceal in ourselves recoil uncomprehendingly from the merest flicker of light. If we would free ourselves from the "dire fears and colossal sufferings," as the Bhagavad Gita calls them, of human existence, we must open the hidden chambers of our hearts to the purifying rays of God's light. Concealing nothing from Him, we must pray unceasingly, "I am Thine alone!"

In that effort—seemingly, at first, so difficult!—life in God becomes increasingly easy. Embracing His light, the soul emerges at last from its ancient shadowland, and rises on radiant wings to the realization of itself as, forever, a child of the light.

CHAPTER FOUR

The Incarnation

Probably the greatest mystery in Christian theology is that of the Incarnation. Jesus, though human, is believed also to be the Son of God. An early challenge to the very survival of Christianity centered on this point. It was delivered in the Fourth Century A.D. by Arius, a prominent Greek theologian, who caused a major rift in the church by claiming that Jesus was only a man, and therefore not the Son of God. Had Arianism become universally accepted—and it very nearly was—Christ would have become little more than a legend, and his teachings would have been studied as a philosophy, like the teachings of Epictetus and Marcus Aurelius.

The divinity of Christ has been a problem not only for Christians. The Jews have seen in this doctrine a contradiction of the basic tenet of their religion: *"Hear O Israel, the Lord our God, the Lord is one."* How, they ask, can the one God be also triune? And how can Jesus Christ, a human being, belong to that supposed divine Trinity as the Son of Infinite God? To Jews even today, this teaching is idolatrous.

Sometimes, when one is faced with paradoxes of this kind, it helps to see how they have been treated in other religions. For in wisdom there can be no controversy. As Paramhansa Yogananda put it, "Fools argue; wise men discuss." Two religions may sometimes *appear* to differ on some essential point, whereas a third, approaching the matter from another direction, shows the disagreement to be only a result of cultural conditioning, or a simple matter of definition. The differences, in other words, are not fundamental. People who fan religious controversies are without spiritual understanding. For Truth, like God, is one. Two expressions of truth cannot be mutually contradictory. Differences can appear only in its application, which may vary according to circumstances. If a fundamental contradiction occurs, it can only be due to that most common of human failings: misunderstanding.

To test the truth of a spiritual teaching, ask yourself this question first: "Is it consistent with the high spiritual traditions of the ages?" If the answer is yes, ask another one: "Is this teaching vibrant with spiritual power; does it suggest an 'aura' of divine authority?" Genuinely spiritual works resonate with a divine conviction that cannot be manufactured merely by the skillful use of words. On the other hand, vibrant power is virtually absent from false teachings. They lack conviction, are vague, and suggest no "aura" at all except, perhaps, some sort of grey mist. False teachings, finally, strike one as being intended to impress people, not to uplift them.

Paramhansa Yogananda told the story of a man, without naming him, who wrote a religious treatise under the "inspiration" of a strong imagination. Desirous of having his treatise accepted as scripture, he buried it under a tree and then bided his time. Fifteen years later, announcing that he'd had an angelic visitation, he guided people to that spot, dug with a spade, and "discovered" the manuscript he himself had buried years earlier. By now the writing had acquired a certain patina. "A revelation!" the man cried, and his followers, awe-struck at this "miracle," grew numerous. Their "faith," however, was but a pious presumption; it in no way validated the manuscript.

Anyone who desired to write a new scripture couldn't go far wrong, of course, in telling people to be humble, honest, and loving to all. It would be virtually incumbent on him, in fact, to include injunctions of this sort in his treatise. One feels safe in assuming, however, that this "revelation" contained more than mere truisms; otherwise, why would he have gone to all that trouble over it? He must have felt he needed to add a few "extras": the more startling, the better. His "scripture" soared, one imagines, into the rarefied atmosphere of pure fantasy, including, perhaps, detailed descriptions of heaven and of the "lifestyle" there, in "eternity." One wouldn't expect the manuscript to give such practical advice as how to progress spiritually, or how to transcend phenomena and experience union with God. Minds that find inspiration in etheric wonders find little to excite their imagination in spiritual practicality.

It is important to test spiritual claims by the yardstick of how well they agree with sacred traditions. Jesus for this reason frequently quoted scripture. He demonstrated not only that his coming had been foretold in the ancient prophecies, but that the teachings of the prophets coincided with his own. He did not actually need the prophets to corroborate his teachings, which he'd received directly from God Himself. He quoted them to convince people who wanted outward reassurance that his teachings were rooted in tradition.

True religious teaching is similar to modern science in several respects. Both, for example, are devoted to truth. Both also rely on direct experience rather than on hearsay evidence. Tradition, moreover, is important in both disciplines; novelty is viewed skeptically until it has been proved by the test of experience. From this point on, the two disciplines go their separate ways. For religion insists that true knowledge depends not on progressive discovery, but on eternal wisdom. Divine truths, unlike scientific facts, are not phenomenal but changeless, existent forever at the very heart of being. The teachings of Jesus Christ may have been "news" to the spiritual illiterates of his day, but they were not revolutionary. As he himself put it, *"Think not that I am come to destroy the law . . . : I am come not to destroy, but to fulfill."* (Matthew 5:17)

Nowadays, people have become increasingly aware of other cultures and spiritual traditions, and of the fact that many of the teachings of Jesus Christ, and of Judaism, are fundamental to the tenets of other religions also. Indeed, it is becoming evident that the major religions agree with one another on most issues.

What, then, of those issues on which they disagree? Are the disagreements only apparent, or are they actual? Are they fundamental, or merely superficial?

The Jewish challenge to Christianity on the divinity of Christ is certainly a case in point. As we shall see, this disagreement is only apparent. It is a question of definition. Indeed, once the Christian claim is rightly understood it becomes clear that it excludes no other religion.

A search for fresh insight outside the Judeo-Christian tradition turns up a solution in the scriptures of India. The Hindu teachings in no way contradict the Christian belief in the divinity of Jesus Christ. Nor do they contradict Judaism's objection to that belief. What the Hindu teachings do is broaden the teaching; they show that divine incarnation is a universal truth, and that it in no way opposes the doctrine, "The Lord is one."

"Allah ho akbar!" cry the Muslims: "God is one!" The Bhagavad Gita said it long ago: God is one, without a second, formless, and indivisible. That scripture goes on to declare that the Supreme Spirit takes on the *appearance* of form in creating the universe. Everything in existence is a manifestation of God's consciousness. There is nothing, anywhere, except that consciousness. Creation is born of an infinity of thoughts at the surface, so to speak, of the Creator's mind.

The divine light shines at the heart of matter, somewhat like sunlight shining on an infinite number of window panes. Certain of the panes are blackened by the soot of inertia and are virtually opaque. The only evidence left of the sunlight is the warmth on the window panes.

Gradually, through the process of evolution, the soot is rubbed off, and awareness begins to shine through the panes.

In the early stages of evolution, awareness is still

dim. The cleansing process is therefore slow. The keener the awareness, the more accelerated the process becomes. At first, the sunlight is visible in the windows not as light, but only as a diminution of darkness.

Evolution gradually removes soot from the glass. Thus, awareness manifests itself with steadily increasing clarity. Instinctual expression in the lower animals evolves to greater degrees of intelligence, until finally, in mankind, it becomes egoic and keenly self-aware. Until human beings develop spiritual awareness, however, their "window panes" remain clouded, their glass translucent but not transparent. The glass seems to shine with its own light. Thus, the intelligent awareness of human beings seems entirely their own.

As one develops spiritual awareness, however, his window pane becomes transparent. To those of spiritual sensitivity, then, it is evident that the expanded consciousness of the saints cannot be only theirs.

A symbol of the divine grace filtering through human consciousness is the stained glass windows in Christian churches. Ego-consciousness, suggested in the coloring of the panes, thins finally, in the case of great masters, to transparency. The masters transmit the full effulgence of the sun's light.

To most people, a master seems much like other human beings: a window opening, merely; that is to say, a physical body. They usually sense in him, however, some greater-than-ordinary power. Those who are themselves developed spiritually behold in him that light which "lighteth all men." The light may appear as an actual halo around his head, as in classical paintings of the saints, or even surrounding his whole body.

Paramhansa Yogananda described Sri Yukteswar's aura once as filling the entire train in which the great guru was traveling.

The Bible, somewhat obliquely, expresses the same truth. In the first chapter of St. John's Gospel, Jesus is described in his essential nature as *impersonal*. John describes him later on as also human, showing that the impersonal and the personal are aspects of the same reality. In verses 6–14, John states:

"There was a man sent from God, whose name was John. The same came for a witness, to bear witness of the Light, that all men through him might believe. He was not that Light, but was sent to bear witness of that Light. That was the true Light, which lighteth every man that cometh into the world. He was in the world, and the world was made by him, and the world knew him not. He came unto his own, and his own received him not. But as many as received him, to them gave he power to become the sons of God."

The distinction here between John the Baptist, the saint, and Jesus, the Christ, is fundamental. John had attained a high level of spirituality. His consciousness was absorbed in contemplation of the inner light; he could therefore "bear witness of it," which is to say, speak of it with authority. John had not yet so merged his consciousness in that light, however, as to behold himself as having no existence apart from it.

Jesus, on the other hand, had reached the state of absolute perfection. Inwardly, he had realized himself as one with the light of God. His self-awareness was therefore infinite; Jesus, the man, was united in consciousness to the omnipresent Christ.

It is important to understand that conscious one-ness with God was not uniquely the case with Jesus Christ. What he represented, rather, was the eternal potential of every soul. Divine union is the eventual destiny of us all, as His manifestations. Outside of God, there can be no other reality. Jesus was sent not to strike awe in people's hearts at his greatness, but to remind them of their own potential greatness, in God.

The distinction between Jesus, the man, and the infinite Christ consciousness is explained further in this passage. For though human nature feels a natural attraction to Jesus, the perfect human being, the Gospel emphasizes that he was far more than what he appeared to be. *"That which lighteth every man that cometh into the world was the true light."* Because the divine light "lighteth every man," each of us has the divine responsibility to realize in that light the essence of his own being.

It is significant that this passage doesn't name Jesus, while it names John the Baptist. *"He was in the world, and the world was made by him, and the world knew him not."* The "world" knew Jesus, the man. What the Gospel is saying is that Jesus, in his divine reality, was not that which the world saw with physical eyes. People beheld him as the son of Joseph and Mary: Few could recognize him as the Son of the Infinite Father. It was people's limited perception of Jesus that prompted him to say, on one occasion, *"Before Abraham was, I am."* (John 8:58)

Jesus said also in another passage, *"He that hath seen me hath seen the Father."** This statement was made

* John 14:9.

60

in reference not to his human body—which everyone, even his judges and executioners, could see clearly—but to his soul. Only someone who was spiritually advanced could perceive him in his spiritual nature, for which the body was but a cloak. Only a few persons, then, were ever blessed to see him as one with the Father.*

"He came unto his own, and his own received him not." Who—one asks—were "his own"? Since ancient times the Jews had considered themselves "God's chosen people." This didn't mean they were special favorites of God's, though some of them may have believed so. They had been chosen, rather, because of their own desire to serve God. Paramhansa Yogananda said, "God 'chooses' those who choose Him." The Jews had elected as a people to place God first in their lives. It was this choice that separated them from other peoples. Those peoples, if they were interested in such matters at all, prayed for the fulfillment of their worldly desires, and gave little thought to serving God, unless by doing so they could gain a bargaining position with Him.

To be chosen of God doesn't mean basking in heavenly blessings from then on, while others (to quote from the musical, *Showboat)* "tote dat barge" and "lift dat bale." Far from it! Instead of finding an alleviation of life's normal tests, one may well find their severity increased. To choose God means to accept willingly the

---

* The writer recalls to mind, in this context, a brother disciple of his who was reprimanded on this point by Paramhansa Yogananda. The disciple had fairly papered his room with photographs he'd taken of the guru. One day, Yogananda said to him, "Why do you keep taking pictures of this body? Get to know me in meditation, if you want to know who I really am."

task of self-purification, so that one's soul may soar to spiritual heights. It means purging the heart of every earthly desire and attachment. God's will for us is that we reclaim our eternal state of oneness with Him.

This is not to say that living for God is, spiritually, like a sort of Charge of the Light Brigade or a Japanese kamikaze mission. Countless blessings come on the spiritual path. Even the tests become increasingly easy to bear.

Often there is, at first, a spiritual "honeymoon" when the soul experiences a constant flow of grace. Usually, then, there comes a "middle ground" when the seeker finds he must work hard on himself. Only later does the flow of grace return, and, with it, unceasing sweetness. From this point on, the tests themselves seem almost inconsequential.

Once a person dedicates himself to God and refuses any longer to worship the "idol" of materialism, the course of his life changes dramatically. For God asks that he offer to Him everything he has and is. The process is exacting. Spiritual novices may not realize how little ego-reassurance they are going to receive. For God's plan for us is what Jesus expressed in his command to the disciples, *"Be ye therefore perfect, even as your Father which is in heaven is perfect."* (Matthew 5:48)

If our love for God is sincere, He will help us to rid ourselves of every delusion, so that we become impersonal in outlook even as He is; non-attached to the things of this world; and infinite in our love.

The devotee naturally asks, How can I "love God with all my heart" and at the same time love Him impersonally? Paramhansa Yogananda explained this apparent paradox by saying that we must look upon any aspect of God that we hold dear as an expression of Infinity. Behold infinite consciousness, he said, in the eyes, especially. To develop "infinite-mindedness," offer back to God any blessings you receive from Him, and don't hug them, even in gratitude, to yourself.

History describes the Jews as a stiff-necked people. It was, of course, they who wrote the history; self-deprecation is a notable Jewish trait! There may, however, be another reason also for their stubbornness. For the emphasis in Judaism on the absoluteness of spiritual law must have had a stiffening effect also on their will.

Stubbornness was at the same time, however, their virtue. For their loyalty to truth inspired dedication to the *supreme* Truth: God. To the extent that their stubbornness was also a shortcoming, it made them excessively reliant on divine law, and inadequately surrendered to divine love. In time, they came to equate truth with theological legalisms. Thus, their intuitive heart-feeling was left under-developed; they became intellectually brittle, the result of too much reasoning.

When reason lacks the guiding hand of intuition, it tends to roam about freely, like an unbridled horse, and often ends up grazing among the brambles of doubt. The problem is not that intuitive feeling is an obstruction to clear reasoning. Quite the opposite! Reason itself, rather, cannot develop clarity unless it is balanced by intuitive feeling. Reason alone, deaf to the promptings of intuition, inclines to depend on concrete facts for its conclusions. Preoccupied with material evidence, it often develops a materialistic outlook. Intellect, if unbridled and unguided by intuitive feeling, strays on endless bypaths of questions and rationalizations.

The teaching of Jesus was a bold challenge to such intellectual meandering. Instead, what he declared frequently, and powerfully, was the need to base one's faith on actual experience.

His mission occurred at a time in history when the Jews were at a crossroads. It was time for them to reemphasize their divine destiny. Jesus told them, in effect, "Return to the way of intuitive love. Hold yourselves humbly open to the channels God sends you, and be not proud in your intellectuality, lest you lose touch with God's grace."

Mosaic law had commanded them to reject idolatry. Over the centuries, however, they had embraced it anew, as a golden calf of a new kind: that of material attachment. It was the rabbis' materialism, not their faith in God, that caused them to reject as false a messiah who preached the supremacy of love, and who wandered penniless among the common people rather than parading in regal splendor. The shout went up at the end: "Crucify him!" The rabbis had forsaken devotion, and were more interested in the clever splitting of theological hairs. Insensitive to the divine greatness in Jesus, they saw in him merely a rabble-rouser and a threat to their priestly authority.

Excessive dependence on material security is not compatible with divine faith. As God in the aspect of the Divine Mother once said to Paramhansa

Yogananda, "Those to whom I give too much, I do not give Myself."

What the Jews expected of a messiah was a great and powerful king, who would drive out the Romans and return Israel to its erstwhile glory. Instead, what they got was far more than a king: a very king of kings! The teachings of Jesus, the spiritual master, were destined eventually to conquer Rome. He never played the role others expected of him, however. What did he care for their expectations? It was God he served, not the idol of popular approval! He rejected a majestic role, and showed himself as unlike a warrior skilled in the martial arts as anyone could imagine. The priests especially, blinded by theological legalisms, were unable to appreciate his spiritual refinement. For only the pure in heart can appreciate, or even perceive, greatness in simplicity. Most people consider greatness to be demonstrated by worldly power. Jesus had come as God comes to the soul: *"like a thief in the night."** Not surprisingly, considering the rabbis' excessive intellectuality, *"They received him not."*

Nevertheless, the Jews at least *wanted* to abide by God's ways. For their rejection of that one whom God had sent to them, they suffered. The Law in which they believed so exactly had to exact its own price. Human beings cannot dictate what the law shall do. Every aspect of life is governed by divine law: the law of cause and effect, or *karma.* This law is infallible, whatever man's misunderstanding of it.

Whatever trials we receive in life are those, always,

---

* I Thessalonians 5:2.

which we attract to ourselves. In our souls we recognize the lessons we need to learn. Indeed, on deeper-than-conscious levels we invite them. The Jews' adherence to divine law was focused too narrowly. They were unaware of the law's balancing aspect, which is love. Therefore, they became scattered abroad.

Fortunately for them, however, they retained their commitment to divine truth. Moreover—to their credit, if also to their misfortune—they retained their strong will. They needed, as a people, to become more sensitive to the sweetness of divine love. God, however, never turns away from those who seek Him earnestly. The very tests the Jews received through the workings of divine law were meant to nudge them toward eventual wakefulness in Him. It was their destiny to suffer until they could declare with humility, as Jesus told them they must do: *"Blessed is he who comes in the name of the Lord."**

What the Jews needed, and still need as a people, was to learn the kindlier, more self-giving path of devotion. Today, instead of determinedly carving out a nation for themselves and claiming that it is theirs by divine right,† they need to understand that the true "promised land" was always inward, and only symbolized outwardly in a "land of milk and honey." Jesus pointed out this truth to them in the words, *"Neither shall they say, Lo here! or, lo there! for, behold, the kingdom of God is within you."* (Luke 17:21) It was to some

---

* Matthew 23:39.

† It is astonishing, in view of their belief in a divine destiny, how many Jews today declare themselves to be atheists.

extent, alas, his very insistence on this truth that made them reject him so violently.

It must be understood that the Jews were by no means unique in their confusion of spiritual with worldly glory. Christians—not all of them, certainly, just as, quite as certainly, not all Jews—have been as guilty. Majestic cathedrals have been raised so as to impress people with the majesty of the Christian religion. For centuries, popes schemed for worldly dominion. Christianity has traveled far, in these two thousand years since its inception, from the true "kingdom" promised in the Bible. Most Christians, while glorifying God outwardly with solemn processions and loud hymns of praise, have all but ignored His inner glory in their souls.

Paramhansa Yogananda once remarked, "Whenever I hear the expression 'Praise the Lord!' I get the mental impression of God as a rich, pampered lady wanting people's flattery!" God is above all pleased with humility, from which come restfulness of heart and expanded soul-identity. He never imposes on our free will, however. Christianity, early in its history, forsook the practice of inner communion, and concentrated instead on ceremonial pomp. Prelates gazed down with priestly self-importance on the bowed heads of their flocks, and everyone thought in terms of how their numbers might be increased. The divine law has no favorites. As Paramhansa Yogananda said, those who seek honor in the eyes of men shall receive dishonor. The relative unimportance of the priestly profession today is due not only to the materialism of this age, but to the self-importance of priests in former centuries.

Paramhansa Yogananda once visited a famous church in America. Gazing around him, he marveled that so much artistry had been deemed necessary for worshiping God. All at once, he heard the divine inner voice saying, "Would you rather have all this, and a congregation of thousands, but without Me? Or . . ." (he was shown a vision of himself seated on the ground under a tree, a handful of disciples gathered around him) ". . . would you rather have this, with Me?"

"Lord," he replied fervently, "I want Thee alone!" He often said to people, "I prefer a soul to a crowd, though I love crowds of souls!" By "souls" he meant lovers of God.

India, too, is not blind to the attractions of pomp. The abbots (called *mahamandaleshwars*) of great monasteries move in grand procession on the backs of elephants, surrounded by all the panoply of maharajas. Perhaps they justify this display in their own minds as a proclamation that God is the mightiest of all monarchs. Their motivation, however, seems no different from that of their priestly counterparts in the West.

It should be added that such ceremonial pomp is not the norm for India. The author had occasion in 1959 to meet the hereditary leader of millions of Hindus in South India. This man was simply garbed, seated unostentatiously on the ground beneath a palm tree. There he received rich and poor alike with equal kindness, and displayed concern for the wellbeing of them all. Although bound by his position to uphold the authority of the scriptures, his way of doing so was fresh, sometimes gently humorous, and always wise. Never pedantic, he demonstrated a complete lack of pretension.*

Architecturally, the spirit of India has been captured beautifully in a little shrine on a hilltop above the town of Ranchi. Its four sides are open to the panorama below; its roof is crowned with the simple Sanskrit character, AUM. The over-all impression is one of unassuming simplicity.

Many times in the history of religion has God appeared in response to the loving call of His devotees. In the Bhagavad Gita, Krishna states:

"Unborn, changeless, Lord of Creation and controller of My cosmic nature though I am, yet on entering Nature I am dressed in the cosmic garment of My own maya [delusion].

"O Bharata, whenever virtue declines and vice predominates, I incarnate on earth. Taking visible form, I come to destroy evil and re-establish virtue."

This passage speaks of the mystery of divine incarnation as a repeated event in history. In Christian theology, Christ's incarnation is considered unique; scholars therefore have given little energy to pondering how the event might have taken place; for them, it suffices that it was miraculous. In Hinduism, however, because the teaching is that God incarnates repeatedly,

---

* An example of the simplicity with which this man, the Shankaracharya of Kanchipuram, expressed himself was an answer he gave to the question, "How long does it take to escape delusion?" He replied, "That depends on how much one still has to overcome! When a nail protrudes from a board, you can't say how much of it is still left buried in the wood. All you know is that the way to get it out is to keep pulling at it. If you live earnestly for God, He will free you in His time from delusion's bondage."

greater interest has been shown in the actual process. Even so, most Hindus confuse Krishna's use of the personal pronoun, here, with his human personality, which they regard as an incarnation of God in the form of Vishnu. Vishnu, in his turn, is thought of as a personalized aspect of God. Only at the pinnacle of Hindu wisdom have great masters explained the process more exactly.

A divine incarnation, they say, is a manifestation of infinity. It is personal only in the sense that human beings receive personal benefits from it, and not because God is a person.

It may seem incredible that the Infinite Spirit should be concerned with mere human needs. Nevertheless, that Spirit—mostly through AUM, the Divine Mother aspect of God—has shown tender concern for mankind many times, and in many ways. The infinite Creator of countless galaxies is also the loving Father/Mother of each one of us. Moreover, He acts *through us* in His cosmic dream, and is therefore, in this sense, personal also. God answers every sincere prayer. Jesus Christ expressed God's concern for us in his well-known saying, *"The very hairs of your head are all numbered."* (Matthew 10:30) Indeed, omnipresence implies infinitesimal smallness as much as infinite immensity.

God has revealed Himself to saints in vision throughout history, in every religion. He has come to them as Father, Mother, Friend, Beloved—even, as we read in the account of Moses, as a burning bush. St. Jean Vianney, the humble parish priest of Ars, France, once declared, "If you only knew how much God loves you, you would die of joy!"

God has manifested Himself phenomenally on earth also, without actually taking physical birth. He has appeared to sincere devotees during moments of danger, when, unexpectedly, Someone came who steered them in the right direction. Seconds later, when they turned to express their thanks, their benefactor was nowhere to be found. Such stories as these may be dismissed as pious myths, but the author has heard accounts like them from people whose truthfulness was, in his opinion, beyond question.

Physical manifestations of this sort are transitory, however. The Lord would not controvert His law, which He Himself established. Nor would He bypass normal channels to incarnate specially in extra-legal perfection.

Visions, like all divine experiences, are means that He uses to inspire sincere devotees. No vision, however—and, by extension, no divine incarnation—is meant to limit people's devotion to that one form alone.

God already "incarnated," in a more impersonal sense, in the manifestation of His creation. He is manifested most openly of all in those saints who have realized Him. Sometimes a great master is born, in accordance with the divine will, who has already won soul-release from delusion in former incarnations.

The doctrine of reincarnation is not addressed in either Jewish or Christian theology. Both the Old and New Testaments teach it, however. Some of the references are obscure out of respect for those who were not ready for it. Nowadays, people have become more or less accustomed to hearing about it, and many accept it as, in the words of Hume, "the only explanation to which philosophy can hearken." An in-depth investigation of the doctrine at this point would divert us from our theme. Nevertheless, the biblical passages are so pertinent that a few examples, at least, must be included here. The following references should suffice for now.

In Matthew 17:12–13, Jesus says, *"Elias is come already, and they knew him not. . . . Then the disciples understood that he spake unto them of John the Baptist."* It had been prophesied that Elijah (Elias, in Greek) would come again. Christ's comment here is unequivocal.

Again, in Matthew 11:13–14, Jesus says, *"For all the prophets and the law prophesied until John* [the Baptist]. *And if ye will receive it, this is Elias* [Elijah], *which was for to come."* These words, "If ye will receive it," suggest that the concept of reincarnation was, for the people at that time, controversial.

In Genesis 9:6 we read, *"Whoso sheddeth man's blood, by man shall his blood be shed."* Paramhansa Yogananda pointed out that objective circumstances, and the "thwarting cross-currents of ego" as he called them, may prevent the law from being fulfilled immediately. It is not uncommon, in fact, for the boomerang effect of a sin to be activated in another lifetime. Assassins, for example, sometimes die of natural causes, and may seem thereby to have cheated the law. St. Paul, however, said, *"Be not deceived; God is not mocked: for whatsoever a man soweth, that shall he also reap."* (Galatians 6:7) The working of karmic law may be observed in deaths that, according to human understanding, have seemed unjust. Life is not unfair. The law, indeed, is infallible. The justice it exacts, however, takes no account of human expectations. It has nothing to prove. It simply *is*.

Again, in Job 1:21, we read, *"Naked came I out of my mother's womb, and naked shall I return thither."* Job could not have "returned naked" to the womb, except by becoming once more an embryo in the womb of his next mother.

Jesus, in the Book of Revelation, is quoted as saying, *"To him that overcometh will I grant to sit with me in my throne, **even as I also overcame, and am set down with my Father in his throne.**"* (Revelation 3:21)

Divine incarnations like Jesus are born in the full realization of God. Such masters, by their words, and by their magnetically uplifting influence, bring a "special dispensation" to mankind: the power of divine love, which alleviates the heavier exactions of karmic law. To sincere disciples of those great masters comes the grace of redemption.

No wave can express the vast ocean in its entirety. No human being, similarly—not even a divine incarnation—can define the totality of God. Were God Himself to incarnate directly, that manifestation would *of necessity* be limited also. Finitude can never define infinity.

Moreover, according to the divine plan our own consciousness must be expanded to infinity. Were the Supreme Spirit to materialize on earth and declare, "I am God!" it would suggest—amusingly—that God had stepped in just when a few of His children had attained perfection and were able to serve others in a divine way—when they were able, that is to say, to "come in

His name"—and announced: "I liked it when you all were bungling everything, but now that some of you are wise I think it's time I took control."

God acts through conscious instruments. This is true even in the case of each one of us. "God helps those who help themselves." It is God's will that we develop by our own effort, but with His help, and in attunement with His will.

A simple story tells it all. A certain Irish priest visited a farmer and was given a tour of his farm. When the tour ended, the priest exclaimed, "What a grand farm you and God have created here!" The farmer, pleased with this encomium, but not so happy at the thought of sharing the credit with anyone else, replied, "Father, you may be right, but you should hae seen this place when God had it all to His self!"

Without God, man can do nothing. Without God, we could not even breathe. God acts *through* us, not *around* us, to accomplish whatever we ourselves want to accomplish. If we do a job badly, it is because we have not attuned ourselves sensitively enough yet to His energy and wisdom. Nevertheless, whether consciously or unconsciously, we live by God's power all the time.

Is it not, indeed, more inspiring to think that salvation can come to us through one who, after prolonged effort, has achieved it himself? Is it not in the perfect fitness of things for us to learn from one who has walked the path himself and experienced its difficulties personally? one who, as a result of his own experience, is familiar with the pitfalls and shortcuts on the journey? What inspiration for our own striving would there be if guidance came to us from some Divine Manifestation, automatically omniscient and omnipotent, and bearing no laurels of a hard-won victory? Such a divine "Superman" would give us little incentive to work for our own redemption. Instead, more likely, we would depend on Him to do all the work for us.

If people's devotion were drawn to such a manifestation outwardly, they would not be inspired to seek God where alone He can be realized: in the Self. This was the truth Jesus emphasized in saying, *"The kingdom of God is within you."* All the scriptures proclaim the same truth. God must be sought first of all *within,* and only secondarily in Nature, in places of worship, and on pilgrimages. Even service to our fellowman is not an act of devotion, unless it is rendered with love for God. Lacking this attitude, the good that we accomplish cannot but be limited, for it will lack true spiritual power.

The author had a little set-to on this point several years ago with a Dean of the Church of England. The two of them were on a panel of speakers. The Dean, who spoke first, urged the members of the audience to dedicate themselves to social upliftment. In what can best be described as a diatribe he shouted angrily, "You've got to serve the poor! the prostitutes! the destitute!" Perhaps his intention was to persuade people that the church is still relevant in this age of heightened social awareness. The author's turn to speak came next. He surprised even himself—for normally he tries to support his fellow speakers—in saying, "Follow your own divine guidance. If in fact you feel that God wants you to render social service, then do so by all means, and with your whole heart. But don't do it merely because someone tells you to. Pick up leaves in the park if that is what you feel God wants of you. The Bhagavad Gita tells us it is better to fail in the performance of one's own duty than to succeed in the performance of someone else's." The author would have liked to add, but didn't: Religion lays a heavy burden of guilt on people when it tries to order their behavior, instead of encouraging them to seek their own guidance from God.*

The Dean, it remains to be admitted, was not happy.

Devotees—it remains to be said also, in the Dean's favor—should strive to express whatever degree of spiritual understanding they have achieved so far. Perhaps the Dean was being true to his own "inner understanding," though it is also possible that the opinion he expressed was simply an "in" thing to say.

Do your best, above all, to follow God's *will*. It is important to understand that perfection is not something that can ever be achieved outwardly. The most ideal Eden will always harbor the serpent of potential suffering. In serving others, then, think of them as altars of the divine. And try to serve them as a channel, yourself, of divine inspiration.

Above all, heed God's call within. Give to Him always, not to His creation, your first love.

Christians who truly love Jesus, and Hindus who

---

* Frank Laubach, the great Christian missionary, once campaigned in America to persuade more ministers of religion simply even to *mention* God in their sermons!

truly love Rama, Krishna, or some other divine incarnation, should realize that they honor those incarnations most truly who seek to realize the Christ consciousness *in themselves.* For Christ resides there eternally, in their own hearts.

CHAPTER FIVE

"The Only Begotten" —Why?

"And the Word was made flesh, and dwelt among us, (and we beheld his glory, the glory as of the only begotten of the Father,) full of grace and truth." (John 1:14)

Much of Christian theology is based on this statement that Christ is "the only begotten" Son of the Father. How ought the teaching to be accepted? Certainly, if interpreted too literally, it is unpalatable to non-Christians; everyone believes his own religion is at least the equal of any other.

Belief in the unique divinity of Jesus, the man, was conceived during a time when people could imagine God Himself as an old man with a long, white beard, seated somewhere in the sky on a throne of gold, and wholly preoccupied with the affairs of mankind. People in those days thought they lived in a cozy universe, with a flat earth situated at its center. Creation, they believed, took a mere six days to complete. The time span between the creation and the birth of Jesus Christ was actually calculated in the Nineteenth Century at 4004 years. An anthropomorphic concept of God was far more acceptable before the astronomical discoveries of Galileo than it is today, when we know the universe to be inconceivably vast. All the stars the naked eye can see belong, we are told, to only one out of countless billions of galaxies. As recently as 1918 it wasn't even known that other galaxies exist. In that year, the astronomer Hubble discovered the supposed "nebula" in Andromeda to be a complete star system—an "island universe," it was called. The horizons of human knowledge have continued to expand with the aid of increasingly powerful telescopes. The earth, far from holding a central position in the universe, spins its relatively insignificant way near the outer fringe of our "Milky Way" galaxy. Its age, moreover, is no longer computed in the thousands but in the billions of years.

It is not possible any longer for thinking people to assign to the Creator of this immensity the shape and mentality of a human being. Nor is it reasonable to believe in Jesus, the man, as the only offspring of such a Creator.

Paramhansa Yogananda explained that the expression, "the only begotten of the Father," refers not to the man, Jesus, but to the infinite Christ consciousness with which Jesus was identified in spirit. Jesus himself tried repeatedly to get people to see him not only in his human form, but in his subtle, divine reality. *"Where two or three are gathered together in my name,"* he said, *"there am I in the midst of them."* (Matthew 18:20) Had he been identified with his human body, he could not have promised to be simultaneously present in the midst of the thousands of congregations that would someday be gathered "in his name."

Jesus tried to get people to see in him not only his divine reality, but *their own highest potential.* In John 14:12 he declared, *"Verily, verily, I say unto you, He that believeth in me, the works that I do shall he do also; and greater works than these shall he do; because I go unto my Father."* And when the Jews, accusing him of blasphemy, said, *"Thou, being a man, makest thyself God,"* he answered, *"Is it not written in your law, I said, Ye are gods?"* (John 10:33,34)

The Christ consciousness is called "the only begotten" because its presence permeates the whole of cosmic creation. Christ is the unmoving stillness at the heart of every spinning atom.

God, the "Father" beyond creation, may be likened to a sun upon which all things depend for their existence. The Word, or Cosmic Vibration, may be compared, then, to the light emanating from that sun. And the Christ consciousness is the still "reflection" of that light on whatever is touched by it.

The sun, the light emanating from it, and the light's reflective power are aspects of one and the same thing. In this sense, although triune, they are one.

Our analogy is not perfect, of course. Analogies never are. For what we must suppose here is a sun that is conscious, and light that is conscious also. This vibration of conscious light has the power to condense itself into thoughts, which in turn manifest the illusion that is cosmic creation. The divine light is invisible to scientific instruments, but is beheld in the calmness of deep meditation.

The mind cannot but ask: How can vibrations produce anything as solid as a rock? The answer is that rapid vibrations often give the illusion of having substance. The band of movement created by the tines of a tuning fork may appear solid, if their vibration is broad enough. The blades of a propeller or of an electric fan, similarly, though distinct and separate when they are at rest, appear as a solid wheel when they rotate rapidly.

In similar fashion is the universe manifested. An infinite number of rapid vibrations give the illusion of being substantial. It is all an illusion. There are, in this case, no actual objects at all—no tines, no blades to be set in motion: There are only vibrations of thought, and of the thoughts that respond to those vibrations.

In the motionless Spirit, and in the primordial vibration of light and sound, and again in the motionless reflection of Spirit at the center of that vibration, are defined the Trinity: Father, Holy Ghost, and Son: AUM, TAT, SAT they are called in Sanskrit. Christian theology describes the Holy Trinity as "One in Three, and Three in One."

The Sanskrit writings, like the Christian, personalize these three aspects of God with a view to making them more comprehensible. They describe the Supreme Spirit as the masculine principle: the Father, in Christian tradition. AUM, or Cosmic Vibration, is the feminine principle, which "begets" the universe. AUM, therefore, in Hindu tradition, is the Divine Mother, who receives power from the Father to manifest cosmic creation. The union of these two principles produces the Son, "only begotten" because His reflection of the Spirit is omnipresent in creation.

This third aspect, the Christ consciousness, is not separate from the other two, but is an aspect of the same Truth. Cosmic Vibration would be incomplete without the stillness of Spirit subtly reflected at the center of all movement.* In order for cosmic creation to be truly vibratory, and not helter-skelter movement in all directions, it needs to be centered, not at some point in outer space, but at the heart of every vibration. From that center, movement begins. AUM is an emanation of Spirit, and reflects at its own center Spirit's motionless consciousness. Thus the Bible says, *"And the word was God."* For that vibration manifests, in its very motion, the motionless Divinity at its center.

At the heart of vibration there is stillness. The soul, on its journey to enlightenment, communes first with AUM, the Cosmic Mother, as sound or as light. With deeper meditation, it perceives AUM not only in the body, but throughout the universe. Next, it communes with the unmoving Christ consciousness in the body, then in omnipresence. When the soul realizes its oneness with the Christ consciousness, it perceives its deeper reality as the state of oneness with the "Father" beyond creation.

The author once asked Paramhansa Yogananda at what stage of realization one becomes a master. The guru replied, "To be a master, one must have attained Christ consciousness." A master can withdraw his consciousness into the Supreme Spirit at will. As long as he is active in the world, however, he manifests the Christ consciousness rather than the remote-seeming and watchful state of the Father.

People tend to react to any new truth with emotional resistance. Inertia prevents them from weighing the evidence impartially. They prefer their cocoon of

---

* A verse from a song of the author's reads, "Without silence, what is song?"

habit-woven opinions. Protestant Christians oppose worship of the Mother aspect of God, condemning it as "Roman Catholic idolatry." They point out, not unreasonably, that the scriptures don't describe Mary as being one with the Father. In condemning this "popish" dogma, however, they close themselves to God in His motherly aspect: Her sweet concern for humanity, Her kindness, Her compassion. The Jews similarly, in rejecting the idea that Jesus—to them a mere human being—could have achieved soul-union with God, reject that potential also within themselves. Thus, they deprive themselves of having a self-expansive relationship with Him.

It would help everyone to understand that the Mother aspect of God is not limited to a specific form, any more than God the Father has the form of an old man with a beard. Mary was the mother of Jesus, but she also symbolizes, and may be thought of as expressing, the Divine Mother of the universe, whose Son is the Infinite Christ. A Bengali saint of the Eighteenth Century, Ram Proshad, worshiped God in the aspect of Mother. He wrote, however, in a song that is still known to every peasant, "Oh, it's true, and thousands of scriptures declare it: She whom I worship as my Divine Mother is beyond all the limits of form!" (*Nirakara,* "without form.")

Jesus in his divine nature was one with the omnipresent Christ consciousness. Thus, meditation on the relationship of Jesus and Mary to each other can help Christians to attune themselves to a deep truth, but one that is otherwise difficult to conceptualize. Whatever be a person's belief regarding the spiritual stature of Mary, to worship her as the Infinite Mother is expansive, and cannot but touch the heart of the Divine Mother Herself. Those, also, who worship her human form, and don't think of her as formless and infinite, are not mistaken in doing so. The Madonna has appeared in countless visions to humble devotees whose hearts were pure. And whereas no scriptural teaching actually equates Mary with the Divine Mother of the universe, the mere fact that she was selected for the role of mother to Jesus Christ suggests that she must indeed have been a very exalted soul. Dogmas aside, then, it is perfectly acceptable, even for devout Hindus, to consider Mary a *conscious* instrument of the Motherhood of God.

Yogananda once referred, in the author's hearing, to a vision he had received of the Divine Mother. He had been inspired by that vision to write one of his most beautiful poems, "The Lost Two Black Eyes."* On that occasion he quoted the Divine Mother as saying to him, "I have suckled thee through the breasts of many mothers. This time, She who suckled thee was I, Myself." He repeated with emphasis, "This time, it was She, Herself."

Krishna says in the Bhagavad Gita, *"In whatsoever form people worship Me, I Myself accept their offering."* Such worship is not idolatry. Idolatry means worship with selfish motive instead of offering one's self to God with expansive aspiration. To worship even a stone is

---

* The author wrote a song inspired in turn by that poem, and by his guru's deep love for the Divine Mother. The song is called, "Dark Eyes." Its melody was later recorded by the famed Irish harpist Derek Bell.

not idolatrous if, through that symbol, one invokes God, and views the stone as a *reminder* of the Infinite Lord. To reject images outright in the name of worshiping only God is to be left with an arid heart, and a mind drifting on a dark sea, directionless, through fogs of abstraction.

Guru Nanak, the first of the Sikh gurus, pointed out to Muslims that, despite their belief in rejecting form altogether, they bow four times daily to Mecca, the birthplace of Mohammed. "Don't you see?" he remonstrated with them, "as human beings you cannot even conceptualize formlessness!" We are surrounded constantly by forms. Abstract concepts do not come naturally to the human mind. The soul goes beyond form when it enters the higher ecstatic states, but until then, to deny form in favor of abstraction is like stepping off a cliff into nothingness.

Idolatry is of the mind; it is not images placed on an altar. Idolatry is of the heart especially, for there it is that our desires are churned, like milk, to produce the butter of outward fulfillment. In this sense, clearly, few human beings—which is to say also, few Muslims—are not idolaters!

Physical forms, on the other hand, can help to inspire devotion to God. God doesn't much care that our theology be exact, any more than the parents of a little girl care much that the love she displays for her dolls is not logical. The important thing is that she develop her ability to love. And the important thing for one who would *know* God rather than merely theorize about Him is to develop devotion. Attempts to define God exactly are doomed to failure in any case! It is devotion that supplies the wings the soul needs, to rise above egoic limitations.

In Christianity today there is a noteworthy movement that emphasizes the need for developing a personal relationship with Jesus Christ. The adherents of this movement do not reject church affiliation, nor Bible study, but they claim that if one doesn't also seek a personal relationship with Jesus he is missing the true meaning of Christianity. This movement represents an important step toward emerging from the stone-enclosure of *Churchianity* into the experience of *Christianity* as a living religion. Jesus constantly urged his disciples to attune themselves to his spirit. He also discouraged mere doctrinal squabbling. Only by direct experience can one attain wisdom. Indeed, lacking inner experience, one can twist scripture itself to conform with any bizarre notion one fancies. "Even the devil," as the saying goes, "quotes the scriptures."

Attunement with Christ must be sought more and more deeply in the silence of meditation. It is not enough to seek personal blessings for oneself and one's loved ones. The fulfillment of divine love comes from the utter gift of one's self. Jesus, like all true masters, represents a bridge to Christ consciousness. If, in our prayers, we clutch him to ourselves,* what this means is that we want him to cross over to our side of the

---

* This is a natural devotional sentiment. In a much-loved Bengali song to Krishna, *"Gokula Chandra,"* Radha, his greatest woman devotee, sings, "Although I know my Beloved's consciousness is as infinite as the ocean, still, if I find him, I will bind him with my sari and drag him home with me!" To hold him to oneself is good, but only if in so doing we do as Radha did: merge our consciousness entirely in him.

ravine: to relate to us as human beings, rather than to our souls. The mission of every master, however, is not to make our human lives more comfortable. As Jesus put it, *"Think not that I am come to bring peace on earth; I came not to bring peace, but a sword."* (Matthew 10:34) Using the sword of discrimination, we must sever the Gordian knot of delusion itself!

Consider, again: If your baby is playing in a mud puddle, won't you at once lift him out of it? It would be a strange parent indeed who decided to clean up the puddle instead, so as to make it more comfortable!

If we want truly to know God, we must raise our hands to Him and allow Him to lift us out of our mud puddle of worldly attachment. We must cross over to His side of the ravine, and leave behind us forever the land of egoic limitations.

Self-transformation is, of course, far more difficult than crossing a bridge! Indeed, our spiritual tests begin in earnest only when we decide to give our lives entirely to God! Satan tries to hold us, Prodigal Sons that we've been, on this side of the chasm. Tests are also God's way of asking us, "Are you ready to forsake everything for Me alone?"

The first chapter of the Gospel of St. John states that those who receive Christ are also given *power* "to become the sons of God." The noun here is plural: "sons." Divine Sonship is the potential of all souls.

We saw in the last chapter the Bhagavad Gita's description of the Supreme Spirit as unborn, changeless, and cosmic—*"dressed in the garment"* of universal appearances. Krishna states in Chapter Seven that the manifested universe is the Spirit's "lower" aspect. In

Its "higher" aspect, he says, the Spirit is the true Self of all beings. *"O Arjuna, my higher nature is . . . the self-conscious life principle that sustains the [entire] cosmos."* This is the "Krishna," or Christ consciousness: the motionless reflection of God, immanent in all creation.

Krishna, like *Christ,* is not a name, but a title. Many words in other languages have their origins in Sanskrit. The author recalls a Roman Catholic priest once challenging him in India with the question, "What do you mean, when you call these Indian gurus, 'saints'?"

"My reference," the author replied, "is to the Sanskrit word, *sant,* from which our word *'saint'* is derived." (Thus was nipped in the bud an invitation to an argument!) The same etymological connection exists between Krishna and Christ—or, in the original Greek word, *Christos.* Indian teachers often emphasize this connection by transliterating *Krishna* as *Christna.* The two words are pronounced almost identically.

Krishna is the *Kutastha Chaitanya,* the unmoving divine consciousness present throughout the universe. It is this consciousness which is born on earth in great Saviors such as Jesus Christ, Gautama Buddha (the "Enlightened One"), and Krishna.

Paramhansa Yogananda gave the following explanation of the stages of spiritual awakening: A master, having shed every vestige of ego, merges his consciousness in God. At this point he becomes what the Indian scriptures term a *jivan mukta:* one who is free in spirit even though living in a physical body. Such a great soul, no longer trapped in delusion, has won release from the bondage of desire. His reality, now, is God alone.

A *jivan mukta* still carries in his subconscious,

however, the memories of his past, ego-motivated deeds. These memories must be expunged also, released into cosmic consciousness. The *jivan mukta* must realize that the Infinite Dreamer has ever resided at the heart of his human actions. He was their central reality, merely obscured by egoic ignorance.

That divine presence must be realized in even the most mundane memory. Even criminal actions are but veils the ego casts over its inherent divinity. An enlightened master, having released into soul-freedom the last of his karmic memories, becomes a *param mukta,* or fully liberated soul. Such freedom is rarely achieved on this material plane of existence, but it does occur.

When a fully liberated master is reborn on earth, he comes in response to humanity's spiritual needs. In this case, he is an *avatar,* or divine incarnation. Through him, God radiates a power greater than even that of a *param mukta.* One who is fully liberated in this life can save his direct disciples, but a divine incarnation can bring to God as many as come to him with devotion.

At this point it may be asked, "Why even go to lesser saints, if one can tune in to an *avatar?*" The answer is that every channel of truth deserves our reverence, in God's name. Be grateful to God for whatever He sends you. At the same time, seek direct contact with Him above all, through any human channel He sends. He will give to you according to your spiritual needs. It is His decision what help He will send you, and when. In the normal course of events, God subtly leads the beginner to books, then to someone who can set him on a spiritual course in life. *Avatar*s are very few. Even to approach them in spirit usually requires personal contact with a living channel. Any saint, moreover, who has attained the state of *jivan mukta* is eminently fit to be a true, or *sat,* guru; his limitation lies only in the number of souls he can bring to God.

An ancient saying puts it perfectly: "When the disciple is ready, the guru appears."

An *avatar*'s blessings are not limited by his physical presence. Any devotee of Jesus Christ, for instance, can as surely commune with him today as he could have two thousand years ago, while Jesus still lived on earth. One who wants to "have his life" in Jesus Christ will probably be guided for training, in time, to a living and relatively advanced disciple of Jesus Christ. It is always important in any case to have at least one contact with a living channel.

Finally, it will be helpful for abstract teachings like these to be given the immediacy of daily practice. Whatever you do, try in every thought and action to express inner, divine inspiration. Visualize grace as flowing through you from AUM, the Holy Ghost or Divine Mother.

The best way to express this inspiration is to listen inwardly to AUM, first, or to listen *for* it if you cannot yet hear it. Listen in the right ear, which is the positive side of the body. When you hear that sound, thrilling to the soul, expand your consciousness with it until it fills your brain, then your entire body. Your creative efforts will become attuned to the highest source of inspiration, and will no longer merely express your own personal tastes and feelings.

A further practice is to feel at the center of every movement, whether physical or mental, the stillness of Christ consciousness. By dwelling on this thought of stillness, you will find yourself becoming more aware of the inspiration that flows from AUM. Expand your consciousness with AUM, in the stillness of Christ, until the divine consciousness permeates your whole being.

A technique for attaining this inner stillness is mentally to watch your breath. Concentrate on the stillness *at the center of* the breathing process. Don't control your breathing, but particularly enjoy the pauses between the breaths. Be aware of the eternal stillness, of the Christ consciousness at the center of this gentle movement, until the pauses, like a pendulum slowly coming to rest, are united in breathlessness. In this way, you will deepen your attunement with the Only Begotten, in which, you will discover, you live and have your eternal being!

CHAPTER SIX

Receptivity: the Key to Spiritual Development

"But as many as received him, to them gave he power to become the sons of God." Thus states the Gospel of St. John, Chapter 1, Verse 12.

We have discussed this verse before as it relates to the meaning of the expression, "sons of God." The verse contains other vitally important teachings for the spiritual seeker. One of these is the first phrase, "as many as *received* him." Another is the concept that one needs *power* to become a son of God. Both concepts are central to the teachings of Jesus Christ.

What is the meaning of those first words, *"received* him"? The average Christian takes them simply to mean that, in order to be saved, one must *accept* Jesus Christ as his only Savior. Acceptance, however, implies only a mental attitude and, usually, passivity. It doesn't imply the kind of soul-dedication one would think necessary for attracting divine power. Acceptance may imply belief, but not that dynamic faith which "can move mountains." To say of someone, "I believe in him," suggests that we expect good of him, but not that we would necessarily give him the key to our treasure chest. He must demonstrate himself reliable in the face of life's tests before we can say with conviction, "I have *faith* in him."

For centuries, acceptance was all that was required of a Christian. *"Credo!*—I believe!" Even today, this statement is most people's declaration of faith. St. Paul said, of faith, that it is *"the evidence of things not seen."** If faith is *evidence,* then it cannot be blind. It must be the fruit of some actual experience. Belief that hasn't been tested by experience is vulnerable. If, for example, people only believe in the Crucifixion as an atonement for the sins of mankind, they have nothing concrete on which to rest their faith. History offers only weak support for that claim. During the first centuries of the Christian era, mankind seems on the whole to have become more hardened than ever in sin. (Think of the blood-lust at the "games" in the Roman Colosseum.) Even so-called "believers" do not seem, by their behavior, to have become exactly "sons of God." (Think of the cruelty of the Spanish Inquisition, and of the Salem witch hunts.) Christian history is not unqualifiedly edifying, though unquestionably it has affected millions of lives for the better.

On the other hand, there have been Christians in every century who clearly *did* receive Christ—not mentally only, but with their entire being. These people were the saints. Other Christians of their times, to whom religion meant the simple declaration, "I believe," resented and sometimes persecuted them. Tepid "faith" always views sanctity as a silent reproach—indeed, as an embarrassment—to itself.

* Hebrews 11:1.

People who lack any personal desire for spiritual transformation often consider it even presumptuous for others to be more devout than themselves. Such people think of Jesus as one who mixed with the common people—who identified with them, in other words, and with whom they could identify in return.

"Normal" Christians like these, who want to be good but not *too* good—or, like St. Augustine, "not yet"—respond instinctively to any saints they have the inconvenience to meet by denouncing them as hypocrites, or—if that mud won't stick to the wall—as madmen or fanatics. Only after a saint has been safely dead for years does his church, sometimes, praise him as holy. Usually, in that case, it claims credit for his holiness—not wholly unjustifiably, moreover, since persecution is known to be a path to sanctity. The broad highway of religion is too noisy for anyone in that jostling throng to heed Christ's call to "receive him" within, in the soul.

People no longer view belief of any kind with the trust they once did. Too many concepts, formerly accepted as valid, have been disproved by modern science. Some of them were mentioned in the last chapter: the relative smallness of the universe; the earth's central position in the universe; the relatively recent creation of the earth; its flatness. In many ways, science continues to contradict the very evidence of our senses. It has found, for instance, that the density of matter is only an illusion. The space between the atoms of our bodies is as great, relatively speaking, as that which separates the stars. Since Darwin's publication, in 1859, of his book, *The Origin of Species,* more and more people have come to ask themselves, Is there even a meaning in life, in evolution, in *anything?* Members of non-Christian religions, moreover, whom believing Christians once considered pagans, have been found on association with them to be no more pagan than themselves. While there have been Christian saints, by every proof of sanctity there have been great saints in other religions as well.

Thus, people now view belief itself—religious as well as mundane—with skepticism. What they demand are proofs.

Science has taught us to view dogmatism, especially, with caution. It has taught us to submit hypothetical claims to the test of experimentation—or, where human life is concerned, of experience. Jesus himself encouraged such an attitude. *"By their fruits ye shall know them,"* he said. (Matthew 7:20) St. John said also, *"Test the spirits, to see whether they are from God."* (I John 4:1) To "receive" Christ doesn't mean merely believing in him; it means to *experience* his presence inwardly.

We expect scientific hypotheses to be either proved or disproved. We expect proof also, or at least evidence, in matters of common interest. The taste of a banana, for instance, can be known only by tasting it. It isn't enough to read definitions of its taste. Religious claims need to be submitted to similar tests. If they can't be tested directly by experience, then they ought at least to be tested indirectly by an appeal to comparable experiences.

Do we know whether receiving Christ will give us the power to become sons of God? Perhaps not, but certainly we can see whether receiving him won't give us a degree of inspiration we have never experienced before. A simple experiment could be tried: For one week, or even just for one day, include Christ *minute-by-minute* in your life. Share with him your thoughts, your feelings, your actions, even your most ordinary activities such as walking, eating, and breathing. You may find it helpful to be in seclusion for this experiment, in order to give it your fullest attention. At the end of this period, see whether you haven't experienced some significant change in yourself. Have you ever in your life succeeded in accomplishing anything as meaningful by positive affirmations and resolutions? The question is rhetorical; its answer will be self-evident.

It may not be possible to test every religious teaching directly, but most of them can at least be tested "comparably." Consider the common belief in life's continuance after death. Do heaven and hell really exist? Do souls actually live in them? The evidence may be tenuous, but comparable realities can be tested easily. A person who is generous minded, for example, experiences an inner "heaven" of peace and happiness. One, on the other hand, who is mean spirited builds for himself an inner "hell" of unhappiness, no matter how urgently he tries to justify himself. So infallibly does human life demonstrate these facts that the experiential approach to religious doctrines ought to have been considered long ago. Instead, classical theology has been constructed on the cloudlike framework of carefully reasoned abstractions.

Certain religious claims, of course, are not susceptible

to testing: for example, the dogma of the assumption of the Virgin Mary into heaven. Scholastic theologians once were wont to spread themselves on such subjects. This claim, however, and others like it, no matter how devoutly one believes in them, are not fundamental to spiritual faith. If anything, indeed, they impede attempts to strengthen one's belief.

"I believe!" is, in fact, a meaningless statement. Jesus Christ said to Nicodemus, *"Verily, verily . . . We speak that we do know, and testify that we have seen."* (John 3:11) What about us, when we say, "I believe"? Would we renounce everything we own and are for that belief? If not, we cannot truthfully say that we *know.* Probably, we don't even really believe.

Paramhansa Yogananda chuckled over a story about a famous evangelist, Billy Sunday, who appeared after death at the "pearly gates" confident of being received with joyful cries of welcome. St. Peter, however, on consulting his Book of Life, announced, "I'm sorry, I don't find your name listed here." The evangelist was outraged. "Say, what about all those thousands of souls I sent up here?" St. Peter consulted his book again, then replied, "You may have sent them, but none have arrived!"

Doesn't the statement, "I accept Jesus as my personal Savior!" have a certain ring of presumption to it? Whether or not we accept him, the important question remains: Does he accept *us?* The love of Christ is infinite, but it is not void of discrimination. As Jesus put it, *"Not every one that saith unto me, Lord, Lord, shall enter into the kingdom of heaven; but he that doeth the will of my Father which is in Heaven."* (Matthew 7:21)

Shouting our beliefs from the housetops is no proof of anything. Often, indeed, it is the emotional supporters of a cause who give it a bad name. What proof is it to cry "Hallelujah!" every time a preacher declares something of which we approve? If we announce, "In Christ Jesus I am saved!" we should remember the words of Jesus himself, *"By their fruits ye shall know them."* What are the actual fruits of our belief? Are we more peaceful, loving, forgiving of others, non-attached to the things of this world? To be saved means, after all, to be saved from *something.* Saved, then, from what? from hell? If anyone gives you that answer, ask him: "Are you free from the manifest hells of earth, such as anger, jealousy, pride, and lust?"

"With all thy getting, get understanding," says the Bible.* The contrast between right and wrong ways of "receiving" Christ was well exemplified in the story of Martha and Mary. Jesus reprimanded Martha for her restlessness, but praised Mary, who was quietly absorbing his vibrations of peace and love.

To *receive* Christ means to *tune in* to the Christ consciousness. That consciousness, as we have seen, is omnipresent; it is with us always. Christ consciousness is the potential rest point at the center of all conscious vibration. It is potentially manifest in every pause in activity: at the moment a wave crests, and at its depth, just before it begins its next rise. To "receive Christ" means to be aware of him as what might be called "the stillness at the heart of stillness."

"If stillness is the issue," some may ask, "why don't we simply try to still our minds? Do we need religion

---

* Proverbs 4:7.

to accomplish that?" Well, try it! You may not find it so easy to do. Even so, the point might be valid were stillness the whole issue. The Bible itself tells us, *"Be still, and know that I am God."* (Psalms 46:10) Many people, especially nowadays, imagine that understanding is only a matter of getting a right mental "handle" on things. St. John, however, wrote of the need, in addition, to receive *power*. In Christ lies the power to create the universe. It takes power to become a son of God! Such power cannot be attained by merely viewing things in a fresh light. Divine power is the perspective that accompanies greatly heightened awareness.

No one can achieve sainthood if he clings to his accustomed, human state of awareness. And what concerns us here is not ordinary goodness, but *sainthood*. Millions of people call themselves Christians—or Hindus or Buddhists or Moslems or Jews—but if their devotion is lackluster, and diluted by worldly desires, they do not yet deserve to be identified with those high designations. There are few true saints anywhere, and in any religion. Most self-described Christians, though well-meaning, could not *receive* Christ if they wanted to: They are too busy "receiving" so much else!

It is no easy task to transcend one's individuality. And what is asked of those who would "receive" Christ is self-transcendence. Most people think, "This collection of thoughts, opinions, likes and dislikes, talents, and possessions is who I am." To love God truly means to shatter such self-definitions. We must repeat constantly in our hearts, and mean it fervently, "All that I have, Lord, and all that I am is Thine alone!"

Alas for noble intentions! Individuality is deeply

rooted in human consciousness. We identify ourselves with our bodies and personalities. Most of all, we identify ourselves with this human "I." This sense of selfhood defines us, or so we imagine, as we shall always be. Moreover—just see the irony of it!—our belief is not intrinsically mistaken. For although this little self, the ego, separates us from the ocean of life around us, that very thought, "I," is fundamental to infinity itself. Paramhansa Yogananda described it in his poem "Samadhi" as, "Ever-present, all-flowing I, I, everywhere." The thought, "I," is implanted in every sentient being by God, the one true Self in existence.

If we would truly receive Christ, we must, as we saw in the last chapter, cross the bridge over the chasm that separates our egos from divine consciousness. To "receive" Christ means to absorb him into ourselves, and to allow him to transform us into Himself. Therefore Jesus said, *Whosoever will save his life shall lose it: but whosoever will lose his life for my sake, the same shall save it.* (Luke 9:24) In calm, determined, but never presumptuous self-giving lies the secret of soul-receptivity. In giving ourselves to God, nothing in the end is lost, and everything is gained including eternal life.

How can "receiving him" give us *power* to "become the sons of God"? The answer is that what we receive is his consciousness. Paramhansa Yogananda explained this point further: A little cup, he said, cannot contain the whole ocean: Only an immense basin of land can do that. Our consciousness must expand to become a receptacle for Infinity. We must ourselves, in other words, become infinite. The "power" to know God is the power of self-expansion to infinity.

What, again, is the power of receptivity? It is the gift of love. As Jesus said, *"Blessed are the pure in heart, for they shall see God."* In pure love the heart's feelings are no longer centered in oneself, but in the object of one's love. We assume to ourselves the characteristics of those we love. Actually, what we attract is not so much those characteristics themselves, but the state of consciousness, the *magnetic quality* of each of them. If we love a Christlike master, we may think at first that it is him (or her) we love, as a person. In our attunement, however, we receive the master's state of consciousness, the salient features of which are, first, a complete lack of ego, and, second, divine love, which fills the emptiness. The magnetism emanated by a master lifts his disciples above their egos. Once ego-limitation has been demolished by selfless love, nothing remains to prevent self-awareness from expanding to infinity.

Love is the greatest power in the universe. Never coercive, its compelling force is magnetic. What it awakens in us is a response of sympathetic assent. By the interchange of love between the soul and God, the soul absorbs itself in infinite love.

A bar of steel, in proximity to one that is magnetized, develops magnetism itself. Attunement to the consciousness of a Christlike master, similarly, develops magnetic love in the disciple. Thus, the statement, "to all those who received him," refers not only to keeping oneself impersonally open to infinite consciousness, but also to receiving *the magnetic influence of love* that emanates from a Christlike guru.

A single spark may start a forest fire. The smallest

step toward God can be a beginning in the process of soul-awakening. The Bhagavad Gita says, *"To him who offers Me even a flower or a leaf with devotion, I Myself come and receive his offering."* The smallest expression of pure love can be the spark that ignites a fire of devotion which ultimately consumes the forest of our desires and leaves our consciousness free to soar untrammeled in infinite skies.

Meanwhile, though we find ourselves separated from divine awareness by the yawning chasm of our self-interest, if we will "receive" Christ even as our divine friend, in deepening attunement with him, our consciousness will gradually be transformed into his own.

This is what Jesus meant when he requested baptism of John the Baptist. John demurred that he was unworthy, for the spiritual state of Jesus was higher than his own. Paramhansa Yogananda explained the sublime meaning of that event. Despite John's lower state of Self-realization, he was, from former incarnations, the guru of Jesus. John the Baptist had been, as we saw earlier, the prophet Elijah (Elias, in the Greek). And Jesus was Elisha, the disciple of Elijah. Therefore Jesus answered, *"Suffer it to be so now: for **thus it becometh us to fulfill all righteousness.**"* (Matthew 3:15)

The guru's divine responsibility is to lift his disciples to oneness with God, and not—as ignorant people imagine—to keep them subject to his own authority. Sometimes it happens, as it did in the case of Jesus and John, that a disciple becomes more highly advanced than his guru. The bond of divine friendship between them, however, is eternal. In that spirit, Jesus lovingly honored John as the source of his own enlightenment.

The disciple, by attuning himself to the "ray" of his guru's love, receives the guru's magnetism in return. This is the way to God; there is no other. Jesus therefore said, *"I am the way, the truth, and the life: no man cometh unto the Father, but by me."** His reference was not to his human self, but to divine love, of which he was an expression, and to the need for attuning oneself to that love.

God's love is given equally to all. Never imposing on the free will of anyone, He guides us toward our final liberation through life's various stages: the disillusionment, for example, that comes when wrong desires are fulfilled; the deep inner satisfaction that accompanies generous thoughts and actions; books and lesser teachers, when the first craving awakens for understanding; and, finally, through the guidance and blessings of a Christlike master, when the heart's desire for God grows deeply sincere. A master is a clear channel for God's love. In that ray he bestows soul-expansion on his disciples, an expansion of awareness they, on their own, could not even conceptualize adequately. The deeper one's attunement to this channel, the more clearly one realizes himself, too, to be a son of God.

There is a sequel to the Gospel quotation in this chapter. The verse begins, *"But as many as received him, to them gave he power to become the sons of God"*; it ends, **"even to them that believe on his name."** True belief, we have seen, means not passive acceptance, but a positive commitment of faith. Faith, here, is the willing-

---

* John 14:6.

ness to receive Christ into the very shadowlands of one's being. What, then, of the phrase, "even to them that believe *on his name*"? Belief is the necessary prelude to seeking the experience of Christ's presence. It means that Christ's power is available not only to those who knew Jesus in the flesh, but to all who, in future, would attune themselves to his spirit. Christ's gift of the power to know God need not, cannot, and never has been personal.

The Bhagavad Gita makes the same promise, using the personal pronoun also in reference to both the Infinite Spirit and Krishna as the human channel for the Spirit. *"To those who are ever attached to Me, and who worship Me with love, I impart discernment, by means of which they attain Me. Out of my love for them, I, the Divine within them, set alight in them the radiant lamp of wisdom, thereby dispelling the darkness of their ignorance."* (Chapter 10, Stanzas 10, 11) Divine power, here again, is shown as the one essential for finding God. Human striving alone cannot lift us to the divine realms. God's wisdom and love are two aspects of the same truth: The fruit of true love is wisdom; the essence of true wisdom is love.

Many yoga students make the mistake of thinking they need only will power. They expect by breathing exercises and physical postures to attain cosmic consciousness. Is God, then, some alpine peak to be "conquered" with mountaineering bravado? This is hardly the teaching of yoga! Ego-motivated yoga students lack understanding of their own teaching. Laboriously scaling the heights of self-conceit, instead of soaring on wings of divine love, they gaze about them in a spirit of aloof austerity, and see not their pride as but a dead tree, its brittle branches held self-importantly aloft to be snapped off by the fierce winds of *maya*. How different, their attitude, from the one Jesus Christ and all great masters advise, to become "like little children."

The essence of spiritual development is, by deep calmness, humility, and love to increase our *receptivity*. Yoga practice is in this respect no different from other spiritual practices. Its difference lies in its practicality, and in the awareness it develops of subtle energy currents in the body. This awareness helps one to attune himself to the inner flow of divine grace, enabling him to cooperate with that flow which, otherwise, he might find himself resisting in sheer surprise, owing to his ignorance of it, or to any fear he may have of the unknown.

The work of the spiritual aspirant is, above all, to *receive* God. The Bhagavad Gita tells us how. To "receive" God, Krishna says, we must become attached to Him, relinquishing attachment to the world. We must worship Him with devotion, to rid our hearts of delusive infatuation. We must invite His light into ourselves, and ask it to illuminate the darkest corners of our consciousness. Above all, we must surrender to the power of His love.

Fully to embrace divine love takes heroic courage. Yet only in doing so can we find the fulfillment we all seek in life. Jesus said, *"Seek ye first the kingdom of God, and his righteousness; and all these things shall be added unto you."* (Matthew 6:33)

We can develop divine magnetism by attuning ourselves to God's love, which flows to us consciously through the living channel of a true guru. By perfect receptivity to that savior, we can become—like Jesus Christ and like every great master—sons of God.

CHAPTER SEVEN

Divine Grace vs. Divine Law

This passage is from the Gospel of St. John, Chapter 1, Verse 17:

"The law was given by Moses, but grace and truth came by Jesus Christ."

At the time when God gave the law to Moses, the need was for the tribes of Israel, recently liberated from four centuries of slavery in Egypt, to be molded into a single, homogeneous nation. Basically, the Ten Commandments and the six hundred more general laws were moral guidelines for a God-fearing people. It was as if God had said to them through Moses, "You, as a nation, have chosen to live according to My ways. I now give you rules by which you can be pleasing to Me."

Some of the laws and Commandments can be interpreted more inwardly also. For example, *"Thou shalt have no other gods before me"* is an injunction not only against paganism, but against worldly attachments and desires. These, indeed, are mankind's real idols, regardless of any images people place on their altars. As Jesus said, *"Where your treasure is, there will your heart be also."* (Matthew 6:21) God was telling the Jews, "Give your love to Me alone." Perfect self-offering is possible only in deep communion with the Lord.

In our spiritual evolution, outward observances normally precede inward ones. A person first learns to fear and obey God. Only gradually does he come to love Him.

The Jews took the step, which was an unusual one for those times, of accepting God, not mammon, as their Lord. They resolved to live for Him faithfully and to abide by His law. Thus, Moses gave them a set of disciplinary rules to help them to live in the ways of "righteousness." They were shown how, in living by them, to attune themselves to the divine will.

The history of the many failures of the Jewish people to live by that will, and of their repeated mutinies against it, is not so much a story of faithlessness as of a whole people struggling to emerge from the widespread spiritual ignorance of their times. They were not always successful in that effort. Yet they were a stubborn people: Anyone with strong spiritual inclinations has to be, for it takes will power to dedicate oneself to high principles and to God. Again and again the Jews, unfortunately for them, refused to listen to the prophets sent to them by God in answer to their own plea. It was this tendency in them that Jesus lamented when he cried, *"O Jerusalem, Jerusalem, which kills the prophets, and stones them that are sent unto thee; how often would I have gathered thy children together, as a hen gathers her brood under her wings, and you would not!"*

He added, *"Behold, your house is left unto you desolate: and verily I say unto you, Ye shall not see me, until the time come when ye shall say, Blessed is he that cometh in the name of the Lord."* (Luke 13:34,35) He was speaking here not as Jesus, the individual, but as Christ, the omnipresent reflection of God in the universe.

The most important step on the spiritual path is to make oneself receptive to divine guidance. It is already a great and noble beginning to decide to live by high principles; in this decision the Jews were far ahead of most peoples of their time. They took the next step also, of recognizing that living for God is the highest principle. They *chose* God. For this reason, as the Bible states, God chose them. The age in which they lived, however, was spiritually unaware. The Jewish national character was egoically defiant. Their next step would have been to welcome practical spiritual guidance—not only through written laws, but through enlightened sages who themselves were in tune with God's will. For this step the Jews, as a people, were not ready.

Their reluctance is understandable. It is always more pleasant to have one's wishes and opinions mirrored back to one, however indirectly. People with a religious bent often seek such a mirror in scripture, which they can explain according to their own convenience. (It cannot answer back!) When the ground seems safe, they may also seek the counsel of priests or pastors, who, like most people, tend to endorse the delusions of their times. Even to seek guidance from the lives of saints may be more convenient after they've been safely dead for some years. Still-living saints, in this respect, are likely to mirror back to people the things they'd rather not see. Paramhansa Yogananda in *Autobiography of a Yogi* quoted a great yogi as saying,

109

"Worldly people do not like the candor which shatters their delusions. Saints are not only rare but disconcerting. Even in scripture, they are often found embarrassing!"

Perhaps the mission of Jesus was only to the Jews, and not to other peoples as well, for to the woman of Samaria he said, *"Salvation is of the Jews."* (John 4:22) More probably, however, those words were spoken to test her, for shortly thereafter she, and many others from her city, accepted Jesus as the Messiah. Prophecy had made it clear, however, and so did unfolding circumstances, that Jesus Christ's mission would not be fulfilled, as it might have been, in the spiritual molding of his people. Instead, it had to be to the whole world.

The Jewish people had arrived at a karmic crossroads. Soon they would be dispersed as a nation. They might have been spared that fate, had they turned within spiritually as Jesus tried to get them to do. The challenge they faced was to waken to God's love, and not merely to reaffirm their status as a nation. Jesus brought them what their souls needed, not what their egos wanted. He had come to help them understand that their original "contract" with God was primarily inward. Alas, they rejected his message. Had they heeded him; had they even repented and followed him after the Crucifixion; their diaspora, if still it needed to happen, could have become a generous and loving mission to the world instead of bringing them the suffering which made them cry annually for centuries, "Next year: Jerusalem!"

Instead, the divine commission had to go to others. Unfortunately, other peoples were even less prepared for Christ's teaching of divine love. But at least they didn't obstruct his mission with the prideful thought, "This is ancient teaching to us: We've known it for centuries!"

Referring to the Jews' need for continuing spiritual refinement, Jesus once answered his critics, *"For the hardness of your heart [Moses] wrote this precept."* (Mark 10:5)

Jesus came to teach the Jewish people the true meaning of freedom: not liberation from outer slavery such as they'd endured in Egypt and in Babylon, and were enduring to a lesser degree under Roman rule, but freedom from the tyranny of delusion: from material desires and attachments, from the demands of an arrogant and self-affirming ego.

Of the numerous laws of Judaism, two were, Jesus said, of paramount importance: *"Thou shalt love the Lord thy God with all thy heart, and with all thy soul, and with all thy mind, and with all thy strength,"* and, *"Thou shalt love thy neighbor as thyself,"* (Mark 12:30–31) the second being, he said, *"like unto"* the first.

Several times during his mission he made it clear that it was not his purpose to break with Jewish tradition. We have already seen how he told people, in Matthew 5:17, *"Think not that I am come to destroy the law, or the prophets: I am not come to destroy, but to fulfill."* He hadn't come to establish a new religion, but only to add to the old one the refinement of love, to help the Jewish people to live more consciously in God's grace.

Love supports the law. Yet love also is above the law,

and is the ultimate purpose of the law. Jesus' teaching was not for people who clung to the ancient strictures too tenaciously,* but for those who understood the need for grace, and for an *inward perception* of truth.

The line of development from Judaism to Christianity was not from divine law to devotional love. That would have been the fulfillment of its higher destiny. Unfortunately, God's light cannot reach human consciousness directly, for it must penetrate the dark fog of human delusion. Not uncommonly, even the disciples of a great master alter his essential teachings—sometimes even drastically so. Their action is not deliberate; rather, it is an expression of their very devotion to him. His reality as a person is, for most of them, greater than his teachings. Thus, the disciples of a master whose expression was the sweetness of God's love may, out of loyalty to him, seek to justify his teachings in the eyes of the world by offering scholarly support for them; they end up attracting intellectuals, but not devotees, to his teachings. And the disciples of a master who taught the oneness of all religions may seize upon the very freshness of this teaching as proof that he was unique—indeed, superior to other masters!

Thus, the development of the Judeo-Christian tradition passed from Mosaic law to form-bound definitions that enclosed Christ's teachings in organizational restrictions and dogmatic definitions.

During the early years of Christianity, the importance of a personal relationship with God was widely

---

* *"And no man putteth new wine into old wineskin, else the new wine doth burst the skins, and the wine is spilled, and the wineskin will burst: but new wine must be put into new wineskin."* (Mark 2:22)

recognized. This importance was particularly emphasized by the *Gnostics,* a school of early Christians who were eventually suppressed by those Christians who wanted to establish a formal religion. To church-minded Christians, Jesus Christ would never become a major influence in the world if his message was given too mystical a slant. His promise of salvation to all men would, in that case, remain unfulfilled. They, themselves Westerners, were probably more comfortable with the outward aspects of his message. The Greco-Roman approach to life was radically different from the more-or-less unsystematic teachings of Jesus Christ. "Church Christians" felt that those teachings needed a formal structure, under strict administrative control. Such was the Roman way.

The suppression of the Gnostics constituted, however, a major loss for Christianity. Granted, their more mystical school of thought had its own shortcomings. The self-expression it emphasized was not always rooted in wisdom. A few Gnostics also developed a certain proud aloofness, not unlike those ego-affirming yoga students mentioned in the last chapter. Errors crept into their teachings, including the reasonable, but mistaken, belief that Jesus Christ, being the Son of God, could not possibly have suffered on the cross.

The Gnostics' commitment to an inner experience of the truth was no guarantee of success in achieving that experience. When Gnosticism was suppressed, however, and fixed doctrines were formulated, Christian leadership came wholly under the church dignitaries, who sought to make Christ's teachings uniform in order to strengthen the authority of the church. It was best, they felt, to under-emphasize those aspects of Christ's teachings which might encourage people to excessive inwardness in their devotion, for that would mean too much independence of churchly control.

Thus, "grace and truth" came to be interpreted outwardly. Truth was explained no longer in terms of God-realization, but rather of carefully defined dogmas. Grace no longer meant the actual experience of divine power, but salvation after death for church members in good standing. "Good standing," moreover, came to be understood as "good, better, and best" standing, depending on how much money and worldly power came with the standing. For once a religious organization embarks on a course of placing its members under the control of a central authority, its natural next step is to want increased wealth and worldly power for the church. Such, simply, is human nature.

It is more than likely that the Church, in discrediting the Gnostics, exaggerated their fallacies, and passed lightly over their virtues. Christ's emphasis on inner communion could only have been an embarrassment to it, for it wanted large congregations. That goal made it necessary to emphasize the outer symbols of truth, and to minimize the inner experience of God.

The Jews' rejection of Jesus pushed his followers out into a world where institutionalism had already been developed to a fine art. Church leaders considered it necessary to adapt his message to this alien culture— for most of them, the only culture they knew.

The Jews were not spiritually ready to receive Christ. And the Greco-Roman world was not ready for the "grace and truth" of *inner communion,* which was

Christ's deeper message. Thus, as his mission developed, a better name for it might have been "Churchianity," not Christianity,

Fortunately, those twin principles, "grace and truth," were not lost. Though increasingly defined in terms that were supportive of the church, they still touched the hearts of individuals who accepted the commandment of Jesus to love God with all one's heart, soul, mind, and strength. Jesus Christ remained, for them, not only Someone to be addressed with formal hyperbole during church services, but their own divine Friend, with whom they could commune in a relationship of love. Jesus Christ himself, not church dogma, has been from the start the living essence of the Christian religion.

From time to time in the history of Christianity, there have appeared true men and women of God who, experiencing Christ's actual presence, have infused the Christian religion with renewed faith. Without them, the churches would long ago have come to resemble elegant mausoleums. It also happened, however, unfortunately, that those saints were never given the freedom to join hands with one another over the centuries, and thus to create a coherent spiritual tradition. Always, they had to give primary recognition to the authority of the Church, which insisted that public revelation ended with Jesus Christ and the apostles. Anything experienced since then, it decreed, falls into the category of private revelation. Thus, no tradition ever developed comparable to the ancient yoga tradition in India.

During the first thousand years of Christianity, inner communion was more widely recognized than it has been ever since. The struggle, however, between the church's somewhat grudging recognition of inner communion, and its active encouragement of outer worship, has always been weighted in favor of outer worship. St. Benedict, who lived in the Sixth Century and was a gifted mystic as well as a good organizer, supported the Church by trying to give an outward structure to spiritual attitudes. A hermit himself for some years, and sought out by people from far and near, St. Benedict had the Western quality of systemizing what he believed in. Thus, when others asked to be allowed to join him in his life of prayer, he organized them into a monastery instead of letting them wander about on their own (as monks do even now in India). Thus, the Benedictine Rule brought those who were mystically inclined also under the control of the Church. His Rule is followed even today by most Christian monastic orders, though certain of its quainter aspects have been modified. (It is no longer the practice, for example, for bread to descend at mealtimes by means of a rope and pulley, to remind all that their sustenance comes from God!) Retirement to remote places for a life of contemplation received progressively less encouragement; gradually, society ceased to support the hermitic life.

During the second thousand years of Christianity, Christ's message was increasingly defined outwardly. Less and less attention was given, even in monasteries, to the soul's inner relationship with God, and more and more to outer discipline and communal conformity.

The argument in favor of organized religion is, in its own context, valid. For one thing, the Church at least succeeded in keeping the barbarians at bay. It also

116

strengthened the faithful. Its benefits, in fact, were many, as will be seen later on in this chapter. The Church did not in itself, however, produce saints. This, God alone can do. Saints developed *within* Christianity—often not so much *because* of the church as *in spite* of it. Still, the Catholic Church has honored its saints by canonizing them. The Protestants, on the other hand, have not so much persecuted them as ignored them. In fact, a number of Protestant sects officially insist that *every* Christian is a saint, by virtue of his having accepted Jesus Christ as his Savior. Thus, somewhat through the Roman Catholics, and more so through the Protestants, an important truth has become almost forgotten: that *the saints in every religion are its true custodians.* Spiritually speaking, the effect of this vanished understanding has been enormous. The saints in fact deserve our respect, even our veneration—not for themselves, but because in them we behold our own highest potential. When that respect is absent, religion loses its vitality, and divine aspiration is replaced by reasonable compromise and pious indifference.

In fascinating contrast to Western efforts to institutionalize religion stands the freedom of religious expression in India. God-communion is not viewed there as something to be controlled outwardly. As Jesus himself put it, in reference to the Spirit, *"The wind blows where it wills."* (John 3:8) The contrast between the typical attitudes of East and West was revealed in a question an American visitor put to a saint in India, and in the answer he received. The American asked what might be done to ensure the safety of our planet.

117

The saint replied, "He who created this world, don't you think He knows how to take care of it?"

In India, institutional religious control is looked upon with a certain disfavor, and is virtually non-existent. Admittedly, the Indian temperament tends somewhat toward disorganization anyway. In religious matters, however, this tendency has permitted spiritual genius to flourish. Toleration for eccentricity has prevented the social sanctioning of mediocrity. If a teacher in India contradicts the scriptures, there exists no formal body with the authority to silence him. Consequently, he faces no threat of official excommunication, anathema, or imprisonment. He may be confronted on the issue informally, but his free will, if not his judgment, is generally respected. For the feeling is that error, like a tree growing in barren soil, produces poor fruit anyway. Truth, on the other hand, like a fruit-laden tree, gives sustenance to many and is self-propagating. Truth ultimately overwhelms delusion, as the Christians of Alexandria discovered when they heard St. Anthony declare, "I have seen him!"

Of course, no country has a monopoly on fanaticism, emotion, or mob violence. "Ignorance, East and West," Paramhansa Yogananda used to say, "is fifty-fifty." If persecution is necessary to the achievement of sainthood, India is not wanting in this important ingredient. Emotions, however, like waves, constantly rise and fall. What is blessedly lacking in India is the arctic cold of religious institutionalism, which in effect freezes the waves of understanding with formal, enforceable decrees. Also lacking is the mistaken belief that such control is even desirable.

An attitude of universal tolerance, typically Indian, is evident elsewhere also. It was expressed by Rabbi Gamaliel in The Acts of the Apostles, to other rabbis who were urging that the upstart Christian sect be persecuted. *"Leave them alone,"* he advised, *"for if this counsel or this work is of men, it will fail; but if it is of God, you will not be able to overthrow it, and might even be found in opposition to God!"* (Acts 5:38,39)

There is a further point worth considering here, one rarely taken into account by church officials, whose training is in administrative skills. The tendency of religious officialdom is to look rather condescendingly on people whose temperament is devotional, especially if those people don't show proper interest in stern institutional efficiency. The humble devotee seems, to most administrators, to have his "head in the clouds." Priding themselves on their worldly wisdom, sober "defenders of the faith" seldom realize the extent to which superconscious experience clarifies a person's understanding and his reasoning powers. As Swami Sri Yukteswar, Yogananda's guru, put it, "Divine perceptions are not incapacitating!" Saints, when forced to engage in debate with theologians, prove themselves formidable opponents. Even illiterate saints have emerged victorious from doctrinal attacks by mere scholars.

The way of the saints is not argumentative. What they do is announce the truth calmly and clearly as they have experienced it. In verbal riposte they exhibit the keenest intelligence and, often, a delightful sense of humor. The saints, moreover—unlike their reason-addicted brethren—are in agreement with one another on basic spiritual issues.

Four points are strong arguments in favor of the Indian, over the Western, attitude toward religion. The first—and even Christian missionaries have remarked on this one—is the Indian's extraordinary devotion to spiritual matters, and to God. Indians don't need organizational encouragement to love God.

The second point is that, in India, sainthood is encouraged, not suppressed. Eccentricity is not viewed as a community problem, but is tolerated, sometimes approved, and sometimes even enjoyed.

The third point is that people in India have free access to living saints, and go to them often for guidance, counseling, and inspiration. No official body exists to delay their expressions of devotion until after the saints' death.

The fourth point is that, in India, the saints are seen as the crowning glory of religion, and not as uncomfortable anomalies—worthy of admiration, perhaps, but just as likely to be shrugged off as "a bit extreme!" Radhakrishnan, the first vice president in India after its liberation from British rule, remarked to the author during a private meeting, "A nation is known by the men and women it looks up to as great." In no nation are the saints so revered as in India.

Saint Teresa of Avila once lamented the harm done by spiritually inexperienced counsellors in their attempts to externalize the devotion of spiritual aspirants. The average priest thinks first of binding people to the Church. "You will have time enough for ecstasy in heaven," is their caustic comment. "Meanwhile, be

guided by the monastic rule or by clerical authorities."
Jesus, however, praised Mary's silent inner absorption,
and criticized Martha's restless outwardness. Mary, he
said, had "chosen the better part."

Paramhansa Yogananda said, of his mission to the
West, that it was twofold: "To bring back the original
teachings of Jesus Christ, and the original yoga teachings of Krishna." The West, today, is ready for practical
guidance in meditation and inner communion. The
cultural climate in our time has changed, partly in consequence of science's insistence on tested knowledge
over theoretical deduction. People are coming more and
more to recognize their need for personal experience of
God, and see this experience also as the very essence of
Jesus Christ's teachings.

Of the four gospels, St. John's is the most inward in
emphasis. Certain scholars have suggested that St. John
was influenced by the Greek philosophers. With that
suggestion, however, they reveal their ignorance of the
spirit of discipleship. John was the "beloved of Jesus";
in other words, he was his closest and most highly
advanced disciple. It is inconceivable that he would
have sought support elsewhere for his most fundamental exposition of his master's teachings. Would someone with access to a powerful telescope seek
corroboration from a spyglass? St. John described
Christ in the first chapter of his gospel in terms of infinite truth. Those statements were not philosophical
abstractions. They could only have been given to John
by Jesus himself.

The statement, then (quoting John the Baptist),
"The law was given by Moses, but grace and truth came

by Jesus Christ," must have had Jesus' endorsement also. Its meaning was too deep for anyone else to make that statement without Christ's approval.

The Gnostics were closer, in this sense, to the spirit of Christ's teachings than the churches have ever been. For they emphasized *inner* grace and truth, not outer law and authority. The Gnostic teachings were, in fact, more Eastern than Western in their orientation. The church was a Western imposition on the teachings of Jesus. Jesus, too, in the context of his day, lived in the East.

Things have not changed to such an extent that Western religion no longer needs organization. Paramhansa Yogananda himself founded a religious institution in America, and considered it necessary to his mission. For there exists in America, and in the West more generally, an insufficiency of respect for spiritual authority. This attitude is fed by the supposedly democratic attitude, "I'm just as good as anyone else!" It is also a sign of spiritual immaturity. Dilettantish presumption would have diluted the teachings beyond recognition, had there been no focal point from which to disseminate them.

Yogananda, however, never displayed much enthusiasm for spiritual institutionalism as such. Rather, he seemed to view religious organizations as necessary evils at best: a means of serving truth-seekers, but an obstacle to prolonged, deep meditation. No organization could, in his mind, replace the need for personal communion with God. As he once told his monk-disciples, "You have to individually make love to God."

To the author he said once, with evident approval,

"Those who leave the monastery will someday have groups of their own." He encouraged the author himself to write books. His instruction, as it turned out, required the author's separation from the organization. For his books could never have been written or published within the organization, the primary duty of which was the publishing of Yogananda's books.

"Grace and truth came by Jesus Christ," wrote St. John. The inner experience of both grace and truth is the aspect of Christ's teaching that Paramhansa Yogananda was sent especially to teach again.

A woman disciple of Yogananda's, to whom he'd given work to do outside the organization that was better suited to her nature, once helped to highlight the difference between organizational and spiritual obedience. She was questioning something he'd asked her to do. "Master," she protested, "what will the organization say?"

"Are you following the organization?" he asked her. "Or are you following me?"

The ideal solution to the common, though seldom necessary, conflict between obedience to an organization and obedience to the inner voice of God is to recognize that each fills a need. Each, therefore, has its place.

Organization is like fertilizer for a tree. Genius itself, though always a mark of inner inspiration, could not flourish in a social vacuum. In Florence, Italy, for example, during the Renaissance, a cross-pollination of ideas produced Leonardo da Vinci, Michelangelo, and many more of history's greatest artists. During the Seventeenth Century in France, the over-all social consciousness made possible the appearance of France's great playwrights: Corneille, Racine, and Molière. During Germany's great era of music, it took a musically appreciative society to produce Bach, Handel, Mozart, Beethoven, and other composers of genius. Rarely, if ever, has a work of genius flowered alone, like a solitary plant in the desert, unsupported by a society that could appreciate that genius. Even the desert fathers of the early Christian era could not have embraced their lonely calling, nor been successful in it, without the supportive consciousness of a large society.

For, too, society is an institution, even if it is not organized on managerial lines. India is, in this sense, an institution also. For lack of anything like India's spiritual atmosphere in other countries, people with deep divine aspiration have not felt called to the hermit's life. For lack of general artistic sensitivity, great art has never flourished in a mining camp. And because of the present world-need to strengthen family ties, monasticism everywhere has diminished both in numbers and in magnetism.

Where there is a lack of group understanding, but an over-ridingly powerful inspiration in a single individual, that individual has no choice, if he wants to help many, but to found an institution. Only from that base can his teaching spread. For this reason, Paramhansa Yogananda founded an organization in America. Otherwise, his teachings would have put down only shallow roots in this alien soil.

On the other hand, as Yogananda himself often said, "Seclusion is the price of greatness." An organization can be a means of helping people to attain a certain spiritual understanding, but it cannot itself *produce* understanding. True understanding, whether spiritual, artistic, scientific, or political, comes from within. It cannot be taught: It can only be recognized.

Divine vision, as Yogananda put it, is "center everywhere, circumference nowhere." Every atom is like a magnet, drawing other atoms to itself. Every ego is a magnetic vortex, drawing from Infinite Consciousness the thoughts and inspirations it wants, and with which it feels in tune. Organizations, too, draw power to themselves, and thereby strengthen their members. The vortex of a large religious organization can be powerful, exerting a magnetic influence even on people who are not personally in harmony with it. The thought that a large organization may project is: "There are so many who think as we do. Who are you, to dare to think differently?" This thought, stultifying to intellectual freedom, can nevertheless affect many minds.

We see in the power of group magnetism both the strength and the weakness of religious organizations. When the purpose they serve is good, they give that purpose a shape and focus. True inspiration, however, is not a matter of group endorsement. It is born in the consciousness of an individual. True guidance also, especially in spiritual matters, comes from within. Even a great master can only stimulate responses in his disciples. He cannot impose his insights on them. Merely to be the disciple of a master is no guarantee of spiritual attainment. As Jesus put it, *"Many that are first shall be last, and last, first."*[*]

---

[*] Matthew 19:30.

Thus, even within an organization it is important that the sincere devotee seek his guidance and inspiration principally from within. He should also do his best, in a spirit of willing cooperation, to obey outward guidance. Obedience, however, to someone who is not himself wise is beneficial only in the sense that it may keep one humble. No spiritual gains are made by walking in "lockstep togetherness" with other people. Blind obedience to someone who is spiritually ignorant means courting ignorance in oneself. God, it is said, will guide one through his superiors; if they are wrong, He will correct them. Well, miracles do happen, but to accept guidance that defies common sense can only, as Yogananda said, suppress, and therefore weaken, a person's will power.

Is it, then, good to join a religious body? Why not? if one is in sympathy with its ideals. There is strength, even spiritually, in numbers. To suspend one's own discrimination, however, in the name of that basic sympathy can impede spiritual development, not hasten it. The sentiment, "My country, right or wrong," is admirable if a statement of loyalty, but contemptible if said only to justify obedience to its errors. There can be no spiritual gains in mental numbness. Life imposes on us the need for compromise, but even compromise must be conscious, deliberate, and willing. Otherwise, it is not compromise, but surrender. The "yes-man" is the bane of every institution, for while he gives support, he weakens its integrity.

A person may have, at a certain point, to decide to follow his own star—if not outwardly, then at least inwardly. If such should be the case, he must if possible avoid doing so in a spirit of rebellion. For it is always good to respect and appreciate what one has received from others. If a high school graduate goes on to study at a university, he ought not to damn his high school teachers because they gave him a lower education.

An organization is like fertilizer. This is not written with disrespect, for both are stimulants to growth. An organization can help people in their spiritual development. However, just as too much fertilizer can kill a plant, so an excessive emphasis on organization can paralyze inspiration. "Too many rules," Yogananda used to say, "destroy the spirit." Religious organizations, like vortices of energy, draw power to themselves. A group may therefore develop a sense of its own importance, and a certain indifference to the needs of people, even of those for whose benefit the organization was created. The danger for organizations, then, is institutional arrogance.

The danger for the lone individual, on the other hand, is personal arrogance. For pride easily develops when there is no one to offer correction and check one's spiritual directions.

Group egotism can be combatted by an attitude of service. And personal egotism can be combatted by respecting other ways of seeking God, whether inside or outside of an organization. In both cases, it is necessary to keep alive the flame of generosity by service to others, and by loving them.

What benefits are there for the individual in these two alternative ways? The way of outer compliance offers relative safety from numerous dangers. Their power, moreover, ought never to be underestimated.

The way of independence, on the other hand, exposes the lone "eccentric" to those dangers. The difference between joining an organization and walking alone is like the difference between a plant that grows in a hot-house and one that grows in Nature. The hot-house plant, protected from the weather's inclemencies, may grow large and beautiful. It lacks the stamina, however, of a wild plant. The latter, on the other hand, exposed as it is to buffeting winds and extremes of heat and cold, may not survive.

Would you rather be self-reliant, like that wild plant? or live in the security of an institution? Look well before you make that decision. Yogananda used to say, for the benefit especially of beginners on the path, "Environment is stronger than will power." It takes spiritual strength to stand alone. Look well, then, before you make your choice.

Not every spiritual seeker is able or free to join a monastery. Paramhansa Yogananda therefore proposed a timely alternative. He urged those who were spiritually minded, whether householders or single people, to form communities that they might seek God together. The author has been fortunate in creating several such places—six, so far, in America and in Europe. They are the first communities developed along the lines envisioned by Yogananda. Perhaps, in time, thousands of similar communities will spring up across the world, autonomous models for people who place God first in their lives.

Of his mission, Yogananda said, "The time for *knowing* God has come!" Again and again, as long as even a few souls long for enlightenment, great masters will appear to show them the way. Yogananda was sent to the West to teach the secrets of meditation and inner communion. Jesus Christ himself, Yogananda said, had appeared to Babaji, the first in Yogananda's line of living gurus, and asked him to send someone to the West to teach again the deeper aspects of his revelation. Those teachings are clearly stated in the Bible, but have been overlooked under the pressure of religious organizational responsibilities.

The time has come, Yogananda said, to re-emphasize the importance of meditation—not by denying the benefits of organizational affiliation (though it is important to see that these benefits are secondary), but by helping people to achieve true communion with God. He often said that, instead of dogmatizing people, teachers should encourage them to seek true joy in meditation. As he put it, instead of "dyed-in-the-wool" Christians he wanted to see people "dyed in the wool" of their own divine experience, through Kriya Yoga.

We live in a new age. "Self-realization," Yogananda declared, "will someday be the religion of the world." People everywhere will realize that the essence of religion is true "gnosis": knowledge of the inner Self.

The Bhagavad Gita emphasizes also the need for personal experience of God, rather than blind obedience to outer rules. In the final chapter of the Gita, Krishna, in the poetic translation of Sir Edwin Arnold, says:

> *Nay! but once more*
> *Take My last word. My utmost meaning have!*
> *Precious thou art to Me; right well beloved!*
> *Listen! I tell thee for thy comfort this.*

Give Me thy heart! adore Me! serve Me! cling
In faith and love and reverence to Me!
So shalt thou come to Me! I promise true,
For thou art sweet to Me!
  And let go those—
Rites and writ duties! Fly to me alone!
Make Me thy single refuge! I will free
Thy soul from all its sins! Be of good cheer!

Krishna is referring here to a path higher than that of formal observances such as fasting, rituals, and good deeds. The path he recommends is that of inner communion with God. In no way is he belittling those who strive valiantly to abide by outer rules. Discipline is necessary, up to a point. There comes a time, however, when the devotee naturally transcends the need for it. A path should not be confused with its goal. The purpose of religion is to guide people out of egoic limitations, not to impose on them a new thralldom.

There is a higher purpose to every scriptural commandment. Consider the commandments of Moses, for example. One of these, *"Thou shalt not kill,"* may be compared to a teaching in the Indian scriptures: harmlessness, or non-injury. By following this principle to perfection, say the Indian scriptures, one realizes his oneness with all life. Life, then, provides him in return with loving support.

"Thou shalt not steal" says Mosaic law; and again, *"Thou shalt not covet."* Non-covetousness is taught in the Indian scriptures as well. By following this principle to perfection, one attains a state of centeredness in the Self. One's every need, then, is met without effort on his part.

"Thou shalt not bear false witness" declares Mosaic law. Non-lying, again, is taught in the Indian scriptures. By perfect adherence to truthfulness, one becomes attuned to the great symphony of life. One's simple word, then, is binding on the universe.

If we pay too much attention to outward law, however, we become distracted from loving God deeply. The deeper our communion with Him, the less outer forms of religion seem important to us. For divine love makes it impossible to desire to harm anyone, to covet anything, or to be untruthful under any circumstance.

Grace—and truth. What more does one need? God's grace in our souls, and complete acceptance of the truth that, eternally, we are His own.

CHAPTER EIGHT

Can God Be Known?

"No man hath seen God at any time; the only begotten Son, which is in the bosom of the Father, he hath declared him." This passage, the eighteenth verse from Chapter One of St. John's Gospel, ends Part I of our book, the focus of which has been on the divine basis for Christ's mission.

St. John, up to this point, has described the descent of Divinity into matter. His description might be compared to the Vedanta "philosophy" of India,* which treats of the nature of the Absolute. St. John presents truth here in its impersonal aspect: *"In the beginning was the Word. . . . The light shineth in darkness. . . . All things were made by him."* At the same time, he brings that truth to a focus in the incarnation of Jesus Christ: *"The Word was made flesh and dwelt among us, full of grace and truth. . . . The law was given by Moses, but grace and truth came by Jesus Christ."* He explains how, by attunement with Jesus Christ, the soul can come to

---

* "Philosophy" is put in quotes here because *Vedanta,* though often described as a philosophy, is actually revealed wisdom. Literally, *Vedanta* means "the end, or summation, of the *Vedas.*" The other, complementary systems of spiritual teaching are *Sankhya* and *Yoga. Sankhya* explains the importance of escaping worldly involvements and seeking a higher truth. *Yoga* explains techniques and practices necessary to the aspirant in his spiritual search. *Vedanta* explains the nature of Truth.

132

God. Verse Eighteen is the final "vedantic" insight presented in this portion of the Bible.

To recapitulate, John's explanation has been of truths that are knowable to the soul, but not to the ego. His words, "No man hath seen God at any time," do not mean that God cannot ever be seen and known, but only that such knowledge is impossible in ego-consciousness. Jesus made statements that might seem contradictory to this one of John's, but that in fact only clarify it. His words, *"Who hath seen me hath seen God,"* referred not to those who had seen him in the flesh, but to those who had realized him in the spirit as a manifestation of the Christ consciousness. His "beatitude" in the Sermon on the Mount stated, *"Blessed are the pure in heart, for they shall see God."* Thus, Jesus clearly indicated that God *can* be seen, but only by those whose hearts are not attached to the things of this world. Christ and God are one. Their nature is spiritual, therefore, not material. So long as we identify ourselves with our physical bodies, our vision will be physical, and we shall be unable to see God. St. Simeon, however, who lived in the Tenth Century (but is still known by the sobriquet, "The New Theologian"!), declared that at the moment when the heart's feelings become purified, the soul beholds God.

In the second part of our passage, John states, *"The only begotten Son, which is in the bosom of the Father, he hath declared him."* It is the Christlike guru, or savior, who "declares" the Father, by transmitting his awareness of God to those who are attuned to his consciousness.

God, in His essential nature, is without form and

infinite. In this sense He may be compared to electricity, or to an ocean. Suppose a person announces after a day at the beach, "I have seen the ocean." What has he actually seen? A minute portion of its surface, merely. Does he really know that it was even an ocean? Judging from his experience, it may have been only a large salt-water lake. For anyone to experience the ocean in its entirety, he would need to *become* it. And for anyone to experience God in all His vastness, he must become one with Him. Confinement in an ego makes oneness impossible.

To see God means more than seeing a little light in meditation. To "comprehend" the light—using St. John's earlier expression—means to merge in it. Thus, John describes Jesus, in his oneness with the Christ consciousness, as being *"in the bosom of the Father."*

Krishna makes an identical point in the Bhagavad Gita. To Arjuna he says, *"Thou canst not see me with mortal eyes. Therefore I now give thee sight divine."* The scripture goes on to say, *"Hari, the exalted Lord of Yoga, revealed himself to Arjuna in His infinite form."* Arjuna then saw God as *"thousand-armed, without beginning, middle, or end* [infinite and eternal, in other words], *irradiating the whole universe!"*

Perfect purity of heart can be achieved only by abandoning ego-attachment. We are not the physical body, but the soul, made in the perfect image of God.

Earth is prized when it is out of doors in a field, because there it nourishes the plants. On arable land it is called soil. Indoors, however, in a kitchen or on a temple floor, it is deprecatingly spoken of as dirt. Our hearts' feelings should be centered in God, for they belong there. There, they are pure. When the heart is cluttered with desires for anything else, however, that which it seeks is foreign to its true nature, and its feelings are therefore impure. Desires, like dirt on a temple floor, sully the shining reflection of God beheld in soul-intuition.

"Hari," says the Gita, "revealed himself to Arjuna." The literal meaning of *Hari* is "thief": "Thief of Hearts," in other words. God's love is all-absorbing. It steals away everything except love for Him. The Indian scriptures describe Him as *rasa:* the most relishable.

The divine consciousness cannot be described in terms that are even remotely understandable to man. It must be exemplified for us in someone who, though in a human body, is united inwardly to that consciousness. By loving association with a spiritual master, we can attune ourselves to his perception of God.

How can a master be recognized out of millions of unenlightened human beings? Not, it must be said first, by outward "signs and wonders." Miracles are evidence of a mighty, but not necessarily a godly, spirit. Physical looks, too, can be deceiving. In a certain tribe of gypsies in Romania, the men bear a striking resemblance to the popular image of Jesus Christ. Those men are reputed, however, to be criminals, not saints. Outward beauty is another misleading factor: It can conceal the heart of a devil. And there have been saints who were physically unremarkable. St. Francis of Assisi—with what truth it cannot now be said—described his appearance as resembling that of a hen. Purity is of the heart. It is in a saint's attitude toward life that his spiritual greatness is first revealed. His attitude is evident from his behavior, and especially in the calm gaze with which he views the world. People of spiritual sensitivity sense around him above all a palpable divine aura and experience in his presence an extraordinary upliftment of spirit.

It is apparent, from the behavior and attitudes of a master, that the things of this world have no effect on his consciousness. He is unalterably even-minded, free from likes and dislikes, joyful in himself, and well disposed toward everything and everyone. Above all, those who are sensitive recognize in his love for others a manifestation of God's love for them.

The secret of wisdom lies in a person's power of abstraction. To the wise, opposites such as pleasure and pain, success and failure, are but waves that rise and fall on the surface of the sea without affecting the ocean deeps. They are the waves of delusion. A person of true wisdom discerns in all life the changeless consciousness of the Divine.

Abstraction is the ability to separate or distill what is changeless from mere things, which forever change. Isaac Newton saw an apple fall,* and, recalling other objects falling, he suddenly realized that in their movement there existed a single operating principle: the Law of Gravity.

Newton's discovery was of historic importance. All of us, however, have abstracted universals of many kinds from diverse phenomena. A baby whose only experience of flatness and roundness is a tabletop and a tennis ball will identify flatness with that tabletop, and roundness with that tennis ball. With passing time,

---

* The story is apocryphal, but what of it? It helped to popularize and thereby give life to his discovery.

however, his experiences diversify, and he notices other flat or round objects also. Thus, he learns to abstract flatness and roundness from the objects that express them, and to see shape as an abstraction—a mental concept, he realizes at last, quite distinct from any specific object.

Consciousness itself is the ultimate abstraction. Other abstractions, without it, would not exist. It is in the mind that flatness and roundness are recognized. Even someone so dull-minded that he is incapable of defining anything is, at least, conscious, and conscious of being conscious! It is our consciousness that convinces us of our existence. René Descartes, the French philosopher and scientist, was mistaken in his famous statement: "I think, therefore I am (*Cogito, ergo sum*)." Thoughts can only *express* consciousness, more or less as a tennis ball expresses roundness. Descartes, searching for the key to existence, thought it necessary for him to have an object to study. Consciousness, however, is not an object, but the subject of anything seen. It is not something to study; rather, it is that which studies. Consciousness is the universal constant, irreducible to any other abstraction.

Happiness also is irreducible. It is expressed in countless ways. We may experience happiness in the fulfillment of a long-cherished desire, or in release from suffering. Happiness is, to varying degrees, expressed by all life: in gazelles leaping gaily through the long grass of an African veldt; in the glad chirping of sparrows around a basin of water; in the excitement of a dog anticipating its dinner. Though most people identify their happiness with specific circumstances, it is a constant of life, underlying all our experiences. Sorrow is not such a constant. Happiness, on the other hand, is subtly, watchfully present even at times of great tragedy.

For happiness is not so much the result of something attained, or acquired, as of impediments *removed.* Desire creates in us a sense of want, which constrains the natural joy of the soul. That impediment is removed when that desire is fulfilled, and leaves us happy again. Happiness is a state of mind; in the last analysis, it depends on nothing external at all. The happiness we experience in things depends on the welcome our hearts extend to them.

Divine wisdom is evident in a master's ability to distill or abstract consciousness, existence, and joy from the cloud wisps of gladness and sorrow. He is unaffected by loss or gain, failure or success, tragedy or reprieve—even by death itself.

Did Jesus, then, suffer on the cross? Yes, in his human nature. His suffering, however, had to have been for people's ignorance. "Father," he prayed, "forgive them, for they know not what they do." In his Christ consciousness, he could not have been touched.

No matter what circumstance in which a master finds himself, in his soul he remains blissful. He would not be a master, otherwise. Divine Joy, like consciousness, is irreducible. The two co-exist, and are identical.

Existence, consciousness, joy (or bliss): These abstractions cannot be defined, for it is they that must do the defining. No line of logic will ever "prove" their reality: They must be experienced. Therefore the *Sankhya* teaching of India declares, "*Ishwar-ashidha:*

God cannot be proved." Therefore also Swami Shankara gave this description of God: "*Sat-chid-anandam,* Existence-consciousness-bliss."

One can appreciate Descartes' difficulty! No effort of intellect could ever have resolved the riddle of his existence. The solution to that riddle depended on his attaining divine enlightenment. For this reason, the spiritual search is said to be the sole activity worthy of mankind. Sukdeva, a great sage of ancient India, declared, "All time is wasted that is not spent in seeking God."

All of this is to say that, when it comes to finding God, we are confronted with an abstraction which the mind cannot even begin to conceptualize. Even such simple abstractions as flatness and roundness are difficult enough: We need at least some mental image to understand them at all. Again, how are most people to understand joy as the changeless constant beneath all misfortune? It takes a human Christ to evidence—or, as the Bible puts it, to "declare"—the existence of an immutable, infinite consciousness in this ever-fluctuating universe. If lesser abstractions are difficult to conceptualize, that supreme abstraction, existence-consciousness-bliss, is impossible! We need a master, with realization pure and unaffected by any passing circumstance. We need to attune ourselves to his realization. A master's state of consciousness is absolute, not relative. And it is absolutely beyond every possible human experience.

The example and assistance of a master can bring us that perception of truth which, as Jesus said, "*shall make you free.*" (John 8:32) Only such a person can lift us, as if on a flying carpet of Arabian legend, above human understanding to the ultimate abstraction which is divine consciousness. He alone whose spirit is united with the Christ consciousness is a true guru.

Most of us have experienced receiving insight and inspiration at some time or another in our lives, by association with someone whose experience of things was deeper than our own. The skeptic might scoff, "I don't need anyone to inspire me! I get my inspiration from within myself." None of us, however, lives in a vacuum. We are inextricably bound to all existence. The deeper our attunement to a reality greater than our own, the more likely we are to find inspiration in any undertaking.

The guru's role is to inspire his disciples, and share with them his realization of the Truth. His influence is magnetic in the sense that he awakens them to the awareness of their own soul-center. In this respect he resembles Ariadne of Greek legend, who gave Theseus a spool of thread as he was about to enter the labyrinth and encounter the Minotaur. Unwinding the thread as he went, he was enabled to follow it back out of the famous maze. The "thread" of attunement with the guru serves a double purpose: It awakens in those who are receptive a soul-recollection of their true being. Even more important, it gives them the power to know God. Together, these gifts transform the disciple from an ordinary human being to a living master. Paramhansa Yogananda emphasized this truth in a line of his poem "Samadhi": "By deeper, longer, thirsty, *guru-given* meditation," he wrote, "comes this celestial samadhi."*

The disciple, with the help of his guru, communes with AUM. Gradually, merging in AUM, he expands his consciousness into oneness with the ocean of cosmic sound, the Word. He then passes beyond sound to oneness with the Christ consciousness, and with the Father.

The ego resists submitting itself to what it considers merely the will of another human being. We have seen how the Jews resisted submission even to the will of God. People whose lives are guided by desires and by likes and dislikes imagine that, because it was they who initiated their desires, their desires are an expression of who they really are. The truth is, desire affirms an identity with something we are not, and can never be. Wise is he, then, who accepts guidance from someone who can bring to him the realization of his own reality: the Self of all selves!

This, finally, is the lesson in this passage of St. John's gospel: not merely to inspire us with awe at the greatness of Jesus Christ, but to help us to understand—indeed, to be in awe of—the potential greatness of our own selves! The end of striving is consciousness and bliss absolute. There is no relativity in this final abstraction. Relativities cease to exist, there. St. John took pains to show the universality of Ultimate Truth, a truth "beyond imagination of expectancy," as Yogananda described it. This truth can only be realized

---

* *Samadhi* is the highest state of cosmic ecstasy, oneness with God. It comes when the soul, released from bondage to ego, expands and embraces infinity.

by actual experience. It cannot be confined narrowly by creeds and dogmas. If anything, anywhere, is abstract, the Supreme Spirit can only be described as the ultimate abstraction. The devotee, forever unable to visualize that state of being as it really is, should visualize it in its concrete expressions, as Jesus Christ or some other master—or, if he is blessed to have one, his own guru—and pray mentally, "Make me aware of *your* consciousness within and around me. I offer myself up to you for transformation, for you alone see my divine potential. May my thoughts become your divine inspirations; my consciousness, your infinite bliss. Introduce me to God!"

In India, it is customary for the disciple to touch his guru's feet on meeting and on taking leave of him. This gesture is deeply symbolic. The feet represent that part of the body which is farthest removed from the person's state of consciousness. The guru represents one's physical link with the Divine. He may be compared to an inverted pyramid, of which the body is the tip. The pyramid extends upward and outward from that tip to infinity. To touch the guru's feet is a way of saying, "Every part of you is holy to me, for what I see before me is my gateway to Christ consciousness." Thus, a song of Paramhansa Yogananda's contains these words: "Think in your heart the lotus feet of your guru, if you want to cross the ocean of delusion."

Meditate daily on the vastness of God. Attune yourself to the guru's, or Christ's, consciousness of infinity. Visualize that presence as a light residing at the very center of your heart, shining with purity. Mentally expand the light until it fills your body. Then visualize it expanding beyond the body, surrounding you with a golden aura. That aura, not your physical form, is your true body.

Go on expanding the light. Visualize it filling the room in which you sit; the countryside; your neighborhood; your nation—all the continents and oceans of Earth. From the center of your expanded awareness in your own heart send rays of pure light and love in blessing to all beings, everywhere!

Release your light, finally, from its earthly confines. See it streaming outward in bliss to embrace the solar system, the Milky Way galaxy—the universe!

Meditate daily on this expansion of pure light and love, until you find your consciousness soaring on wings of inspiration to God. As the Bible says, *"My thoughts are not your thoughts, neither are your ways my ways, saith the Lord. For as the heavens are higher than the earth, so are my ways higher than your ways, and my thoughts than your thoughts."* (Isaiah 55:8,9)

May His consciousness of bliss, light, and love become at last the realization of your own Self!

PART II

The Instruments
of Recognition

CHAPTER NINE

How to Study the Scriptures

*"Then he opened their minds, **so that they might understand the scriptures**."* (Luke 24:25)

Man finds himself forever mentally divided. On deep levels his soul whispers, "Return to stillness, where you belong. Return to the bliss of your own being." Ignoring this inner call, however, he allows himself to be drawn out of himself by the noise and excitement of the world. Thus, the call to perfection remains a dim memory, which he thrusts into the recesses of his mind while he pursues more immediate interests: a comfortable home, a loving life-companion, a happy family, a secure bank account, the respect of his fellowman—reassurances to his ego, in short, that his earthly existence is not really the gamble he subconsciously knows it to be.

This dichotomy is present also in his religious life. The scriptures indicate the way to inner perfection, but he reads into them a message of worldly fulfillment. Perfection, he tells himself, will be attained through religious rites, religious structures, and outward rules of religious behavior (without, however, a corresponding change of consciousness). In his soul, if he is spiritually inclined, he longs for divine love. He believes, however, in the power of outer systems to establish divine love on earth, their structure a stone statue as it were, beautifully posed.

Where religious rules abound, love grows dry, peace is held at a distance, and soul-inspiration appears still-born in people's lives. Devotion then hardens into methods for winning divine favor. Bartering attitudes develop which, though perhaps suitable in the market-place, make a travesty of the soul's eternal relationship with God.

If we want truly to please the Lord, we must commune with Him in inner silence. The reward for divine communion—sufficient to our every need if only we knew it!—is bliss. Every spiritual master has emphasized again and again this simple truth.

Buddha declared the need for personal effort, as opposed to supine dependence on divine grace. The people of his time had grown too dependent on outer rituals.

Krishna stated in the Bhagavad Gita, *"Those who worship the lesser gods go to their gods, but those who worship Me come to Me."* By these words he also meant name, fame, and other temporary fulfillments for which "the lesser gods," usually, are but symbols. Such "gods" may be attained, eventually, after arduous effort and countless disappointments, but after that—what? The soul will not know peace until, as Saint Augustine put it, it seeks rest in God. Outside the Self, fulfillment is a sham: It simply does not exist. Expectations of it lead only, in the end, to its desperate affirmation as people tell themselves they have indeed achieved it, because others tell them they have. Those others, meanwhile, give their reassurances with the implied expectation of being reassured in return. People in this respect are like tourists at a modern art museum who glance about furtively to see how others are reacting to some particularly baffling monstrosity, praising it only if that labor of confusion appears to meet with general approval.

To understand the scriptures, one must already understand something of what life is all about.

The Gospel of St. Matthew tells us, in Chapter 15, *"Then some of the scribes and Pharisees from Jerusalem came and asked Jesus, 'Why do your disciples break our ancient tradition and eat food without first properly washing their hands?'"* The same question might have been put to him by priests in India, where the codes of cleanliness are every bit as strict. Right conduct *is* important; no master would flout the rules governing it if he didn't have some important lesson to teach. Error arises only when people define religion outwardly but forget its inner spirit.

The Biblical account continues: *"Then [Jesus] called the crowd to him and said, 'Listen, and understand this thoroughly! It is not what goes **into** a man's mouth that defiles him. It is what comes **out** of it that makes him common and unclean.'"*

To the disciples afterward he remarked, *"They* [the Pharisees] *are blind guides. And when a blind man leads another, both of them end up in a ditch!"*

Jesus, not surprisingly, was opposed by the narrowly orthodox of his day: the pedants and the prelates whose understanding was enclosed in high walls of dogmatism. They condemned his fresh perception of truth, inspired as it was from within and expressed spontaneously, with joy and wisdom. Scholarly minds prefer the measured phrase, carefully couched in such qualifications as "if," "however," and, "from this, therefore, it would seem. . . ." Yet when the theologians tried to engage Jesus in debate, he parried their thrusts effortlessly. It was simply not his way to argue. As Paramhansa Yogananda remarked wryly, "Fools argue. Wise men discuss."

When Jesus Christ quoted scripture, he encouraged people to use their common sense, first of all, to understand it. He quoted scripture also to show that it endorsed his teachings. *"You search the scriptures,"* he told the Pharisees, *"imagining that in them you will find eternal life. And all the time they give their testimony to me!"* (John 5:39)

The New Testament makes it clear that Jesus considered intellectual knowledge greatly inferior to spiritual insight. Primarily, he urged people to seek the source of their inspiration *in themselves.* (*"The kingdom of God,"* he told them, *"is **within**."* (Luke 17:21))

He also urged the necessity for love, and emphasized this point again and again. One time he told his carping critics, *"But I know you. Ye have not the love of God in you."* (John 5:42) He encouraged people to rely on the natural and generous sentiments of the heart as guidelines to understanding. The Pharisees once asked him, *"Is it lawful to heal on the Sabbath day?"* Jesus answered: *"If any of you had a sheep and it fell into a ditch on the Sabbath day, would you not take hold of it and pull it out? How much more valuable is a human being than a sheep? **Of course** it is right to do good on the Sabbath day!"* (Matthew 12:11,12)

Again, he pointed out that motives are even more important than the deeds they motivate. One time, accepting the devoted ministrations of a woman of low character, he answered his host's unspoken criticism by remarking, *"Her sins, which are many, are forgiven, for she loved much: but to whom little is forgiven, the same loveth little."* (Luke 7:47)

Calm feeling, from which springs spiritual love, is the secret of intuitive understanding. This understanding cannot be learned; it comes only by recognition. Intuitive understanding is the universal key to the scriptures. Words, on the other hand, can do no more than echo that understanding. Words are incapable of expressing fully the ideas one wants to convey. For one thing, they create different mental and emotional associations in different people. Language, moreover, evolves. Where ancient writings are concerned, particularly, the meaning of a verse may become quite distorted by time. In translation, moreover, subtle nuances are often lost. The Italian language has a colorful expression for this process: *"Traduttore è traditore:* To be a translator is to be a traitor." Add to these problems the fact that, until the invention of the printing press, every sentence had to be copied out laboriously by hand, and we see that endless possibilities existed for error. The intellect alone is woefully inadequate to the task of penetrating behind that linguistic veil to the heart of a scripture, to perceive its true meaning.

Consider this not-unusual example of the problem with words. Everyone knows the saying of Jesus, *"It is easier for a camel to go through the eye of a needle than for a rich man to enter the kingdom of heaven."* (Matthew

151

19:24) Many people must have wondered why it even occurred to Jesus that one would want to pass a camel through the eye of a needle! In recent decades, a Bible scholar discovered that the word in the original Greek was *camilos,* not *camelos:* "rope," in other words, not "camel."

Words are mere symbols of communication. They cannot express the whole of one's intention, and that intention cannot encompass the whole of what one knows. What one knows, moreover, is never the whole truth, unless one has attained divine enlightenment. The writers of scripture—to say nothing of their translators!—were by no means all of them enlightened. It is important therefore to understand, first, the meaning *behind* their words, then the truth behind their meaning. The reader must then relate both words and meaning to his own experience of life, to see how well they resonate with what he actually knows. For all of these reasons, intuition is essential to true understanding.

Meditation and deep, *listening* prayer are the way to develop intuition. Before even reading a scripture, meditate; then read it in an uplifted state of mind. Offer up the thoughts you encounter in that passage to the spiritual eye in the forehead, and pray to be guided in your understanding of them. Above all, seek that intuitive insight which only the heart can provide.

Intuition is the soul's power of knowing truth. When intuition springs from the soul, it is infallible. Usually, however, it is filtered by the mind's restlessness, preconceptions, and prejudices, which make it unreliable. Insights one believes to be intuitive should always be tested on the litmus paper of common sense.

And what is common sense? It is understanding born of actual experience, and uninfluenced by emotional predilections. When we defy common sense, we sever the cable that holds the mind anchored to reality.

Dogmatic rigidity is the coward's defense against the new and unfamiliar. People who fear an expansion of consciousness, and prefer the false security of the familiar, are the sort of "believers" to whom Jesus referred when he said, *"Nobody tears a piece from a new coat to patch up an old one, for by doing so he would ruin the new one, and the new piece would not match the old."* (Luke 5:36) Fresh, new insights are not for pedantic minds, the faded fiber of whose intellects has been rubbed thin by long association with old ways of thinking. Jesus didn't even try to convince such people of threadbare understanding, but left them to gather dust like old clothes with the comment, *"He that hath ears to hear, let him hear."*

Again and again he emphasized the importance of common sense, and urged people not to accept dogmas indiscriminately. He also stressed the need, however, for guiding common sense by love for God, and by charity to others. For whereas common sense can protect one against gullibility, it can also blight with skepticism the green shoots of inspiration.

Scriptural misunderstanding occurs most often at opposite ends of people's spectrum of response. The first end is gullible superstition; the second is automatic denial.

Gullible superstition ignores the cautionary voice of reason. It takes every scriptural statement as the solemn pronouncement of the Almighty. In the opinion of gullible believers, Jesus meant quite literally the words, *"The hour is coming, in which all that are in the graves shall hear his voice, and shall come forth."* (John 5:28,29) The gullible mind, like a horse with blinders, thinks linearly. It is like a child, incapable of appreciating the subtlety of symbolism. To the blind believer, "graves" means quite literally those pits where corpses are laid. Such naiveté, it should be added, is not wrong in itself; it is simply a stage through which the ego passes on its way to enlightenment. The natural stages, beyond gullibility, are doubt, followed by disillusionment, cynicism, and, finally, charitable recognition that it is after all not possible to confine truth in a straitjacket.

Common sense spurns a literal reading of this passage. "What about all those people," it asks, "who are never buried at all? Are they excluded from Christ's promise? What about bodies that are cremated, or utterly demolished in explosions? The atoms of the body, moreover, are eventually reabsorbed into the earth. Even during a person's lifetime they move on— perhaps even to inhabit other human bodies. How many corpses 'in their graves' will be able to respond to Christ's voice, and for how long?"*

It takes very little imagination to realize that by "graves" Jesus meant worldly minded people, "deathlike" in their spiritual ignorance. He used this image on another occasion also, when, to the man who said he wanted to go bury his father before returning to

---

* Common sense cannot but ask, further, "Why didn't Jesus say, '*my* voice' instead of '*his* voice'?" The obvious answer is that, in his deeper consciousness, he never thought of himself personally.

become a disciple, he said, *"Let the dead bury their dead."*

Common sense is an invaluable tool for understanding. When it takes the form of automatic rejection, however, it is like gullible superstition in that it merely obstructs understanding. For common sense can be *too* common: that is to say, too grounded in the commonplace. Automatic negation fills the fountain of inspiration with sand, and reduces its refreshing spray to a muffled gurgle. People who vaunt their "down-to-earth" realism often ridicule anything out of the ordinary, labeling it "impossible." Our life experiences, however, should guide us to further possibilities.

A three-year-old boy may not easily imagine himself with a beard and a low voice. Experience, however, tells him he has grown already. Perhaps he has seen older boys who have entered puberty. And he is aware that grown men aren't like himself. It requires no great leap of faith on his part to accept that he, too, will be a man someday, with the characteristics of a man. Thus, experience that informs common sense may be, and often is, vicarious. Common sense can make its assessments on the basis of reasonable assumptions, drawn from what experience has already taught one.

Common sense, when sense, not "commonness," is what is emphasized, opens the mind; it doesn't close it. When a sensible but sensitive person hears of higher-than-ordinary states of consciousness, he doesn't dismiss them scornfully with the words, "Well, I've never experienced anything like *that!*" Rather, he recognizes in human beings a broad spectrum of awareness, from alcoholic stupor and sheer stupidity to intellectual brilliance and genius. On reading descriptions of spiritual exaltation, he responds, "Why not?" Not much imagination is needed to realize that lofty states of consciousness may at least be a possibility.

Common sense is less useful as a guide, of course, when it has no experience to guide it. Most "sensible" people, for example, dismiss miracles out of hand, or perhaps explain them away as allegorical. The Resurrection of Jesus has been shrugged off even by many intellectual Christians, who consider it either a pious myth, or self-justifying propaganda, or an allegory of the body's death and the soul's resurrection in heaven. To weigh this miracle on the scales of common sense, however, one needn't compare it with experiences that one has lived personally. For though common sense restrains and directs the imagination, the general experience of mankind is convincing evidence that many things await discovery in the familiar.

Consider that wonder-drug, penicillin, which was discovered in prosaic mold. Advances in modern science suggest that similar substances, considered ordinary today, will yield other marvels tomorrow. Common sense should be directed, then, toward broadening our experience of life, not toward entrenching us in the humdrum.

Jesus is reported to have multiplied five barley loaves and two small fishes and fed five thousand people. Ordinary experience declares that such a feat is impossible. As a song from the operetta "Porgy and Bess" puts it, "The things that you're liable to read in the Bible: They ain't necessarily so!"

On the other hand, one noted Biblical apologist explained this particular miracle—not *away,* exactly, but into the ground. What happened, he suggested, was even more inspiring: It was a "miracle" of sharing. Jesus, he claimed, asked his disciples to share with others nearby them the five loaves and two fishes that "a lad" in the multitude happened to have with him. Everyone, inspired by this example of generosity, was soon sharing whatever he'd brought with others. This spirit of sharing, inspired by Jesus Christ, became so general that no one remained hungry.

Common sense, when the idea of commonness is emphasized, has a tendency to minimize the possibilities while maximizing the commonplace. Had that author been possessed of more imagination, he'd have realized that his explanation rested not on the generosity of Jesus, but on that of the "lad" from whom the first loaves and fishes were obtained. Indeed, a little imagination might awaken in us, too, the suspicion that if this event was the result only of a simple act of kindness, it probably would not have made history. Would it not have been extraordinary if those people, after being inspired by Jesus Christ, had *not* shared their food with others who were without any? After all, this was no ordinary sports event, where the thought of sharing with one's neighbors and, possibly, rival fans is much less likely to arise.

When common sense refuses to peep out of the rut it has worn in the ground by its habits of thought, it may easily persuade itself that that rut contains all there is of reality. In the present instance, however, the explanation seems less probable than the miracle itself.

Common sense should exercise a little imagination and try to visualize a scene clearly before it projects such an unrealistic alternative. A person of true common sense, instead of offering this lame "apology," ought to suspend his disbelief until he knows more.

Gullible superstition insists that miracles like this one prove the divinity of Jesus Christ. What is it that distinguishes gullibility from honest belief? Perhaps only the expectation of receiving something for nothing: grace, for instance, without personal effort or merit. Jesus emphasized the need for personal effort. *"Why call ye me Lord, Lord,"* he said, *"and do not the things that I say?"* Martin Luther claimed that faith alone is necessary, but at least his faith was heroic, not passive. In Luther's day, "free hand-outs," whether governmental or divine, were unheard-of. Regarding miracles, Jesus said, *"The works that I do, [ye] shall do also."* (John 14:12) His miracles, then, suggest the possibility of untapped powers within ourselves, to which all of us have access if we will develop them conscientiously, as the scientists did in discovering penicillin.

A brother disciple of the author's tells of a time when he was with the Master and several guests. The Master offered them a drink of carrot juice, which the community was producing in its processing plant where the disciple worked. The young man went to fetch some, but to his dismay found only enough juice to fill a small glass. Apologetically he gave the Master this small amount. "Never mind," the Master said. "Pour what you have there." Then, seeing that only enough was being poured to give each visitor a mere sip, he added: "No, fill up the glasses."

"Well," the disciple explained afterward, "what could I do? I figured, 'Mine not to reason Why!' So I filled the first glass, then the second, then the third. I filled *all* the glasses, and at the end the pitcher was completely full! Master said nothing about it, but I know there hadn't been nearly enough juice for everyone, nor was any more available to make up the difference. The guests had no idea what had taken place. They exclaimed only that the juice was delicious!"

How are people whose experience of life is not remotely unusual to accept miracles like these? To accept another person's word for them is not faith, though one may believe in what that person says. To develop true faith, one must deepen one's own contact with God. Miracles are not, in themselves, very important. Their value lies in the incentive they give us for seeking—not powers, but the awareness of God's infinite love.

When studying scripture, bear in mind that its true purpose is spiritual instruction and upliftment. Its focus is on inner development. Man's nature is, however, threefold: physical, mental, and spiritual. Balanced scriptural teachings, therefore, are threefold also. Though life's highest goal is spiritual enlightenment, true scripture includes all three of these aspects in its teaching. Thus, when the detractors of Jesus tried to trap him into denying one's social responsibilities, he replied, *"Render . . . unto Caesar the things which are Caesar's, and unto God the things that are God's."* (Matthew 22:21)*

---

* Some people have called Jesus a revolutionary. This statement is his sufficient answer to that misunderstanding.

Perfect self-transformation is, of course, spiritual, but to attempt it without heeding the steps along the way to it is like mounting a darkened staircase from which a few steps are missing. If the body's needs are ignored, the result may be illness, which can hinder spiritual progress. If the mind is restless or confused, to attempt prayer with concentration is like trying to light a fire with a wet match. If in our hearts we hold unkind feelings toward others, to expand our consciousness in meditation is like trying to inflate a balloon that has a hole in it. And if we want Nature to support us, we must live in harmony with her laws. The Bhagavad Gita teaches that the human state cannot be transcended until we accept our present realities and deal with them accordingly.

Thus, the scriptures endorse the need for right diet and physical exercise, for wholesome attitudes, and for loving everyone, along with the supreme need for knowing God. However, as the Indian scriptures declare also, "If a lesser rule conflicts with a higher one, it ceases to be a rule." Ill health, usually, is an obstacle to spiritual development, but if reasonable efforts to attain good health are unsuccessful, one should not make health his priority. The search for God is our highest duty. No obstacle, moreover, is insuperable. Indeed, many a saint has endured illness all his life, and sometimes it was actually because of his illness that he found God. Illness forced him to try harder than he might have, otherwise. Jesus said, *"Seek the kingdom of God first, and all these things shall be added unto you."* Good health will surely be yours in time, if you desire it, but don't devote your whole life to sweeping out your temple. Take the time to sit in it and meditate. The way of wisdom is to fix one's priorities, and refuse to let anything deflect one from them.

Jesus issued a stirring summons to the highest adventure there is: the quest for truth. By his example he challenged everyone to deepen his experience of life until he stands face-to-face with Truth itself. Thus, to Nicodemus he said: *"Verily, verily, I say unto thee, We speak that we do know, and testify that we have seen."* (John 3:11) The challenge Jesus gave us was to make truth our own. *"Ye shall know the truth,"* he said, *"and the truth shall make you free."* (John 8:32) By "truth" he meant the intuitive perception of our essential nature, which is one with God.

The Bhagavad Gita suggests that unless the ship of life is anchored in devotion to God, it will drift with every current, to be flung at last on rocks of suffering and disillusionment. *"The intellects of those who lack fixity of spiritual purpose are inconstant,"* Krishna says, *"and their interests, endlessly ramified."* (II:41) True understanding comes only by intuition. And reliable intuition comes only by one-pointed spiritual purpose.

In the absence of intuition, the best "fall-back" position is common sense. This gift of Nature cannot take us to the spiritual heights, but it can keep us in touch with fundamental realities, and limit our imagination's tendency to distort them with fantasy. To seek the guidance of experience while at the same time keeping ourselves open to ever-greater experiences is, admittedly, a balancing act of skepticism on one side, and hope on the other. This effort is necessary, however. The seeker must soar high while never losing his

161

earthly bearings. Truth is cosmic, but its principles are applicable as well in the marketplace. Truth is eternal, but it is also forever fresh and new. The very simplicity of truth is what confounds the theologians. As Jesus said, *"Thou hast hid these things from the wise and prudent, and hast revealed them unto babes."* (Luke 10:21)

If Jesus sometimes scolded his disciples, it was to urge them to deepen their spiritual insight. Thus, when Peter asked him why it isn't what goes into the mouth, but what comes out of it that defiles a person, Jesus answered, *"Are you still unable to grasp these things? Don't you see that whatever goes into a man's mouth passes into the stomach and then out of the body altogether? But the things that come out of his mouth come from his heart and mind. It is they that really make him unclean. For from a man's mind arise evil thoughts: murder, adultery, lust, theft, perjury and blasphemy. These are what make a man unclean, not eating without properly washing one's hands!"* (Matthew 15:16–20)

The Bhagavad Gita states that the first requirement for the development of intuition is one-pointed concentration. Peter's request for an explanation on a question that should have been clear to someone as spiritually developed as he, showed how powerful prior conditioning can be. His thoughts wavered between the mores on which he'd been raised and the ever-new truths that were being taught him by Jesus Christ.

Study the scriptures calmly, with deep concentration, and in a spirit of lofty aspiration. Otherwise, even scripture may cause you to wander endlessly—from one interpretation to another, from one teacher to another, and from one spiritual practice to many others. Without inner commitment, the babbling brook of released emotions and the swirling eddies of intellectual excitement may exert more fascination than the calm river of wisdom. Surges of emotional enthusiasm spend themselves, however, leaving the mind face-to-face yet again with the need for painstaking effort. When dedication falters, and when spirits droop, it is important to remember the basic guideline for the spiritual aspirant: steadfastness. "Be even-minded and cheerful," Yogananda used to say. The promise of quick and easy results is the spiritual equivalent of "get-rich-quick" schemes so breathlessly offered in thousands of advertisements.

"Outsiders come," Paramhansa Yogananda once said to a group of disciples, "and see only the surface. Sooner or later they drift away. Those who are our own, however, they never leave."

Jesus seldom, if ever, explained his meanings either to the Pharisees or to the spiritual wanderers. It was to his disciples that he clarified them, even when their understanding fell short of his expectations of them.

There was even a time, as we read in Chapter 6 of St. John, when *many of his disciples went back, and walked no more with him.* To his chosen few he then said, *"Will you also leave?"* Peter answered for them all: *"Lord, to whom shall we go?"* This episode occurred as Jesus was nearing the end of his earthly mission. He was weeding out the shallower spirits from among his followers, whose inability to tune in to his spirit made them unfit to transmit his teachings to others.

He made it clear for all time that he alone is a true disciple who cannot be shaken by doubts,* and whose intellect has no need for exacting definitions to clarify the divine mysteries. Intuitive understanding, he wanted his disciples to realize, is the key that unlocks the door to spiritual awakening. To confuse wisdom with mere knowledge is to roam endlessly from doubt to doubt, from one intellectual explanation to another, forever thinking, quoting, and debating the pros and cons of everything. Intellectual vagrancy is for superficial minds.

Krishna, in the above quote from the Bhagavad Gita, and Jesus Christ, in his emphasis on intuitive understanding, urged us to fix our minds on God alone. Only thus will our discrimination fly like an arrow, straight to the heart of Truth.

---

* Not one who never doubts, be it noted, but one who cannot be shaken by doubt.

CHAPTER TEN

Finding a True Teacher

We have already noted that common sense is an important asset in the search for truth. It would be well also to understand more deeply how and when it ceases to be an asset. For while common sense can keep the mind grounded, it can also (as we saw in the last chapter) prevent the balloon of consciousness from rising, when it is ready to soar.

Jesus Christ was united with the Christ consciousness. He constantly endeavored to lift others to that state of consciousness as well. In emphasizing common sense, then, his purpose wasn't to keep people earthbound, but to urge them to seek truth and not lose themselves in abstract theories and untested dogmas. "Be down-to-earth," was his message of spiritual realism, "but don't be earthy."

There were teachers in his day, as there are today, who boasted an exalted spiritual state from no loftier motive than to attract a worldly following. Jesus warned against accepting spiritual claims blindly. "Test what you read, and what people tell you," he said. "Theological dogmas may be the fruit only of abstract reasoning, and not of Self-realization." Another point to consider is that no matter how carefully a dogma is worded, it can always be misconstrued by people whose own reasoning powers are weak, or whose desire for the truth is tepid. Spiritual utterances, if not inspired by inner vision, lack spiritual power.

In the Gospel of St. Matthew, Chapter 7, Jesus stated: *"Beware of false prophets, which come to you in sheep's clothing, but inwardly are ravening wolves. Ye shall know them by their fruits. Do men gather grapes of thorns, or figs of thistles? Even so every good tree bringeth forth good fruit; but a corrupt tree bringeth forth evil fruit.*

"A good tree cannot bring forth evil fruit, neither can a corrupt tree bring forth good fruit. Wherefore by their fruits ye shall know them."

By "good fruits" Jesus meant more than miracles that are temporarily beneficial, like physical healings. His greatest miracles endured beyond the grave, into eternity. They were the changes he effected in people's consciousness. His physical healings were few, relatively, but the people he transformed spiritually numbered thousands.

The teachings of a "false prophet" need not necessarily be altogether false. He may quote scripture to convince people of his piety, and may don the mask of holiness. His real "teaching" in any case will not lie in his words, but in the vibrations of his consciousness.

He may urge people to be charitable, for example, but if his voice contains a harsh tone, or if the impression he conveys is one of inner tension, his piously expressed sentiments will be only a sugar coating on a poison pill. Sensitive people will discern behind his most artful concealments a distortion of the truth, even though his arguments superficially seem sound. False teachers may even, as Jesus said, *"show great signs and*

166

wonders; insomuch that, if it were possible, they shall deceive the very elect." (Matthew 24:24) The "elect" to whom he referred are those who, by clear intuition, can sense a person's vibrations and know whether they are pure and emanate genuine love, or impure and emanate ego and self-interest.

The errors in a teaching can be subtle, and may even be convincing when rationally analyzed. It is by the vibrations that a teacher's depth can be sounded. If he is spiritual, a sensitive person will feel, especially in the heart, a deep calmness, and an upliftment of spirit. If he is spiritually shallow, as false teachers are likely to be even if they reason brilliantly, the sensitive person will feel in him a certain agitation and unease.

The "fruits" of which Jesus spoke are generally reflected outwardly also: in the eyes, in the timbre of the voice, in a person's very gait, and posture. The eyes of a true teacher shine; they are always calm. His voice contains an undercurrent of sweetness and joy. His gait suggests a determined but relaxed spirit; its strength radiates outward from a center of stillness in his spine. His back is straight, and his posture, upright.

The eyes of a false teacher, by contrast, are restless as well as dull. His voice, usually, grates on the listener's ear. His gait suggests inner tension. And his posture indicates a mind that is centered not in himself, but in the world around him.

These signs, whether positive or negative, are to varying degrees evident in a teacher's disciples also. Therefore Jesus likened the disciples to the fruit of a tree. It isn't that a good tree necessarily produces only good fruit. A good fig tree (to use his example) may produce a few bad figs, owing perhaps to some accident of nature and not to the quality of the tree itself. The greatness of a master must be judged by his worthy disciples, not by the failures among them. Indeed, out of very compassion a true master may accept people of unsettled spirituality. Judas Iscariot betrayed Jesus Christ, yet the greatness of Jesus was not thereby compromised. Rather, it was enhanced by his very calmness confronting that betrayal.

A master's disciples come to him with their own karma, good and bad. The test of the master's greatness, then, is how much those disciples who submit themselves to his influence change for the better.

A true master produces saints. His level of spirituality is reflected in everyone who is in tune with his consciousness. A tree's best fruits are those which receive the most sunlight, not those which cluster densely together in leafy shade. "Seclusion," Paramhansa Yogananda often said, "is the price of greatness." The light that emanates from the teacher reaches those most clearly who, in their hearts, stand alone before him and "receive him" without the admixture of any other influence. Disciples who spend too much time in the company of fellow disciples, and rely less therefore on their inner attunement with the guru, receive less of his silent inner guidance and inspiration. And those students, finally, who merely append their names to his roster of followers receive even less. It must be added, however, that these last students receive also blessings that are life-changing.

Indeed, the vibrations of a great master spread into the world like waves, leaving no one in the inner recesses of his consciousness unaffected. Christians who insist that Jesus brought God's revelation on earth once and forever little realize how very great is humanity's need for repeated divine manifestations on earth. Waves on the sea subside after a time, unless the water's surface is repeatedly stimulated by wind—in this case, the winds of divine grace.

There was a woman student of Paramhansa Yogananda's whose eyes revealed an outwardly happy nature. After she'd been with him about a year, she met another teacher—a wonder-worker, in her opinion at least—and decided to follow him. The woman went to Yogananda and told him she'd accepted this man as her guru. "Very well," the Master replied respectfully, "I withdraw my ray from you."

She returned several months later for a brief visit. Friends who formerly had been happy in her happiness were saddened to note that none of her erstwhile light remained.

The vibrations of a false teacher reveal a lack of clarity in his thinking, a confusion and self-contradiction—like ripples on a lake that move every which way in the changeable winds. His vibrations affect with confusion also anyone who tunes in to them. The Indian master Sri Ramakrishna humorously offered another analogy for the power of such influences: "When you peel an onion, your hands smell!" A false teacher, hoping to impress people with his piety, may urge upon them spiritual qualities such as humility, non-attachment, and inner freedom. What he instills in those who listen, however, is the "smell" of his own bewilderment: the hypocritical humility of a Tartuffe,* the boasted non-attachment of one who hopes to detach *others* from their wealth, and the illusory freedom of a fool who leaps confidently from a high bridge in the belief that he can fly. The vibrations projected by a false teacher contradict any noble sentiments he may outwardly endorse.

Some self-deluded teachers go so far as to encourage their students, in the name of a "new" spirituality, to enjoy morally debased behavior. Disciples, glad of the excuse to be as sensual as they please, flock to him.

Outward behavior, though it seem spiritual, is not in itself a proof of saintliness. Poverty, for example, though many extol it as the example set by St. Francis of Assisi, is a virtue only if it is inspired by a spirit of inner freedom. St. Francis was poor in things that mattered to him not at all: money, worldly position, and material possessions. He was rich, however, in the only thing that did matter to him: the joy of God. St. Francis never adopted what many today label "poverty consciousness." Rather, he embraced "Lady Poverty" in silent protest against the arrogance of the wealthy merchants and aristocrats of his day. Poverty is a virtue only if it is embellished by the simplicity of inner freedom. If it is thought of as a burden, it will probably be just what most people consider it: a sign of material and spiritual failure.

Outward signs of spirituality, to be valid, cannot be divorced from inward states of consciousness. People often make another erroneous assumption: that glow-

---

* The main character in a comedy by the French playwright Molière, and the epitome of the false spiritual teacher.

ing good health is a proof of spirituality. They scorn the sincere spiritual seeker who is in poor health, claiming he demonstrates a lack of spirituality. In fact, they are right in one sense, for good health *is* a sign of good karma. There are other, far more important signs, however. A person may be healthy and have no inner light. Another person may be in poor health, and yet be a true saint. It is love for God that makes one a saint. A saint's health may be poor, moreover, only because, out of love for others, he has assumed onto his own body some of their bad karma. This, indeed, was what Jesus did in accepting death on the cross.

By "good fruit," then, Jesus meant three things above all: first, the degree of Self-realization attained by a true teacher's advanced disciples; second, the inner happiness and radiance manifested by his other disciples, those who might be described as his "grade school" students; third, his quantitative impact on the mass consciousness of his times.

Great masters each represent a particular "ray" of the infinite light. The rays of that light are without number. A master manifests the particular vibrations that are needed by people in his times, and by his particular "family" of disciples. No manifestation defines him inwardly, however: In himself, he *is* the infinite light.

No ray of divine manifestation is "better" or "worse" than any other. One master expresses more divine joy; another, more divine wisdom; another, God's energy and strength; still a fourth, the sweetness of devotion and of surrender to God's will. These qualities are manifested also, to varying degrees, in a master's disciples. Indeed, it is often possible to tell who a disciple's guru is by simply sensing the disciple's vibrations. Paramhansa Yogananda used to remark, "All of Krishna's soldiers were like Krishna."

This isn't to say that the disciples of a great master are "rubber-stamped" images of their guru. The personality of each one differs from all the others, and increasingly so as they advance spiritually. For meditation develops one's inner power. As the sunlight, shining through a stained-glass window, brings out its many colors, so the spiritual light in people who meditate gains in brilliance and highlights every aspect of their nature, the bad as well as the good. This, indeed, is a little-known facet of the spiritual life, and not always a comforting one for those who keep the spiritual aspirant company. Certainly, an increase of inner light, though inconvenient for those who find it more restful to be around people whose light is dimmer, has the advantage for the aspirant himself of making the qualities he must work on dynamic to his awareness. If, for example, his nature tends toward a certain brusqueness or intolerance of others, after years of meditation he may find those qualities fairly ablaze in him until he can recognize how incongruous they are in contrast to his more spiritual ones.

If, on the other hand, as his negative qualities become stronger, some of them seize his imagination and look attractive to him, he may fall spiritually. He may even, for a time, become a false teacher. No delusion is permanent, of course. Unfortunately—well, would any story be interesting without its ups and downs, its complexities of plot?—if such a person becomes a spiritual teacher he will be the sort to whom Jesus referred (in Matthew 24:24), when he said that they might deceive even "the elect."*

Worldly minded people, having little or no inner light, are like stained-glass windows at twilight. Their spiritual energy may be so weak that their virtues and defects are almost indistinguishable from one another. If such a person impresses others as kindly, it may be only because he hasn't the force to express his true feelings clearly.

It is not in their personalities, then, that disciples show a resemblance, but in their inner attunement.

There are universal traits, of course, that all masters manifest, and that are present to varying degrees in everyone who is spiritually inclined. These traits may be delineated as follows: a spirit of dispassion; the conviction that life, without truth or God, has no meaning; a spirit of selflessness; an absence in everything one does of the ego principle; inner freedom—whether relative or absolute—from personal desires; detachment of feeling; calmness and evenness of mind in prosperity and adversity; simplicity of tastes; cheerfulness; equal and impersonal good will to everyone, whether friend or foe; indifference to praise or blame; firmness even at great personal cost where *dharma,* or righteousness, is at stake; respect for all; charity in one's dealings with

---

* One example of a "fallen angel," as here described, was Rasputin, the evil genius of the Russian imperial court before the revolution. Rasputin was a man of considerable and well-attested spiritual powers. Yet he emanated also what many people considered an aura of evil. His influence on the Tsar and Tsarina was in some ways directly responsible for the downfall of the Russian empire. Rasputin was, obviously, a false teacher.

others; sympathy for others' sufferings; fervor in the divine search; unflinching truthfulness; great power of concentration; dynamic will power; and divine devotion.

One master may manifest more of certain divine rays than another. The same may be said of his disciples. Even so, every member of a master's spiritual "family" will emanate something of the same spiritual vibration, to a greater or lesser degree depending on the depth of his attunement.

Thus, the surest sign of a true teacher lies not in anything he says or does outwardly, but in the vibrations he emanates, and in the vibrations others emanate who are in tune with him. These vibrations may be too subtle for the average person to sense, but most people will at least "feel good" in such a person's presence, or when recalling that presence to mind. There are exceptions in this reaction, of course, as we see from the enemies Jesus Christ attracted. For if a person doesn't resonate sympathetically with genuine spirituality, he may react negatively—even to the extent of feeling anger or hatred. Powerful spiritual vibrations make a strong impression. Reactions to them tend to be definite and deeply felt. Thus, the Pharisees, who were weaklings spiritually speaking, hated Jesus Christ. And Saul, before Jesus appeared to him and softened his heart, persecuted the Christians with increasing fervor.

The vibrations of a false teacher, and therefore of his disciples, are dark and unclean like muddy puddles, impure with passion, arrogance, and self-interest. These vibrations may suggest specific negative qualities: personal attachment; sensual obsession; inner tension; a tendency to see everything in a personal light; a mean spirit, quick to revenge; self-conceit regarding one's accomplishments, whether valid or imaginary; a love for opulent display; vacillating moods; a tendency to separate people into rival camps, either hostile or friendly; disrespect for others and a lack of charity toward them; indifference to people's sufferings; carelessness of the truth; special affability toward those who show promise of advancing one's own interests; dryness of heart; and unkindness to others—even, when the mood strikes, to one's friends.

Will power is a quality of human greatness. A person can be great in a human sense, however, without necessarily being spiritual. A strong will awakens inner energy. Energy, in turn, generates magnetism. Without a combination of these three qualities—will power, high energy, and strong magnetism—no one will be a teacher to whom anyone listens. If, however, a person is magnetic enough to attract students, it is important to ask oneself: "Is his magnetism uplifting? or is it degrading?"

Fortunately, if the bond with a teacher is degrading it will be relatively short-lived. Because delusion is false, it is also impermanent, like the varying shapes of clouds coasting on a light breeze. The bond between a true teacher and his disciples, on the other hand, is eternal, and is forged over many lifetimes. Not unusually it develops out of a shared discipleship. As Paramhansa Yogananda once said, "Those who fall by the wayside will be picked up by my devotees." This bond is forged on a soul level, and may be very ancient.

Inevitably, each disciple, when he transmits his guru's vibrations to others, acts as a filter for them. For his individual nature is uniquely his own. He may be quite free from egoic pride; even so, he will add to the vibrations he transmits a hint of something peculiarly his own. Successive generations of disciples who would reflect the spirit of their founder must meditate on him directly, and not only attune themselves to his living representatives. On the other hand, to succeed in this process it would be a mistake to try to bypass those more experienced than themselves in that tradition, for these can help them to focus their attunement.

Christians today who would be true disciples of Jesus Christ can tune in to him directly and thus become his disciples in very truth. Nobody, however, lives in a vacuum. Christians in every age are influenced by others of their own times. To the extent that the followers of Christ have kept his vibrations alive on earth, advanced souls will continue to be reborn with the mission of deepening people's attunement with him. Even his own direct disciples may return to earth from time to time, to revitalize the manifestation of his spirit.

Jesus urged people to use their common sense before embracing a teaching, and to let their critical faculties be guided by their own experience of life. His recommendation was the very opposite of dogmatism, which demands unquestioning obedience to authority; and of the impositions of a false teacher who tries to suspend his students' ability to think with such mind-numbing logic as, "Eat the coconut, or it will eat you."

It may be stated as a formula that *fanaticism*

increases in direct proportion to a person's inability to prove his point. The greater the likelihood of a theory's being tested, the less voluble the fanatic's insistence on it becomes. This has been science's chief contribution to mankind: its insistence on testing a theory by its results.

Of course, modern science has only popularized the scientific method. The obvious way of getting at the facts of any matter has always been by experience, not by deduction. In ancient Jerusalem, the decision on the right price at which to sell a weight of figs was determined by practical experience in the marketplace, not by abstract theories on economics. If the people of those days didn't think of applying "common" sense to such abstruse matters as the shape of the earth or the apparent geocentricity of the universe, it was simply because they had no way of getting at the facts. Modern science began when Galileo used the telescope, which some say he invented, to study the planets. Since his day, science has discovered that virtually everything our senses tell us about reality is a pure fiction.

The scientific method, then, is only a refinement of that normal attribute of reason: common sense. Jesus Christ too, in this sense, was scientific. He urged people to submit their spiritual assumptions to the test of experience. Some of his claims were extraordinary—even more so than the up-to-the-minute claims of quantum physics. In his teaching, however, he began as every scientist does, and must. He asked, "Where is the proof?"

Science could only have made its amazing discoveries by proceeding systematically, from simple and obvious studies to others that transcended "common" sense altogether. Scientists first investigated such prosaic data as mass, weight, and motion. Jesus, too, told people to be guided by what they actually knew of life, and not to accept vague, imaginary claims or finely spun webs of untested deductions.

Science asks, "Does it work?" Jesus told people to ask this same question of spiritual teachings. If someone questions the truth of a scientific assertion, he is told to perform the experiments to find out for himself. Jesus said, "This has been my experience. Do what I've done and see whether your experience isn't the same." Like any scientist, again, he urged people to study the effects of his teachings. In effect, what he said was, "If you don't want to commit years to the experiment I propose, then study its fruits in the lives of others."

In fact, this grand "experiment" has been carried out far more thoroughly than any in modern physics: uncounted thousands of times in every century, in every great religion, and in every country on earth. Unlike the experiments of science, this one has never been contradicted, never changed or qualified, and in every case has been proved beyond every possibility of error. Moreover, the truth it demonstrates is of more vital importance to humanity than any mere law of physics or chemistry, for it concerns people's own lasting peace and happiness—not in some nebulous and undemonstrable after-death state, but here on earth—*now*, in the present lifetime.

To Nicodemus Jesus stated, as we've already seen, *"Verily, verily, I say unto thee, We speak that which we do know, and testify that which we have seen."* He then asked, *"Art thou a master of Israel, and knowest not these things?"* His obvious implication was that truth must be experienced, and not merely believed. Far from keeping anything a secret, he made it clear that he both expected *and wanted* everyone to *experience* the truth. He asked of people only that they keep their hearts and minds open to it, and not confuse rational deductions with intuitive perception.

To the woman of Samaria, in the fourth chapter of St. John, he said, *"We know what we worship."* He added, *"But the hour cometh, and now is, when the true worshipers shall worship the Father in spirit and in truth: for the Father seeketh such to worship him."*

When people accused him of being an instrument of Satan, citing as evidence the fact that he cast devils out of people, he referred his accusers back to things with which all of them were familiar: *"Any kingdom divided against itself is bound to collapse. Nor can any household divided against itself last for long. If Satan were expelling Satan,* [it would signify that] *he was divided against himself. How, then, could his kingdom continue?"* And again he reminded them, *"You can tell a tree at once by its fruit."* (Matthew 12:25,26,33)

It should be noted, incidentally, that although Jesus warned against false prophets, he didn't warn people against *all* prophets. He was not, in this sense, like the woman psychic who said to a sister psychic, "Ah no, my dear, I'm afraid you're mistaken. You were not Cleopatra." "What makes you say that?" the other demanded indignantly. "Why, because—*I* was!"

One of the notable features of common sense is a good sense of humor. This trait arises from a sense of proportion. People with a keen sense of the absurd find it natural to view the particular in its relation to the whole. They are keenly aware of the absurdity of disproportionate attitudes: the self-importance, for instance, of the petty bureaucrat, who is accepted by many at his own inflated evaluation. The surest sign of a fanatic, often, is his inability to see things in proper relation to one another. His sense of the ridiculous, if he has any, is seldom kindly, and is not infrequently cruel. What his laughter lacks above all is the spirit of joy. He views everything in grim relationship to himself and to his own interests. Things loom large or small, important or unimportant in his eyes depending on how closely they touch him personally. This attitude deprives him of happiness, for it shrinks his awareness inward upon himself. Fulfillment, to him, lies forever just over the next hill. To the fanatic, even the most trivial challenge to his beliefs is a summons to do brave battle against the very powers of hell.

An ancient description of Jesus, attributed to the historian Josephus, is that he was "a man never known to smile." Such a notion would be acceptable only to people who themselves were completely without a sense of humor. Actually, numerous gospel passages show Jesus in an altogether engaging light. Can anyone who reads them with imagination and clearly visualizes the scenes that are described fail to picture him as at least smiling with quiet humor, if not sometimes actually laughing out loud?

No gloomy preacher, surely, sighing mournfully over the sins of the world, could have attracted the enthusiastic crowds Jesus did! The fulfillment sought by all human beings is happiness, not sorrow. What people desire, and the quality they find most engaging in others, is joy. Would Jesus have won the hearts of thousands had it been his custom to gaze at them lugubriously, as he is so often depicted, compassionating them for their sins? Ridiculous!

Consider the skill with which he lightheartedly dismissed the charge of being Satan's instrument. Consider again his amusing word-portrait, in the sixth chapter of St. Matthew, of hypocrites who, when bringing alms to the temple, hired trumpeters to precede them with the purpose of drawing attention to their pious munificence. And don't we imagine him smiling with quiet irony as he remarked, *"Verily, they have their reward!"*?

Jesus offered his followers the gift of divine joy—a joy which, as he put it, *"No one will be able to take from you."* (John 16:22)

Finally, remember also his parable of the talents. In that well-known story a man returns home from a long journey to find that two of his servants have wisely invested the money he left in their keeping, and have doubled it. After praising them, he dismisses a third servant who buried his share of money in the ground "for safe-keeping," and put it to no use.

A "talent" was an ancient unit of money. From this word we have the meaning Jesus ascribed to it symbolically in this parable: the gifts with which every human being is endowed. Jesus was saying, "Put your talents to good use and don't suppress them." Some people imagine that God considers it presumptuous to develop one's native intelligence. (Consider the old argument,

"If God had wanted us to fly, He'd have given us wings.") Jesus in this parable was telling people to use their God-given "talents," and to deepen their understanding of life and of truth. In other words, he was saying once again, "Submit my teachings to the test of experience. Offer up to God the best that is in you."

Common sense helps us to keep our feet on the ground. We ought not, however, to anchor them there. Jesus, in telling us to invest our talents, was saying, "Soar in the balloon of consciousness. Soar in a spirit of divine adventure! Offer all you know of reality into ever-expanding vistas of understanding." Infinity is no more than suggested to us by the glimpse we get of it when it is framed in the doorway of the scriptures. When a great master teaches, it is from the fullness of direct perception. What he teaches is necessarily consistent with the scriptures, but it also, necessarily, transcends them. The first question the Pharisees put to Jesus was, "What is your scriptural authority?" He answered, "God is my authority. It is from Him that the scriptures derive their authority."

Krishna, in the second chapter of the Bhagavad Gita, put it this way: *"The sage who knows God has as little need for the scriptures as one might have for a pond when the whole land is covered in flood!"*

St. John's Gospel finishes with a further reference to the infinity of truth: *"And there are also many other things which Jesus did, the which, if they should be written every one, I suppose that even the world itself could not contain the books that should be written."*

Common sense is a way of clarifying reason. Reason alone, however, can only infer its conclusions;

it cannot achieve certainty. Superconscious insights, on the other hand, though sometimes they appear to defy common sense, convince the mind by simply transcending ordinary experience. As Paramhansa Yogananda put it, "He who knows, he *knows:* naught else knows!" Truth is infinite. Common sense is like the husk of a seed. Jesus, in one of his best-known parables, described a mustard seed that grew and in time became a mighty tree. The seed could only begin to grow, however, by first shedding its husk.

What should people's response be to a spiritual teacher?

First, they ought to consult their *calm*—not their excited—feelings. Above all, they should ask: "Are these teachings spiritually uplifting?"

Second, people ought to ask whether his teachings correspond to *reality* as they themselves have experienced it.

Third, they should ask themselves: "How well does his teaching correspond with the scriptures?"

Fourth, they should judge the teacher by his "fruits," asking themselves, "What has he actually accomplished?" A further, vital question follows: "Is this teacher's influence calming? or is it exciting?" Calmness brings us closer to God; excitement drives us farther away from Him.

Fifth, and most important, they should ask themselves, "Is this teacher interested in drawing people to himself? or is he trying to awaken devotion to God alone, and to people's own Self-realization in Him?"

It was to false teachers that Jesus referred when, in Chapter 10 of St. John, he said, *"All that ever came before* *me are thieves and robbers."* He wasn't speaking of the prophets who had lived before him in time. Indeed, he said elsewhere, *"Think not that I am come to destroy the law, or the prophets: I am come not to destroy, but to fulfill."* (Matthew 5:17) Those words, then, "all that ever came before me," referred to spiritual teachers who sought to promote their own importance instead of giving all importance to God. The false teacher is a "thief," for he diverts to his own coffers, so to speak, the gold of devotion that the heart owes to God alone.*

Truth and error: Both need time to reveal themselves for what they are. Be open to the truth whatever the form it assumes. And don't be like those "purists" who scoff at new teachings, dismissing them with the indictment: "This teacher isn't like Saint So-and-So of the Twelfth Century"; or, "This explanation differs from the dogma as stated by Pope Such-and-Such."

Jesus made a very interesting statement, one that is rarely emphasized or even quoted: *"Other sheep I have,"* he said, *"which are not of this fold."*† (John 10:16) The

---

* People who prefer to read a personal meaning into these words are not wrong in doing so, for no master, having attained oneness with God, can excel any other in spiritual greatness. It would, in other words, be spiritually wrong to place any teacher or master above Jesus Christ. Anyone who knew the truth would never presume to do so.

† This verse continues: *"them also I must bring, and they shall hear my voice; and there shall be one fold, and one shepherd."* Proselytizing Christians interpret these words to mean that *Jesus* Christ himself had appeared, or would appear, elsewhere on earth. Books have been written on purported legends that Jesus Christ himself "walked the Americas." His use of the pronoun "I" in the above passage refers, as it does repeatedly throughout the New Testament, not to Jesus the man, but to the infinite Christ

ways to God are many. It isn't likely that anyone will feel attracted to all of them, or even to every true teacher. It is enough to be sincerely attracted to one of them. Every human being is uniquely endowed, and should accept that fact as his own special destiny.

Everyone has his own teacher also, whose destiny it is to bring him to God. His loyalty should be to that teacher above all. Error arises only if he defines his loyalty in exclusive terms. Love for one's own mother, for example, is not demonstrated by hatred for other women. Rather, that love is ennobled if it makes one appreciate more deeply the very principle of motherhood.

Out of countless millions of Christians, no two ever hold exactly the same beliefs. For even their recital of the Credo awakens in each of them different insights and different associations.

Truth is like a vast ocean. Into that great body of water all the scriptures, and all the teachings of the great masters of the world, flow like so many rivers. Our attitude on approaching truth should be with an uplifted mind, kept in a state of reason to safeguard against fanaticism, and at the same time with openness to the possibility of ever higher revelations. To fall short of this attitude would be to betray the ideal that our own souls hold eternally before us.

consciousness. "One fold," then, referred not to one Christian church, but to an understanding that all who love God, whatever their outward affiliation, will eventually realize their souls' oneness with Him.

CHAPTER ELEVEN

How to Relate to a Master

The following passage is from the Gospel of St. Matthew, Chapter 16, Verses 13–18:

"When Jesus arrived at the district of Caesarea Philippi, he asked his disciples, 'Who do people say that I the Son of man am?' And they replied, 'Some say thou art John the Baptist; some, Elijah; and others, Jeremiah, or one of the other prophets.'

"Then he asked them further, 'But who do you say that I am?'

"And Simon Peter replied, 'Thou art the Christ, the son of the living God.'

"And Jesus turned to him, saying, 'Blessed art thou, Simon, son of Jonah: for not by human nature was this truth revealed to thee, but by my heavenly Father. And I tell thee this also: Thou art Peter, which is to say, a rock, and upon this rock will I build my church, and never will the powers of darkness overwhelm it.'"

The subject of reincarnation, which this passage touches on at the beginning, has been discussed in an earlier chapter and will be gone into again later in this book. Meanwhile, important to our immediate subject is the contrast presented here between many people's view of Jesus the "son of man" and Peter's recognition in him of the infinite Christ consciousness, the Son of God.

A saint in India was wont to say, "I'm like a drum: As you beat me, so I sound." A master is not what he appears to human eyes. Yet his human appearance is, for all that, an aspect of what he is. The distinction lies in the fact that he is infinitely *more* than what he appears. Thus, for those who see in him a great and wise teacher, he is that. For those who see him as a dear friend, he is also that. He appears differently to every person: as a gracious and charming individual; as a wonderful raconteur of wise stories; a delightful humorist; an inspired lecturer; an invincible opponent; a powerful crusader; a guileless child; a stern disciplinarian; the truest friend one could ever have. He is infinitely more than every possible definition of him, and more than the sum of all concepts of him—more even than people's capacity to understand.

A master is like a mirror: Whatever qualities we present to him, he reflects back to us: not our errors, needless to say, but what our own souls perceive in us from their level of deeper wisdom. To each of us he represents the reactions of the eternal Self. Thus, even if people view him as the personification of kindness, he never fails to correct them, even sternly, if that is what they need at the moment. At the same time, behind each of those reflections he remains ever the same: wise, kind, all-forgiving, humble, firmly resolute, and forever incapable of compromising the truth. He is whatever each of us, in his soul, wants him to be; at the same time, he is beyond our mental concepts, unshakably centered in infinite consciousness.

187

The author recalls once addressing a saint in India lovingly, "How tirelessly and selflessly you have given of yourself to others all your life!"

The saint, gazing at him with calm eyes, replied, "Is that how you see it?"

Whatever else a master is, he is also a person of extraordinary magnetism. Thus—inevitably so—he attracts people to him though his one desire is to draw them to God, not to his humanity. Devotees who love God one-pointedly enjoy more than others do the charm and inspiration of a master's nature. Nor is it wrong for anyone to do so. Indeed, it is his magnetism that carries the soul on a "magic carpet" up to the Infinite Light. The devotion a master receives is directed by him to God alone. And he patiently teaches others to direct their love to God also, viewing him as but a window onto infinity.

One of the chief signs of a true master, indeed, is the impersonality of his love: impersonal where he himself is concerned, but not where others' needs are concerned. He knows, however, and others know also, whose perception is intuitive, that without the inspiration they receive from him their very devotion would become only a sputtering flame.

Thus, disciples often focus their devotion on the master as a catalyst for their love for God. By devotion to him as a conscious instrument of the Divine, they open themselves to the flow of divine love. The magnetic presence of a true master, far from impeding their spiritual progress, greatly accelerates it.

In like manner, people in general are lifted to higher levels of consciousness by associating respectfully with people who live more in wisdom than they themselves do. The young, therefore, are well instructed to show deference to the old, whose longer experience in life has (or should have) given them greater wisdom. It is good, indeed, to serve any human being whose magnetic influence can raise one to higher levels of awareness. To work even as a servant in the home of people who are socially above oneself can be a karmic boon for someone whose family background is coarse and uneducated, for it can help him to become more refined. Even pets who are loved by their owners receive an impetus through that association in their own spiritual evolution.

Thus, association with a great master, even for those with only dim awareness of what he is, can bring priceless spiritual benefits. Of course, the more aware one is, the greater the blessings he attracts.

Much grace comes through association with a great master, even for people who are only vaguely aware of the gifts they are receiving. The benefits vary, depending on the disciples' understanding and receptivity. Few disciples are as intuitively attuned to their master as Peter showed himself in the above story to be. Most are content to enjoy the master's personality. Thus, they follow him about eagerly, gaze at him avidly, and try mentally to absorb his expressions and gestures as indicative of the consciousness he emanates. His least remark is reported eagerly, and every tidbit of news concerning him is circulated widely: to whom he has spoken, whom he has favored especially, the time he has given to this person or to that. The disciples' attention, in other words, is often directed so much outwardly that they neglect to develop inward communion with him, and think by physical association alone to receive his blessings.

Much of this sort of energy may be seen around the kings and queens in the royal courts of this world. We see it displayed also in this Bible passage in people's fascination with such superficial questions as who Jesus was in other incarnations. It isn't that such questions ought never to be asked, but only that too much of this kind of interest becomes mere gossip, and prevents one from absorbing the master's vibrations and magnetism.

The author once, having noted a number of outstanding similarities between Jesus Christ and Paramhansa Yogananda, asked the guru, "Sir, were you Jesus Christ in a former life?"

"What difference would it make?" the guru replied indifferently. "The Ocean is the one reality beneath all its waves."

Peter had perceived the vastness of Christ. Therefore Jesus said to him, *"Thou art Peter, which is to say, a rock."* On the bedrock of Peter's spiritual attainment, he implied, he would be able to construct the edifice—the "church," as he called it—of cosmic consciousness. Peter, in other words, had demonstrated his spiritual preparedness to receive the supreme gift Jesus had to bestow: God-realization.

There are as many ways of relating to a true master as there are human beings that relate to him. Even a master's own disciples limit themselves in what they receive, as long as they define his greatness in merely human terms. Those who seek their inspiration outwardly receive what eyes and ears can absorb, but not the deeper understanding craved by the soul. This understanding comes only by deep communion in meditation.

Wise, then, is that devotee who looks not only to the master's physical form, but communes with him in his soul. To take inside the inspiration one receives from outward contact, however, is to discover that which truly expands the consciousness.

Herein, then, lies the secret of how to relate to a master. It is a relationship not only of inner communion and of receiving, but of self-giving. It comes not by taking eagerly what one can for oneself. Only in a spirit of mutuality can divine love be developed.

A mistake disciples sometimes commit is to attempt to "figure out" their guru, instead of calmly receiving him in their souls. One of Paramhansa Yogananda's disciples, when referring to him, once told the author, "Every time I think I've understood him, I find he's much more than I thought!" After this remark, the author thought, "Why would anyone even *try* to understand a true guru?"

To understand a master, one must himself *become* a master. Human beings—especially those of intellectual bent, like that disciple—often typify others, trying to mold them according to a variety of set "formulas." This particular disciple was an astrologer. Her profession conditioned her to define everything in terms of planetary and constellational configurations. By reducing people to types, however, she lost normal understanding of them as living human beings who struggled, each of them, to achieve perfection. The result of this analytical attitude was that she herself eventually fell spiritually, her delusion being the belief that, in order to understand others, one need only to cover them with symbols.

True understanding, as Peter showed in the above passage, comes by identifying with others on a soul level as masters do. That disciple failed to see that definitions can never take the place of the thing defined. Human beings, especially, are far more than flesh-and-blood mechanisms. And masters, because they have no personal motivation, are not mechanisms at all. In that disciple's attempt to define others, she placed herself mentally in the position of a judge, and thereby both judged herself and lost touch with normal human compassion.

The benefits gained (or the losses incurred) through association with other people are primarily magnetic, not conceptual. Our Guru had tried gently for years to dissuade that disciple from practicing astrology, for he saw that it would lead her to imagine in symbols a reality greater than people themselves.

Intuition, on the other hand, when it is firmly rooted in soul-perception, is reliable and true. It is by the power of intuition that people know beyond any shadow of rationalization that they exist, and that all beings are essentially divine. It was, on the other hand, to people's lack of intuition that Jesus was referring when, in John 8:43, he said: *"Why do ye not understand my speech? even because ye cannot hear my word."*

Except for his prediction that on Peter's firm intuition he would found his church, we do not find Jesus mentioning the founding of any church. And though he said, *"Destroy this temple, and in three days I will raise it up"* (John 2:19), his reference was to his body and not, as his listeners at first thought, to the temple at Jerusalem. Even granting the claim of many Christians that Jesus in his prediction to Peter was hinting at the foundation of a new religion, the important point would be that this religion was to be built on the bedrock of realized wisdom, not on the sandy soil of dogmas. Divine wisdom alone is a true guide.

In the historic unfoldment of religion, the time has come for sincere spiritual aspirants of every faith to establish their own direct contact with Truth. This they must do not only by the use of common sense, as we said earlier, nor by blindly obeying priestly dictates, but by the intuitive power of the soul. Modern science has conditioned us to remain satisfied no longer with mere beliefs. The time has come for people to do more than believe in God: They must commune with Him! The true "church" of God is, as St. Paul put it in II Corinthians, *"a house not made by hands, eternal in the heavens."* It was to this "church" that Jesus was referring in those words to Peter.

It is urgent also that mankind seek a deeper-than-rational understanding of life. For as human knowledge grows, it encompasses other cultures and other ways of thinking. This expansion of awareness cannot but convince people of the truth and beauty of other great religious teachings. People are discovering that many of those teachings are not the superstitious ravings of savages, as they once thought, but declarations of refined wisdom such that they cannot but wonder, "Of all these teachings, is only one of them true?"

Jesus Christ, by emphasizing the importance of

intuition over intellect, showed how this dilemma may be resolved. In the Bhagavad Gita also, Stanza 53 of the second Chapter, we read:

"When your intellect, at present confused by the diversity of teaching in the scriptures, becomes steadfast in the ecstasy of deep meditation, then you will achieve final union with God."

Krishna was implying that the quest for spiritual enlightenment must be founded on deep, inner communion, otherwise the result will, sooner or later, be intellectual confusion. For even the simplest spiritual truth is susceptible of misinterpretation, if one tries to understand it by the intellect alone.

The basic concern of scripture, therefore, is only secondarily to give careful explanations of the truth. Puzzle-solving is for trudging minds. True scripture is primarily a call to spiritual action. It offers practical suggestions for how actually to realize truth. Its primary purpose is to inspire people to desire this lofty achievement.

Endless theorizing is for pedestrian minds. More pleasing to God than all the scholarship our brains can hold is to open our hearts to His love. If we love, then even though our brains be completely unlettered, it matters not.

The way to know God is to still the mind, by deep meditation. The way to know Him is to live consciously in His blissful presence. The way to know Him is to commune with Him in the inner silence, and to fill the heart, finally, with His love.

This, then, is the way to relate also to a master. We must approach him with the sincere desire to establish an inward relationship with God. Superficial disciples make a show of devotion to the guru, but those who are spiritually deep hold his presence in their hearts, absorb his vibrations silently into their souls, and seek his guidance inwardly rather than outwardly in words.

We should not allow our minds to be swayed by outer circumstances, but keep them fixed on our inner attunement. Here it is that our relationship with a master can be established in truth. All else is like winds on the sea that keep the waves agitated while in the process changing nothing.

One who loves God deeply will speak little of his love, but will listen to the Beloved's silent whispers in his soul. He cannot imagine desecrating that beatitude by displaying it before others.

And the same is true in our relationship with a master. That seeker receives most who communes in inner silence, being little interested in outward speech.

Let us speak little, then, but love much. And let us ever commune ecstatically with the Lord, as the great masters do, in our souls.

CHAPTER TWELVE

Heaven Is Our Birthright!

Jesus Christ said, *"No man hath ascended up to heaven but him that came down from heaven: [even so] the Son of man who is in heaven."* (John 3:13)

This passage comes from a verbal exchange between Jesus and Nicodemus in which Jesus hinted somewhat obliquely at certain deep truths. His words were obviously not intended for those whose outlook on life was too literal, for much of his imagery was poetic and, indeed, symbolic. He said, for example, in addition to the above verse: *"The wind bloweth where it listeth, and thou hearest the sound thereof, but canst not tell whence it cometh, and whither it goeth: so is every one that is born of the Spirit."* Further on he said, *"As Moses lifted up the serpent in the wilderness, even so must the Son of man be lifted up"*: a statement that has been taken as referring to his coming crucifixion, although the context of that exchange was not historical, but mystical. To intrude into this discussion the subject of Christ's death on the cross makes little or no sense considered even in terms of his atonement for people's sins. The statement is meaningful for those only who, during deep meditation, have experienced the movements of consciousness and energy within the spine.

Jesus, when speaking of "heaven," usually referred

to God-consciousness and not to the beautiful world to which good people go after death. The average idea of heaven is a place where people live in bodies much like their present ones, but made of light. Such a "place," so to speak, does exist. What Jesus is saying in this passage could therefore be applied to both levels of reality. His primary meaning, however, is that everyone can find God, for it was from Him that we have all descended. His statement is also true if we apply it to the higher astral worlds, for it is from our astral bodies that our physical bodies were projected. He goes on to state, in effect, "I myself came from there, and live even now in that state of consciousness. Therefore I know from experience what I'm talking about."

Jesus Christ came to reassure people of God's love. The above passage, however, might easily be taken as intended not to reassure, but to discourage, for it might sound as if Jesus were saying that only he will ever go to heaven. It is already an established dogma, in fact, that only Jesus Christ is, and ever will be, one with God. Many Christians consider it a dogma also that, since he tells us in this passage that no one but him ever "came down" from heaven, our normal state after death would be eternal damnation were it not for his atonement for us on the cross. It seems difficult to believe that people could hold such a dismal view of God, who is All Love, but there are those who find a sort of inspiration in the thought that they themselves are fortunate, and that others, by comparison, are unfortunate.

Could Jesus possibly have meant, "I've come down here to tell you how great I am, and how wretched you all are"? Absurd! Even to a criminal who was crucified with him Jesus said, *"Verily I say unto thee, **this day** shalt thou be with me in paradise."* (Luke 23:43)

Again, could he have meant that not even the prophets before him had gone to heaven? Certainly not! In Matthew (8:11) he said, *"Many . . . shall sit down with Abraham, and Isaac, and Jacob in the kingdom of heaven."* Obviously, he was implying that Abraham and those others were "in heaven" already. They must, according to this passage, have descended from heaven in the first place. What did his words mean, then, "No man hath ascended up to heaven"? Obviously, he didn't mean literally that no one before him had ever gone to heaven. Nor did he suggest, then, that in the natural course of events we ourselves would be banned from there.

His meaning is, as we said, subtle. It doesn't, however, support literalist preachings that insist on depicting God as an old man with a white beard seated on a golden throne, with Jesus Christ by his side. What Jesus meant was akin to the parable of the Prodigal Son: that going to heaven means a return to our own true home. No man can ascend to heaven until he has realized that heaven is where he belongs. Patanjali, a great exponent of yoga in ancient India, stated that divine awakening is a process of *smriti,* or remembering. It was this truth that Jesus proclaimed. The very promise he brought to mankind was the declaration: "You are children of God's light, not of darkness and sin." It is not presumptuous on our part to claim heaven as our divine birthright. We came from God, and are forever part of Him. It would be presumptuous only if we claimed that this birthright can be ours for the mere asking ("by faith," is the common expression), and that it needn't be earned by arduous effort.

Jesus is saying that our souls came from God, and that we belong in Him. We have wandered far from that eternal perfection, acquiring many false identities along the way, but that state is our eternal reality. We are God's; He is ours. Any other identity is born of delusion, and false.

Jesus underscored his authority to announce this truth by adding, "the Son of Man who *is* in heaven." This shift in tense from the past to the present is significant. A great master lives simultaneously in the manifested universe and beyond it in the Supreme Spirit. His omnipresence includes all the subtler worlds. It is as natural and easy for him to communicate with the inhabitants of those realms as with the people of earth.

Heaven, here, may indeed be taken as referring also to the higher regions of the astral universe, for it is from them that the material universe, and therefore our own physical bodies, were projected. The atoms of the gross material universe are simply lower vibrations of astral energy. The astral plane actually resembles the material in appearance also.

Our physical bodies, too, are projections of our astral bodies, and resemble them. When a person dies, he leaves his earthly form but lives on in his astral body, and in the astral universe. There, he experiences whatever state of consciousness was predominant in him while he lived on earth. The major difference between the astral and material worlds is that a person's awareness is no longer weighted down by matter. His feelings therefore can express themselves freely, and tend to be vivid—even as one's emotions may be, in dreams. Whatever of happiness or misery has been habitual for one on earth becomes intensified in the world of energy. If his consciousness here was dark, heavy, and steeped in materialism, his negative emotions, there, will be strong. He will be driven by powerful gusts of rage, fear, or vindictiveness. If on earth he lived selfishly, acknowledging no one's needs but his own, he will find himself alone there, and abandoned. Finding nothing external on which to fix his desires, he lives enclosed in a grey fog of self-preoccupation, in many cases believing that nothing but darkness exists. Thus, he experiences, as the Bhagavad Gita puts it, "great fear and colossal sufferings."

If, on the other hand, while on earth he expressed kindness to others, and more so still if he loved God, the joy he knows in the astral regions will be intense.

Jesus' statement in the above passage means that only that part of man can go back to heaven, or to God, which came down from there. Man's physical body could not survive in those non-material realms. His jealousy and pride would make it intolerable for him to be surrounded by radiant love. His ego could never withstand what Paramhansa Yogananda called "the liberating shock of omnipresence."

There are accounts of great souls having been assumed into heaven in their physical bodies. The dogma of the bodily Assumption of the Virgin Mary is, among Christians, a prominent example. Many similar events are described in the Hindu teachings as well.

What those accounts mean is that, with the attainment of perfect spiritual purity, the transition after death is unbroken; one passes on to a higher state without any loss of consciousness. It would not be literally possible, however, to retain one's physical body on non-physical levels of existence, any more than it would be possible in this physical body to stand on a cloud. What appears in heaven is, rather—especially in the case of a liberated being—a transformation of the physical body itself into astral energy.

Jesus, being fully awake in the Spirit, was constantly identified with the subtlest spiritual realms, even while he lived on earth as the "Son of man." Even here, he was simultaneously conscious of himself in infinity. For in the state of union with God (*nirbikalpa samadhi* is the Sanskrit name for it), it is possible to maintain that perfect awareness even while living and acting in the physical body. Thus, Jesus could say that his astral body, too, was even at that moment in heaven.

It is important to realize that heaven is our divine birthright. By heaven is not meant only the attainment of some high astral sphere, but union with the infinite Spirit. As children of God's light, darkened though we are by present matter-identification, there exists a center within each one of us where that divine Truth dwells and can be known.

The truth offered in this passage has been stated many times through the centuries. The Greek philosopher Plotinus said, "Like only can comprehend like." The Bhagavad Gita makes this point even more clearly. It explains also the reason why it is not easy to enter into that beatific state. Krishna, in the fifteenth Chapter, states:

"Seekers of union with the Lord find Him dwelling in their own hearts. But those who, lacking in wisdom, seek Him with impure motives cannot perceive Him, however much they struggle to do so."

To know God, we must first become aware of our "descent from heaven." We must seek God with no other motive than to unite our souls with Him. "Like only can comprehend like." God is Love. Only by pure, self-giving love is it possible to know Him. This is the true meaning of God's commandment to Moses: *"Thou shalt have no other gods before Me."*

Superficial devotees may imagine that, since the scriptures claim we are all children of God, we need only to accept this truth in order to experience it. Like only, however, can comprehend like. It is not by the intellect, but by soul-intuition that we can realize God. Divine attainments are not available to spiritual dilettantes. One's aspiration must be earnest. We must follow inwardly as well as outwardly the rules of right and moral conduct. We must practice yoga meditation techniques or other methods for attaining deep concentration. We must pray with devotion. And we must above all seek divine communion.

Many spiritual aspirants practice the teachings haphazardly, and then wonder why they never seem to "get anywhere." Scriptural reassurances that we came from God are given to encourage and inspire us toward zeal. They are not intended to lull us to spiritual complacency! As long as, in efforts to save ourselves from drowning, we cling to the tiny straw of ego-consciousness, there is no hope of our saving ourselves. We must relinquish our grip on this straw and swim bravely on, full of faith in our divine destiny. As long, however, as we seek even God and Truth from motives other than complete union with Him, we shall never escape the swirling currents of delusion. Death will claim us again and again for its own.

Heavenly happiness—so the scriptures declare—is ours by right. But we must work to achieve it! To find the divine presence reflected in our consciousness, we must diligently rub away from our mental mirrors all the rust of egoism.

It is not enough, then, merely to *read* the scriptures: We must hold their teachings up to the watchful Presence within us, which is our own superconscious Self. For we have potentially within us the power to attain the highest spiritual peak. We need only to make that simple choice to attain it—alas, not an easy one! Remember always, therefore: It was from the heights that, eons ago, you descended!

Every scripture gives a further, and enormously important, caution: Be humble! Know that, as you have the potential to develop spiritual wisdom, so there are countless others who, even at present, are more spiritually advanced than yourself: masters, even, who can say as Jesus did to Nicodemus, *"We speak that which we do know, and testify to that which we have seen."* Don't think of yourself as the lead runner in a pack of spiritual laggards. Think of yourself as the last one among countless devotees before you who have earnestly sought, and have finally attained, the one goal in life that is worth seeking. "Like only can comprehend like." Identify yourself with those who are trying deeply to attain God, not with those who are still deeply asleep and haven't yet realized how spiritually unaware they are. To pride oneself on being more spiritual than they is to identify oneself with them. Identify yourself, rather, with those whom you would join. Be only grateful that you have discovered, however belatedly, the truths you sought for so long, truths that can mean the difference between life and death—for yourself, and for those whom you love. Instead of a foolish "holier than thou" attitude, think what a sluggard you've been compared with countless millions before you!

If you maintain the humility that great saints and masters have demonstrated in their lives, you will in time behold the sun of divine awakening rise in the firmament of your consciousness. Then will the shadows of doubt be dispelled at last, and you will find yourself in the position, not of one who has found a sunken treasure and doesn't want others to find out about it, but of an artist who, having been enraptured by an extraordinarily beautiful sunset, wants to capture it on canvas and share it with everyone.

CHAPTER THIRTEEN

Imperfection Is of the Ego— Perfection Is of the Soul

In this final chapter of the section, "The Instruments of Recognition," that instrument should be considered which is most central to human understanding: the ego. Paramhansa Yogananda defined the ego as "the soul attached to the body." We've been persuaded by ancient habit, through this ego attachment of the soul, that this ego is our very self. Yet some instinct never ceases to hint to us that the ego is as much of a hindrance to us as an incentive in our spiritual development.

Here, for example, is the kind of hint the soul gives: Most people consider boastfulness distasteful, at least when others are doing the boasting! Why? Doesn't almost everybody want to excel at something? Is it only envy, then, that arouses a negative reaction in people when others brag, "I'm the greatest!"? Envy may be some people's motivation, particularly if the distaste they feel is strong, but envy is not everyone's motivation. For the offense is not only to the ego. Often, indeed, it is when one's own ego is least involved that he notices the disparity between what a braggart reveals of himself and what he might be, were he less involved in himself. To observe a flaw in someone else is not necessarily a judgment on him. Rather than increasing a person's importance in others' eyes, boastfulness only diminishes it. Thus, the distaste one feels for bragging may be more particularly a sense of embarrassment for the braggart.

But, again, why even embarrassment? Because, even granting that the ego likes occasionally to preen itself, if one tries too persistently to draw attention to himself he only betrays how narrow his own horizons are. Boastfulness is not only self-limiting: It is self-suffocating.

We all know intuitively that the ego is not something one should revel in. Growing emotional maturity tells us that there are other enjoyments in life: radiant sunsets, beautiful gardens, expansive vistas, and wonderful adventures into the unknown. There are people to whom we can relate meaningfully, learn from, perhaps, and love. The ego is not even our entire reality; it is only, so to speak, our point of departure in understanding, our point of reference. Life takes on more meaning for us if that reference is *outward,* and away from, rather than perennially back to, ourselves. We find fulfillment by serving others and by serving a worthy cause. We find very little fulfillment, relatively speaking, in thinking of what we might get in return, or of what others think of us, or of how they have misunderstood us. Happiness comes when we simply forget ourselves.

All things belong to a whole. All things are therefore related to us—even as islands are connected together by the earth, which projects them. At our center, as John Donne rightly said, "No man is an island." Our separateness is an illusion, for our divine Self—not the ego—knows only unity.

The desire for infinite bliss is our hidden motivation in everything we do. We seek pleasure because, deep inside us, we long for the bliss of our true nature. Pleasure is the distorted reflection of bliss in the mirror of our worldly expectations. Our consciousness of separation from that nature, and from one another, arises only because our attention is superficial. We are spiritually myopic, the consequence of concentrating too exclusively on this one body, these particular feelings, the thoughts in our little brains. But the brain itself can do no more than *express* consciousness; it cannot *create* it. Any attempt to define consciousness can only take one in a circle: "Consciousness is thought, which in its turn is conscious." This is no definition! Nor does thought make us aware of our existence, as Descartes declared, for without awareness one cannot think at all. And in order even to think we must be aware that we exist. "I think, therefore I am," is a fallacy. What Descartes might have stated was, "I am aware of my existence; therefore I find it possible to think." But of course, even this would not be a definition. Neither existence nor consciousness can be defined, for definitions are lower functions of them both.

The fact is, awareness is a soul-intuition. It cannot be either proved or disproved: It simply *is*. Our certainty of this fact is utter; it wells up from the depths of our very being. Assuming we are not so "out of it" that we couldn't think if we wanted to, we are, if anything, *more clearly* aware when not thinking than we are when our brains are busy with a thousand thoughts.

I exist. You exist. Together we share this eternal reality. There is unity, moreover, in that existence, for the consciousness of existence is universal, rather than particular to any ego. In giving joy to others we give joy to ourselves. They and we are one. In loving others we ourselves discover love. Love too is conscious: an aspect of universal consciousness. When we experience universal love, it no longer matters much to us whether we are loved in return. Love's own greatest reward is itself.

If, on the other hand, we cause suffering to others, the pain we inflict on them is inflicted above all on ourselves. A flow of energy is always strongest at its source.

Jesus Christ often emphasized these truths. The Christ consciousness, he stated, dwells in every heart. *"Verily,"* he once remarked, *"inasmuch as ye have done it* [that is, rendered or denied service] *unto one of the least of these my brethren, ye have done it unto me."* In whatsoever way we treat others, we treat also the Christ presence in ourselves.

In the Gospel of St. Matthew, Chapter 5, the 21st and 22nd Verses, Jesus says:

"You have heard that our forefathers were told, 'Thou shalt not kill'; and again, 'Whoever kills shall be subject to condemnation.' But my message to you is this: Whoever is angry with his brother without cause already stands condemned; whoever contemptuously calls his brother a fool shall answer for it to the Supreme Council; and whoever calls his brother an outcast of God* shall be in danger of hellfire."

---

* This phrase is found in some texts, but not in all. From some of them it is omitted. Jesus, however, had a good reason for including

There are many forms of murder, of which killing the body is only the most evident. To kill a person's belief in himself, however, or—worse still—his faith in God and in his own hope of finding God, is an even more heinous crime. It, too, is murder, of a spiritual nature, and is far more blameworthy in God's sight.

Many who proclaim their belief in God imagine that He is pleased with them if they condemn sinners self-righteously as outcasts from heaven. Jesus, however, offered hope to the greatest sinners. He emphasized not the darkness of their sins, but their potential as children of God. Even the worst sinner must return eventually, as a purified soul, to His light.

In the famous story of the woman taken in adultery, Jesus told her simply, *"Go, and sin no more."*

Worse also than physical murder, which denies another person's right to live, is the sin of suicide, which is a denial of life itself. Worse, again, than the condemnation of others as sinful is to condemn *oneself* as a sinner. Self-condemnation is a denial of the very saving power of grace.

As we judge others, so we judge ourselves. If we hate weakness in another, it only means we are ashamed of weakness in ourselves: if not the same weakness, then some other. We hate faults in others only if we have them, too, and want to conceal them— not only from others, but, if possible, from ourselves. If we scorn pride in others, it is because we too are proud, and want to divert people's scorn to them. And if we

---

it. It strengthens, and by no means weakens or alters, the meaning of the whole passage as it appears in all translations.

condemn anyone as a sinner, it is because we know that we, too, have failed to live in God's grace. Perhaps we hope to atone for our sinfulness by standing on the side of the angels, hurling stones of judgment (as we imagine them doing) and thinking thereby to align ourselves with divine grace.

From love for God, faith is born. Charity towards others nurtures love in our hearts. Forgiveness towards others draws an awareness of God's forgiveness. Jesus stated it perfectly in the Beatitude: *"Blessed are the merciful, for they shall obtain mercy."* John Donne put it well also in the line we've already quoted: "No man is an island." Separate from one another though we appear to be, we are all one.

The way to live closer to God, and to perceive more of truth and overcome our own error, is to view Him as our own. He is our loving Father and Mother. Never is He our wrathful Judge. That is the meaning of the well-known Parable of the Prodigal Son: The son was welcomed home by his father instantly and lovingly. Such, indeed, is Patanjali's definition of enlightenment. The soul *remembers* what it has always been: the truth we've forgotten during eons that we roamed in delusion, attached to our petty egos.

In the second Chapter of the Bhagavad Gita, Krishna states:

"This Self is never born, nor does it die. Once existing, it can never cease to be. Birthless, eternal, changeless, it is ever simply itself. Nor is it slain when the body is killed."

Obviously, the Self referred to here is not the one we see in the mirror as we comb our hair in the morning! The senses thrust upon us our awareness of the world around us, making us forget the world within. Thus, we confuse our bodies and personalities with our deeper reality. Even immortality, to the average person, means existence through eternity encased in the ego. That person doesn't think of it that way, of course; to him, this isn't imprisonment. The concept of eternity, however, is too staggering for him to contemplate seriously. He can only think of it in terms of earth-years. Perhaps he visualizes himself over the centuries as becoming increasingly beatific. Otherwise, he can only imagine himself as ever the same: Joe Green with a big smile, strolling through heavenly pastures and plucking a golden harp.

Boring? Well, yes! Orthodox images do incline to be a bit static. Activate this image, however, by the concentrated power of the imagination; bring it mentally to life, and might it not easily pass for a description of hell?

In Luke 9:46–48 we find an instructive episode that is described thus:

"Then there arose a dispute among [the disciples] as to which of them was the greatest. Jesus, knowing what was passing in their minds, took a child and stood him at his side. 'Whoever receives this child in my name,' he said, 'receives me. And whoever receives me receives the One who sent me. For whoever is least among all of you is the greatest.'" Our spiritual greatness, he was saying, depends first on renouncing our little egos. For in this respect we *are* insignificant, no matter how hard we try to make ourselves important in our own eyes and in the eyes of others.

In another Bible passage, John the Baptist says of

Jesus Christ: *"He must increase, but I must decrease."* (John 3:30) His statement applies in the deepest sense to all of us. If we would attain perfection, the Christ within us must increase. It can only do so if we eliminate gradually from our own minds the importance we give to our egos.

Thus, when in scripture we read of our divine potential as children of God, we must understand that this high promise excludes the ego altogether. This is a role which the soul has assumed temporarily.

To know God, we must abandon every vestige of thought that we are apart from Him. Jesus said: *"Whosoever shall seek to save his life shall lose it; and whosoever shall lose his life for my sake* [that is, merge his life in God] *shall find it."* (Matthew 16:25) The eternal life that the scriptures promise is one of eternal joy in God. The astral heavens, though blissful in comparison to ordinary earthly existence, are ephemeral also. Though one abide there for centuries, time passes, and all time must end. Eternity can be experienced as a reality only in conscious union with God. We shall not find life in Him so long as we cling to this ego with the desperation of a drowning man. In any undertaking, nothing great can be achieved unless we are willing to relinquish our lesser interests.

Though the human body undergoes countless changes—not only in one lifetime, but over many incarnations—we remain inwardly ever the same. Though we acquire new traits of personality, we yet retain at the center of our being a Self-awareness that never changes. From this center we gaze outward at the universe around us. Yet we are forever untouched by it.

The world conditions us to a self-definition based on appearances. Such definitions are false, however, because fleeting. Strip away the skins of an onion and what is left? Nothing! The same may be said of our personalities. Strip them away, and nothing—*no thing,* that is to say—is left: only the indefinable reality that is our existence. *No thing* remains but that Self which is never born, never dies, is infinite and eternal. Weapons cannot destroy it though they destroy the body. Calumny cannot bring it to ruin though it destroy a reputation. Death cannot kill it even when the brain itself ceases to be. That, eternally, is what you are.

Sri Krishna in the above passage tells us to live deeply at our own divine center, and not at our periphery.

Give to God the credit, therefore, for anything you do well. And for whatever you do ill, think of Him even so as the Doer, for thus you will free yourself eventually from every compulsion. In Him alone glory awaits you—*God's* glory, not yours, which is to say, not that "glory" which people may attach to your little ego!

Meanwhile, strive daily to know Him. Live in His love. God will guide you on the path, until you achieve union with Him, who is the final goal of all striving.

PART III

Son of Man: Son of God?

(For those who are studying this book week by week through the year, the two chapters constituting Part III may be inserted wherever Palm Sunday and Easter occur. For those who are content to follow the present sequence of the book, these chapters follow also in the over-all development of the book.)

CHAPTER FOURTEEN
(PALM SUNDAY)

"Who Is This Son of Man?"

A question once asked of Jesus by certain "people" (the Bible doesn't specify who they were) draws the reader's attention to an important distinction between Jesus Christ, the Son of God, and Jesus, the "son of man." Their question was a response to a veiled prophecy he had made to the effect that he would be "lifted up"—in other words, "on the cross." The people said, *"We have heard out of the law that Christ abideth for ever: and how sayest thou, The Son of man must be lifted up. Who is this Son of man?"* (John 12: 34)

Paramhansa Yogananda explained that Jesus used the term, "son of man," to refer to his physical body. On the present occasion, he spoke of the divine light, which radiated outward to the world from his physical presence in it. The light, he said, would be outwardly with them only *"a little while [longer]."* He urged his listeners, therefore, *"Walk, while ye have [yet] the light, lest darkness come upon you."*

Jesus Christ, the Son of God, was one in consciousness with the Infinite Lord. All human beings are potentially the same as he. The difference between him and us lies only in the fact that most people have yet to awaken to their divine reality. The law referred to in this passage signifies a truth far beyond anything most of them imagine. They think themselves to be only "sons of men." Jesus, on the other hand, was conscious even as a human being of the indwelling Christ consciousness. He often demonstrated this awareness by his perfect knowledge of people's inmost thoughts and of events distant from his physical body.

Jesus did not come to earth to amaze people with his greatness. His mission was to awaken them to their own potential greatness. All of us are, in our souls, the sons of God. To the extent that Jesus distinguished between himself and others, it was to remind them of their divine potential.*

In John 10 we read that the Jews *"took up stones to stone him"* for blaspheming. He had declared: *"I and my Father are one."* He, however, turned the tables on them with his answer: *"Is it not written in your law, 'I said, Ye are gods'?"* He then told them to study the evidence: *"If*

---

* This is an important distinction—one that priests and spiritual teachers and counselors ought especially to bear in mind. For they often tend to belittle themselves in the hope of establishing a sympathetic bond with others. Humility, however, is not self-abasement! It is self-forgetfulness. The duty of the sincere servant of God is not to emphasize his distance from Christ, but to attune himself with the Christ as a means of rising above his own shortcomings. A sincere effort to be Christlike is very different from boasting success in the attempt! It may sometimes be right to admit that one is still distant from the goal. (Humility is also self-honesty.) To over-emphasize this distance, however, amounts to an affirmation of failure. Worse still, it may convey to those one is counseling the despairing message: "What hope, then, have any of us of transcending sin?"

Indeed, if we are nothing but sinners, we have all the excuse our egos need to go right on living in sin!

I do not the works of my Father, believe me not. But if I do, though ye believe not me, believe in the works: that ye may know, and believe, that the Father is in me, and I in him."

He went on to ask them: Why, if God has said, *"Ye are gods,"* do you say *"of him whom the Father hath sanctified, and sent into the world, Thou blasphemest, for having said to you, I am the Son of God?"* The difference between Jesus and other men was, as he emphasized here, one not of essence but of refinement of awareness. Most people are not awake to their own full truth, whereas Jesus, by the grace he had achieved through incarnations of self-dedication, had awakened in God.

In his Sermon on the Mount he told his listeners, *"Be ye therefore perfect, even as your Father which is in heaven is perfect."* (Matthew 5:48) This supreme challenge was and still is incomprehensible to most people. There are concordances of the Bible that don't even include it, fundamental to his message though it is. For people, drawing support from a self-justifying reading of the Bible, are convinced that all men, themselves included, are inherently sinful, and that only the suffering of Jesus on the cross can redeem them.* *The New English Bible* softens this passage to read: *"You must therefore be all goodness, just as your heavenly Father is all good."* And *The Revised English Bible* states, *"There must be no limit to your goodness, as your Father's goodness knows no bounds."* No translator, however, can avoid the truth that Jesus wanted us to live in the divine way, which is to say, in God. And that is to say also, in perfect surrender of our ego-consciousness.

* There is an obvious question they might ask themselves: Has their belief prevented them from further sinning?

It is not that Jesus divorced his commandment to be perfect from the need to be good in a lesser, more human sense also. Indeed, the commandment follows upon advice to develop good spiritual attitudes: forbearance, patience, and love for one's enemies. Even this counsel was given deeper significance, however, in the words that followed: *"that ye may be the children of your Father which is in heaven."* He was saying, in other words, "Behave divinely, *because your true nature is divine!"* To be truly "children of God" is to become like Him—reflections of the Infinite Spirit. As human beings, we are merely the "sons (and daughters) of man." It is when, in deep meditation, we achieve pure consciousness that we become cleansed of limitations and realize oneness with God. *"Tat twam asi!"* is the ringing statement in the Indian scriptures: *"Thou art that!"* God's perfection is, *potentially,* our very own.

Mere death cannot strip us of limitation. The consciousness of unawakened beings passes after death through a "clearing process," described by the ancient Greeks as *Lethe,* the River of Forgetfulness. The consciousness of an awakened master, on the other hand, is not identified with the vehicles through which it expresses itself. A master remains eternally Self-aware.

Earth-ensnared human beings return to the physical plane many times. Rarely do they remember even fleeting episodes from their past lives. Full memory, however, is retained on deeper-than-conscious levels of soul-consciousness. Every choice a person makes is influenced, far more than he realizes, by subtle impressions from the past: traumas, satisfactions, hopes, fulfillments, and disappointments—including especially his past reactions to them, which above all determine his present personality.

Only his lack of spiritual awareness prevents him from experiencing the perfect state of Self-realization, which Jesus and all true masters have attained. It was to mankind's potential for this achievement that St. John spoke in his declaration, *"But as many as received him, to them gave he power to become the sons of God."*

In oneness with God, relativities cease to exist. Past, present, and future are delusions. There is only the Timeless Now. As Jesus said, *"Before Abraham was, I am."* (John 8:58) He was beyond temporal and spatial relativities. As he said also, *"Where two or three are gathered together in my name, there am I in the midst of them."* (Matthew 18:20) Note his use here of the present tense: not "there *shall I be,*" but, "there *am I.*" Time and distance had no effect on the immediacy of his awareness.

St. Simeon, a great Hesychast saint of the Tenth Century (still known by his early epithet, "the New Theologian"), added that this passage meant also, "When two or three *thoughts* are gathered together in concentration on the Christ." For the Christ presence to be cognized, the mind must be stilled and uplifted.

"Who is this son of man?" the people asked. The reality of Jesus was far more than they imagined. Yes, he ate, drank, walked, slept, and talked like others, but his consciousness was centered in infinity. Like others also, he laughed, but his laughter expressed divine joy, not mere merriment. Again, like others, he wept, but never with human grief; the tears he shed were for the sufferings of others, and were never shed in self-pity.

221

Thus, when *"a certain ruler"* addressed him, saying, *"Good Master,"* Jesus replied, *"Why callest thou me good? None is good save one, that is, God."* (Luke 18:19) He wasn't implying, "I, like all men, am a sinner." Rather, what he meant was, "Don't look to human beings for perfection. The credit for any good that man accomplishes belongs to God alone." Human goodness is relative: It is "good" only to the degree that it manifests God.

Jesus Christ was awake in God. Most human beings, by contrast, are spiritually asleep. This distinction should be kept in mind as a protection against spiritual pride.

Religionists everywhere incline too easily to believe that their own religion is the only way. The best religion, however, is that alone which helps one to know God. This truth is universal. A clear instance of it may be seen in an episode in which John said to Jesus, *"Master, we saw one casting out devils in thy name; and we forbad him, because he followeth not with us."* Jesus replied, *"Forbid him not; for he that is not against us is for us.'"* (Luke 9:50)

Dogmatic Christians often cite another passage in support of their much narrower vision. It is a passage that does, in fact, seem at first to contradict the one above. *"He that is not with me,"* Jesus said, *"is against me; and he that gathereth not with me scattereth abroad."* (Matthew 12:30) His words—seldom quoted in their full context—are paraded triumphantly as proof that Jesus was saying that if people don't accept him as their only Savior, they are "against" him and therefore, by definition, "against" God. When this passage is read in context, however, it supports the first one, and makes it clear that Jesus was referring not to himself personally, but to the eternal truth. The choice offered here was between divine and egoic fulfillment, not between acceptance of Jesus and non-acceptance.

This choice between divine and egoic fulfillment is absolute. In India there is a saying, "Life's path is too narrow for both the ego and God to walk it together." To choose one of these means to leave the other behind. To prefer earthly fulfillment to divine awareness is to reject the true happiness all men seek.

The above verse, when studied in context, provides a very different meaning of *"he that is not with me is against me."* The words that follow make it clear that Jesus was not referring to himself, as a human being, but to the impersonal Holy Ghost. For the passage continues: *"All manner of sin and blasphemy shall be forgiven unto men: but [not that of] blasphemy against the Holy Ghost. And whosoever speaketh a word against the son of man, it shall be forgiven him: but whosoever speaketh against the Holy Ghost, it shall not be forgiven him, neither in this world, nor in the world to come."*

Why is this particular blasphemy the only unforgivable sin? It is because, as Paramhansa Yogananda explained, when we set ourselves against the Holy Ghost, we alienate ourselves from our own true being. Losing touch with that Self, we lose our inner peace, and condemn ourselves to perpetual restlessness of spirit. It isn't God who condemns us: It is we who condemn ourselves. Free will is the birthright of every soul. There is only one way to wash away this supreme sin from our consciousness: We must of our own free will, in prayer and meditation, turn back to God. The process may be slow and difficult, but there is no other way.

To love Jesus truly is above all to love the truth for which he stood. *"Why call ye me, Lord, Lord,"* he asked once (with, one imagines, a hint of exasperation), *"and do not the things which I say?"* (Luke 6:46) To love the truth does not mean formally to become a Christian. One may never have heard of Jesus Christ. Even so, if one loves the Truth which Jesus represented, he cannot but be "with him" in the deeper sense that Jesus Christ himself intended.

Jesus underscored his meaning in this passage by adding that to be against him *as the son of man* is, on the contrary, forgivable. For opposition to him as a human being doesn't necessarily mean consciously to oppose the Divinity within him, and within oneself. Thus, Jesus could pray on the cross, *"Father, forgive them; for they know not what they do."*

To reject the *divine truth* Jesus represented, however, is another matter altogether. Indeed, to reject the divine potential of *anyone,* no matter how unenlightened, is to reject one's own divinity. This denial is related to the supreme sin of blasphemy against the Holy Ghost, for there is only a veil of delusion separating us from others. Jesus said also, therefore, *"Whoever calls his brother an outcast of God shall be in danger of hellfire."*

On another occasion he stated something to which Christians of dogmatic bent ought to pay careful heed, though this passage is, unfortunately, seldom quoted in the churches. *"Other sheep I have,"* he said, *"which are not of this fold."* (John 10:16) Then, to make it clear that this "I" referred not to his human, but to his divine, Self, he continued, *"Them also I must bring, and they shall hear my voice; and there shall be one fold, and one shepherd."* The "voice" of Christ is the mighty sound of *AUM,* the Holy Ghost, the divine "Word," Sustainer of the entire universe. And "one fold" means the state of oneness with God.

On Palm Sunday, the throng joyfully acclaimed him on his entry into Jerusalem. They cast palm fronds before him, and sang, *"Hosanna! Blessed is he who comes in the name of the Lord! The Lord bless the king of Israel!"* (John 12:13) How strange, to reflect that less than a week later he was arrested, condemned, and crucified! Perhaps some even in that throng participated in the historic tragedy that followed, and shouted with the mob, "Crucify him!" Such is the bitter-sweetness of human existence: smiles of welcome one day—insults the next. Christians today still suffer in that memory.

How many realize, however, that Christ's suffering was not for himself, but for them and for all of us: for our rejection, through him, of the Christ who dwells in our own selves? Neither praise nor scorn, acclaim nor rejection could affect Jesus in his divine Self, the "Son of God."

Palm Sunday was a joyful occasion, but it was not one of unalloyed joy. Mingled with the general mood of exaltation was a deeper mood of impending, stark pathos. To those who welcomed him it seemed he was entering the city to be acclaimed King of the Jews. He himself knew, however, and had hinted as much, that his "triumph" would be of a very different sort:

tragedy, yes, but also an affirmation of spiritual over worldly "glory." His was not to be an earthly crown, but opprobrium, condemnation, and crucifixion instead. In a symbolic sense, what his death showed was the destiny of every sincere seeker of God. Death, for Jesus, was indeed "kingship," but of a transcendental nature. His absolute submission to God's will demonstrated the victory of Spirit over matter.

All of us must make this choice, someday: God—or worldly fulfillment. The timing of the choice is forever ours. Until we make it, however, we doom ourselves to an existence that can never give us more of happiness than of sorrow, for it metes out both in equal measure until what we choose is God alone.

The lukewarm devotee always prefers compromise. Tepid, spiritually, he tries to convince himself that Jesus too was, in a sense, "worldly." For didn't he *love* the world? And shouldn't we take him in every respect as our model?

Yes, of course we should: but *foolishly?* "Sons of man" like him? or "Sons of God"? He became human to help us to become one with Christ. To be truly Christian means to live *inwardly* as Jesus did: to love all, yes, but with soul-love, not with ego-consciousness.

People undervalue themselves. That is why they belittle one another. They scrutinize the greatest and the noblest for their faults, and mock any weakness they perceive, or imagine they perceive, in them. Do shortcomings in others justify shortcomings in ourselves? *"Physician,"* Jesus said, quoting an ancient proverb, *"heal thyself!"* (Luke 4:23)

People fear to acknowledge greatness in others,

because subconsciously they feel that if they were to acknowledge *true* greatness (not tinseled fame), they would be forced to recognize their own potential greatness. This prospect, to most of them, is frightening! Far more comforting is it to view everyone and everything condescendingly, as if from the top of whatever little mound of achievement they themselves have managed to climb. "Sure, I know old Sam," they'll say; "People think well of him. But" (laughing) "have you ever seen him on the golf course? What a duffer!" Wouldn't it be better to admire Sam for his virtues than to denigrate him for his shortcomings? What have a person's superficial characteristics to do with his true character? Why not admire virtue of any kind open-heartedly? By denying greatness in others, we deny the potential for it in ourselves.

Every human being is born "trailing clouds of glory," as Wordsworth put it. Even the meanest of us has lived, or will eventually have lived, a story more magnificent in scope than the greatest epic ever written. By comparison, those brief accounts set forth in the dramas of Shakespeare, Sophocles, Racine, and Kalidasa (in India) pale to insignificance. Were it possible to weave a tapestry of the voyage each of us makes in a saga of incarnations, it would display an adventure cosmic in its proportion and significance: anguishing often, no doubt, but as often delightful, wondrous, and thrilling: a sweeping quest for the divine treasure hidden at the center of our very being.

In how many ways on this long voyage do we err—often, how tragically! Even our successes seem so petty and pathetic at last—if only because so ultimately disappointing!—beside the triumph that awaits us. Painstakingly, through eons, we chisel away at our granite block of ego-consciousness until it finally reveals to us who we really are—who we always have been, in our souls.

Such was the supreme drama, imbued with the power of ages, of the life of Jesus Christ. It was a drama even greater than that single, wonderful incarnation we all know, terminated so dramatically by the fury of human ignorance. Jesus was the eternal soul who, after a myriad lives of trial and suffering, had *"overcome."**

The love of Jesus for mankind was infinitely generous and tender. Never sternly critical of human weaknesses, it was, rather, an *affirmation* of life: of life's eternal hope and promise. The love Jesus bore all human beings called them to hold God at the center of their existence. It was an example to live under all circumstances in His joy.

As we imagine that throng on Palm Sunday, it is easy to visualize him also smiling in response to their acclamation. Inwardly, however, how sad he must have been, seeing by what a wide margin the majority of them had missed the meaning of his life!

"O Jerusalem, Jerusalem!" he had once cried, gazing down upon the city. *"How often would I have gathered thy children together, as a hen doth gather her brood under her wings, and ye would not!*

"Behold, your house is left unto you desolate: and verily I say unto you, Ye shall not see me, until the time come when ye shall say, Blessed is he that cometh in the name of the Lord." (Luke 13:34,35)

---

* See Revelation 3:21.

It is indeed right to enjoy life, but with God's joy. And it is not wrong to grieve, but with God's sorrow. Paramhansa Yogananda explained that God *does* sorrow, through our sorrows. In God's sorrow, however, there is also the compassion born of a deeper joy. What God grieves for most of all is man's ignorance of His love. Christ's sorrow was rooted in love, not in self-concern.

Some of the early Christian Gnostics distinguished so austerely between Spirit and matter that they denied *everything* material, including the Crucifixion itself. In that denial, they failed to address the question: Why did Jesus weep for Jerusalem? In speaking of the tragedy of the Crucifixion, they asked, "What was there to weep about? Jesus wasn't his physical body!" Jesus, however, in the fullness of perfection, accepted also man's limited understanding. To him, the world was both real and unreal—real, as dreams are real to those who are asleep; unreal, to one who is awake.

It may seem self-contradictory that great masters—in view of their complete non-attachment to the world—should also affirm human life joyously, and weep in sympathy for those who grieve. A fully liberated master, however, is equally at home in the Spirit and in the mist-lands of delusion. His consciousness can never be tainted. Since to him the world is God's dream, there is nothing for him to cling to; nothing to renounce.

In the Bhagavad Gita, the dichotomy between the "son of man" and the "Son of God" is beautifully described also. Sri Krishna, who represents God in human form, reveals his true nature as infinite and omnipresent. In the eleventh chapter of this great scripture his disciple Arjuna exclaims:

> *O Infinite Light!*
> *Thy radiance, spreading o'er the universe,*
> *Shines into the very darkest abyss!*
> *Thy voice o'erwhelms the roar of cosmic cataclysms!*
> *Lo! the myriad stars are Thy diadem;*
> *Thy scepter radiates power everywhere!*
> *O Immortal Brahman, Lord of all:*
> *Again and again at Thy feet of Infinity*
> *I prostrate myself before Thee!*

Arjuna, overwhelmed by the divine majesty, begs forgiveness for having—so audaciously, as it now seems to him—considered the Lord his beloved friend and counselor. Touchingly, then, he concludes: *"Oh, let me behold once again Thy human form, so forever dear to me!"*

Who is this bewildering, this irresistible, this unfathomable being, this divine son of man? He is, in a sense, just as he appears to be: a divinely radiant, inspiring human being, forever seeking to draw us toward our own divine destiny. But He is infinitely more than that also: beyond time, space, and form—the Lord of infinitesimal atoms and of vast galaxies alike, the Secret Power behind everything in the universe, both cosmic and mundane!

CHAPTER FIFTEEN
(EASTER SUNDAY)

Resurrection, and the Meaning of Divine Tests

The famous story is told in the Gospel of St. John, Chapter 20:

"The first day of the week came Mary Magdalene early, when it was still dark, to the sepulchre, where she saw that the stone before it had been removed.

"Then she ran, and came to Simon Peter and to the other disciple whom Jesus loved, and said to them, 'They have taken away the Lord!' . . .

"That same day in the evening—it was the first day of the week; the disciples had assembled, and the doors were closed owing to their fear of the Jews—Jesus appeared to them. Standing in their midst, he said, 'Peace be with you.'"

The resurrection of Jesus is the final and greatest lesson of his mission on earth. People might, in time, have accepted his suffering and death as the summation of his life, had it not been for that joyful ending.

Tradition, in emphasizing the Crucifixion, has treated the Resurrection as only another miracle, not as a teaching and an example for us to emulate. As a lesson, the Resurrection demonstrates the joyful promise behind all of life's trials: the victory that awaits whoever accepts hardship, not despairingly, but with faith.

The Crucifixion epitomizes the persecution that the world inflicts on those who live for God. For it often happens that, in exchange for divine love and friendship, devotees receive hatred and contempt. Those who are drunk with pride resent any reminder of their unimportance in the general scheme of things: that only their souls are important, as expressions of God.

The Resurrection gives not only the comforting reassurance that heaven does exist, but that love and joy are, in the end, more powerful than hatred. Thus, and very fittingly, the Crucifixion and the Resurrection together dramatize the two essential conditions for knowing God: willingness to face for His sake any test that comes; and faith to accept it with love and courage, firm in the knowledge that all things pass, whereas God's love is ours forever.

"Living for God," Paramhansa Yogananda told the author, "is martyrdom." It entails sacrificing not only the physical body, but even the animating ego.

The cross is universally recognized as the symbol of Christianity. Unfortunately, so completely does it define Christ's religion that many Christians believe also that holiness is demonstrated by the intensity of one's suffering rather than by a serene attitude in the face of suffering. Some people even believe that a joyful spirit is displeasing to God. This belief is utterly contradicted by the example of Jesus Christ. It is also contradicted by the teachings of all true saints. Consider these words by St. Francis de Sales, "A sad saint is a sad saint indeed!" And these by St. Teresa of Avila, "A sad nun is a bad nun!"

Pious over-emphasis on the suffering of Christ has distorted a divine truth. Religion, when lived truly, transforms sorrow into joy. True devotees, especially if they meditate, experience joy—subliminally at least—during even the severest trials. Sometimes they must cling to it determinedly, as if to a lifeline in heavy seas! When the waves subside, however, and calmness returns, they discover that joy was theirs even at the height of the storm.

Human life is in any case burdened with countless woes. The religious life has no monopoly on them. Nor is spirituality demonstrated by the mere fact of a person's suffering. What counts is the spirit in which we meet our tests.

The Crucifixion and the Resurrection are symbols—indeed, *affirmations*—of the faith and courage necessary for salvation. In a sense, Jesus already demonstrated his inner freedom by the manner in which he accepted death: calmly, with unshaken faith, and with concern for others—even for his tormentors. *"Father,"* he cried out in his agony, *"forgive them, for they know not what they do!"* Both his suffering and, later, his resurrection were proofs of an eternal truth: that God loves us all, indifferent to Him though so many of us are. What God asks of those who love Him is not suffering, as such, but a victorious attitude even in seeming defeat. If we can persevere in this attitude, we find that sacrifice itself becomes a victory. By maintaining our joy during outer adversity, our hearts' love deepens. Suffering is only the fruit of ego-centeredness. Joy is the fruit of a life lived for God.

A great Sufi saint once put it beautifully: "He is no true lover of God who does not forget his suffering in contemplation of the Divine Beloved."

In Greece, the author once asked a shopkeeper, "Why do Greek artists portray the Nativity scene with the Virgin Mary suffering? Considering that she'd just given birth to the Christ child, wouldn't she have been filled with divine joy?"

The shopkeeper solemnly replied, "She is grieving because she knows that her Son will die on the cross." How absurd! As if suffering were the underlying lesson of that glorious life!

Jesus brought to mankind a very different message indeed. Its focus was not on suffering, but on eternal bliss, transcendent above all human sorrows. Indeed, one wonders how greatly Jesus even suffered, in the human sense. For a master lives in divine consciousness. What would beatitude signify, if physical agony were capable of overwhelming it? Matter, in that case, would be the fundamental reality, even as materialists claim. Suffering overwhelms one only when his consciousness is centered in his ego.

During the early years of Christianity, much controversy centered on this very point, with scathing accusations and counter-accusations of heresy. Paramhansa Yogananda wrote that (as often happens with sincerely held but conflicting beliefs) both sides were right: the Gnostics (who held that Jesus couldn't have suffered at all) and the institutionally orthodox (who held that Jesus, in his agony, bore the suffering of the whole world), but that both also were wrong.

He explained that when a liberated master takes on a human body, he experiences pain and suffering, as other human beings do, but never personally. That is, he never experiences it in ego-consciousness. Those who are centered in their egos think, "It's to *me* this is happening!" God-centered saints, on the other hand, think only, "This is what is happening." A master assumes the human state voluntarily, motivated by pure compassion for mankind. Thus, he may choose to experience human pain also. On the other hand, if he has no lesson to teach others through pain, he may choose not to experience it at all.

Had Jesus not willingly assumed body-consciousness, his suffering on the cross would have been a mere pretense, and his assumption of humanity a sham. Instead, he was as wholly human as we are. The difference between him and us was that his consciousness, even while suffering, radiated outward *from* himself, and included others in his compassion. The consciousness of most people, by contrast, especially when they are suffering, seeks compassion *from* others *for* themselves. Their awareness, unlike that of Jesus, is centripetal; that of Jesus, and of every great master, is centrifugal, flowing outward, not inward. Divine bliss was, for Jesus, life's abiding reality. He was wholly without man's obsession with self which asks constantly, "What about *me?* What's in it *for me?* What are the risks or benefits *for me?*" Jesus was a channel of divine consciousness. He sought to draw people's attention, not to himself as a man, but to God alone.

Like a clean window, he helped people to appreciate the vistas lying outside their little rooms of ego-consciousness. At the same time, again like a window, he framed that immensity by a human personality, in order to make it comprehensible to their understanding. His very suffering on the cross was only a frame through which humanity might glimpse God's compassion.

Certainly, Jesus was not the "man of sorrows" that most people imagine. Had he been that, multitudes would not have flocked to him as they did. People are attracted by what they themselves want from life: joy, not sorrow; sympathy, not pity, and certainly not heavy sighs for their sinfulness! Jesus Christ was self-giving, as the Bible makes very clear. He was endlessly kind. These qualities in a human being produce happiness, not grim and puritanical self-righteousness. In his agony on the cross he showed that even in suffering he grieved not for himself, but for others and for the ignorance that causes mankind repeatedly to reject—even to the point of wanting to destroy it—the gift of divine love. *"Father,"* he said, *"forgive them, for they know not what they do."*

A liberated master plays out his earthly role transcendently. That is to say, he never forgets his inner freedom. Never touched by delusion, he demonstrates the way to live under the most challenging circumstances in a spirit of inner freedom.

The Crucifixion had a further significance. As we know, it was an atonement for people's sins. Man cannot escape the meshes of ignorance by his own efforts alone: His mind is already infected by the very disease of ignorance that he must dispel! Wrong actions through many lives have woven a mental cocoon around his soul, enclosing it in spiritual darkness. The strands of this cocoon are formed of man's ego-motivated actions and desires, and are woven around the thought, "I—I—I!" Some of these strands, indeed, are almost rope-like, very difficult to sever with the delicate knife of resolution alone. The role of the guru, or savior, is to show his disciples how to sunder those bonds with the axe of superconscious perception.

A master, in order to hasten his disciples' spiritual evolution, may sometimes offer his own body as a shield against the violent storms of delusion.

Egoic action implies self-commitment, and is therefore binding. It is what is known in Sanskrit as *karma,* which brings its own retribution or reward according to the type and intensity of its instigating energy. Karmic retribution gradually makes a person aware of the law governing the universe. Karmic rewards deepen our attunement with the law, and are accompanied by expanding happiness, understanding, and an inner serenity . Karmic retribution, on the other hand, has a darkening effect on the mind until one determines to learn its lessons.

A master may expiate his disciples' bad karma by taking onto himself the punishment that is due them. A window not only opens onto the panorama, framing it like a picture to make it perhaps more suitable to people's tastes: It also lets light into a room. Moreover, it protects those who are in the room from Nature's inclemency. The guru's function is similar. He brings the light of divine truth into the human mind. He protects people from the storms of adversity by taking onto himself karmic blows that might be too severe for them. Finally, his physical presence is a protection against life's "inclemency," raising people's consciousness and making them immune to disturbing influences. In taking karma onto himself, he acts as a strong man may who receives onto his own chest blows that might be fatal to a weaker person.

Jesus in his agony on the cross atoned for the karma of many people. Had he taken upon himself the sins of the whole world, however, as people commonly believe, the world would have been transformed, and its inhabitants, sanctified. History suggests that no such uplift occurred. Rather, people seem generally to have sunk into deeper spiritual darkness. The centuries following the Crucifixion are known today as "the dark age." They exhibited a degree of moral depravity that would have been abhorrent, formerly.

We are told that Jesus died for "all the world." This expression is general in many languages, however. The French say, *"tout le monde,"* which means, literally, "the whole world," though it is thought of as meaning simply, "everyone."

Jesus can only have atoned for the sins of those whom he had been sent specifically to help. This number was limited, as he himself stated.* Many Christians are unaware that others knew God long before Jesus was born. Jesus himself, however, acknowledged the prophets before him, saying, *"Think not that I am come to destroy the law, or the prophets: I am not come to destroy, but to fulfill."* (Matthew 5:17) We cannot accept

---

* *"I am not sent but unto the lost sheep of the house of Israel."* (Matthew 15:24)

literally, therefore, the assertion of St. Paul that Christ's crucifixion atoned for original sin and for the fall of man.

It is natural to ask another question: Did the Crucifixion atone for Judas's betrayal of Christ? Not only was Judas in greater need than most people of expiation, considering the enormity of his sin, but he also did more, by later repentance, to earn redemption. Yet neither the Bible nor tradition suggest that Jesus atoned for that sin by the Crucifixion, nor that Judas was saved by his repentance.

The mystery of who exactly was saved, and to what extent, was never explained satisfactorily by St. Paul, who painted with the broad brush of generalizations. No doubt Paul's intention was to encourage people in their faith. Indeed, without faith one cannot receive divine grace. By grace, moreover, and not by theological niceties, comes salvation. If we love Jesus truly, however, and don't deny him,* the issue of our salvation is for him to decide. To declare that we accept him as our "personal savior" is presumptuous. The best we can ever do is, by devotion to him, *invite* his blessings.

Orthodox Christians believe that the Crucifixion atoned for the sins of those, at least, who accept Jesus Christ. The scars of sin, however, seem as deeply etched in many of them as in others, whether Christian or non-Christian. And the aura of sanctity is as bright around the saints of other religions as around those in Christianity. Insistence that Jesus atoned for the sins of all men is harmless, if it inspires faith in God's grace,

---

* To deny *any* God-known master *in his spiritual nature* is also, in some measure, to deny God.

but it can do harm if it deludes people into thinking that Christianity is, therefore, the only true religion.

What seems evident, on pondering the subject objectively, is that those who were clearly transformed after the Crucifixion were the close disciples of Jesus.

Spiritual complacency, born of passive dependence on Christ's suffering on our behalf, may only perpetuate our ignorance, the root cause of all our suffering. Complacency never fired anyone with zeal to know God.

To extract wisdom from what must otherwise be abandoned as a theological fallacy, this much may be stated as a historical fact: The *Christ consciousness* has sacrificed itself repeatedly through the atonement of great masters for human error.

To return to the subject of the Resurrection, not only have there been other great masters besides Jesus, including many who lived long before him: There have been masters, also, who resurrected their bodies after death. The case of Jesus was extraordinary, certainly, but it was not unique. One marvelous account of physical resurrection is detailed in Paramhansa Yogananda's *Autobiography of a Yogi,* in the chapter titled, "The Resurrection of Sri Yukteswar." Christian saints, also, have been known to appear in their physical bodies to disciples after death.

Jesus Christ's crucifixion and resurrection are lessons, above all, in divine freedom. A true devotee should be willing, as Jesus was, to pay the price even of painful death, out of love for God and in the hope of gaining eternal freedom. Whatever wrongs one has committed must, sooner or later, be expiated. Wouldn't it be better to rid oneself of these debts sooner than later?

What about us, then? When our time comes to leave this world, wouldn't we rather leave it in soul-freedom than in bondage?

Jesus is quoted in the Bible* as saying, *"He that taketh not his cross, and followeth after me, is not worthy of me."* (Matthew 10:38) To "take up one's cross" signifies to accept with faith and courage, and not with self-pity, whatever tests come one's way. Otherwise, merely to live in this world is anyway to bear the "cross" of material existence, with its burdens of fatigue, hunger, and physical and emotional distress. Suffering is familiar to all men. Injustice and cruelty are the common lot. Sorrow and happiness alternate constantly in life. Generally, however, people have no conception of *why* they suffer. They may consider themselves victims of an indifferent destiny, of an angry God, or of hostile forces they are powerless to combat. Lacking either the wisdom or the courage to lift their consciousness from suffering to inner joy, they may blame their difficulties simply on life's unfairness. They may even develop what the French call *"la nostalgie de la boue"*—"nostalgia for the mud," seeking unconsciousness through drugs or alcohol. Stupefaction is one of the sadder symptoms of the disease of spiritual ignorance. (Milder ways of escaping reality are to devote hours daily to watching television, or to spending time in other harmless but time-wasting diversions. Sukdeva, a great saint

* The word "quoted" is used here, instead of, "Jesus said," because it seems unlikely that he was actually referring to the cross. The manner of his death was not yet known. We see in this passage an obvious example of later scholarly tampering.

in ancient India, stated, "All time is wasted that is not spent in seeking God!") To most people, the sufferings they endure are afflictions, not opportunities for growing in wisdom.

A true devotee offers up his trials bravely, even lovingly, to God. He sees every test as an opportunity for spiritual gain. Each test passed brings him an increase of inner freedom, joy, and wisdom. At last he learns to behold God's love behind every trial. No longer do his tests, then, seem like punishment, whether karmic or divine.

Resurrection, in the highest sense, occurs on a soul level. Tribulation, though a "cross" that all human beings must bear, is welcome to those who aspire to attain freedom in God. Joyful submission, indeed, is the way to pay off one's karmic debts without incurring any new ones. Resentment, on the other hand, only adds new debts to the old ones.

Cosmic law is unrelenting. Its purpose is to teach recognition of the underlying unity of all life.

Were inner freedom easy to achieve, it would imply a state not very different from the ego-identity with which all of us are familiar. The "pearl of great price" cannot be bought with debased currency: power, fame, wealth, and bodily and emotional pleasures. Though we may sometimes imagine that God's attention is far away, He is eternally near us—nearer even than the tearful prayers with which we implore His help.

The disciples of Jesus were greatly tested by the Crucifixion. They'd believed that he was going to be declared King of the Jews: Instead, he was seized by fools, beaten, infamously judged, and crucified. For the disciples, there ensued a time of deep spiritual darkness. They assembled in secrecy lest they, too, be arrested and executed. Yet for all that, they did assemble, and with faith. All of them, even Thomas (the "doubter"), came together as disciples.

And all at once, Jesus was standing in their midst. He said to them, "Peace be with you." Those few, simple words epitomized the ending of every test of God's, once it is accepted with love and faith. These attitudes, love and faith, by no means imply passivity. However deep be a person's sorrow, if he offers it up determinedly to God, the divine light must dawn for him at last. God's peace will enter his heart, bringing solace greater than he could ever have imagined. As the lyrics of a song state that the author wrote many years ago when undergoing a divine test:

Every grief, every wrong

Has its ending in song.

Those who in their grief forget God never learn this supreme lesson of life. One, however, who clings to God through every trial finds reassurance at every plateau as he climbs up Mount Carmel. In every reassurance he experiences Easter, and the Resurrection.

"Ah! ye who into this ill world are come—fleeting and false—set your faith fast on Me! Fix heart and thought on Me! Adore Me! Bring offerings to Me! Make Me prostrations! Make Me your supremest joy! and, undivided, unto My rest your spirits shall be guided." Such were Krishna's immortal words in the ninth chapter of the Bhagavad Gita.

Wise alone among mortals is he whose discrimination leads him resolutely toward God: who realizes to the depths of his being that worldly attainments are illusory, and will always bring disappointment—sometimes at the very moment of triumph. No matter how shining with promise this world seems, its fulfillments are as evanescent as the glistening sunlight on a dewdrop.

Divine tests may seem to portend all that we most feared. In the end, however, what they bring is the very opposite! We may imagine that God is testing our endurance: In fact, what He is testing is our love.

Our tendency, beneath adversity's blows, is to close inward upon ourselves like travelers in the desert during a sandstorm, huddled self-protectively within our mental cloaks to shield our bruised feelings. People often emerge only slowly from a siege of suffering. Sometimes it takes years to reach the point where, with renewed trust, they can open their hearts once again to life's gifts. Many, alas, remain embittered all their lives, requiring rebirth into a new body, or perhaps into successive bodies, before they can wash away their subconscious memory of pain. How long the process takes depends on one's own strength, and on his spirit of inner freedom.

Poor, foolish humanity! God Himself cannot help them so long as they determine to shut themselves within thick walls of egoism. Many shoot arrows of outrage and accusation at Him, though He comes to them lovingly, His hands outstretched to help them. Even devotees, during tests, sometimes misunderstand the workings of grace and question God. To all humanity, however, God whispers silently, "Even if you reject

Me, I will wait. Eventually you will understand how deeply, through eternity, I love you."

The true devotee remains inwardly as joyful during life's dark as during its shining moments. His faith, though it tremble sometimes in the storm, remains firmly rooted; he embraces every test as a gift sent to him by his Heavenly Father/Divine Mother. To him, even arduous tests are as precious to his soul—though, admittedly, not to his ego!—as gifts that come wrapped attractively. For the storms of life, though appearing to bode disaster, in fact bring nourishing rain. One's consciousness afterward becomes like a fertile meadow, covered with the wildflowers of heavenly solace.

God is our infinite Beloved. He is our one and only true Friend. His wish for us is our eternal happiness. The tests He sends have only one purpose: to help us grow in wisdom. The sooner we accept them with understanding, the sooner we'll come to realize that His support was with us always—not for our errors, but in spite of them. For we are His own. Even were we made to walk through fire, we would remain unharmed and the flames would be a balm to our souls, burning off impurities that for eons had given us pain.

Have faith in God! Love Him above all else. Surrender your heart to Him. Open yourself to Him even, and especially!, in your darkest hours. For He alone, and not the brief dewdrops of earthly attractions, can give you the peace for which your soul longs.

Christ's resurrection was an outward act, but it symbolized a great inward truth: That person whose love remains firm through all trials finds himself resurrected at last into eternal bliss.

The teaching of the Resurrection applies also to life generally. Resurrection signifies, as Paramhansa Yogananda put it, "*any* beneficial or uplifting change." In this sense, resurrection can be experienced repeatedly throughout life.

Referring to our need for *inner* resurrection, Yogananda often quoted this heartfelt plea from the Bhagavad Gita: *"O devotee: Get away from My ocean of suffering and misery!"*

Offsetting those cautionary words of Krishna's is a promise, and an eternal consolation: *"Arjuna, know this for certain: My devotee is never lost!"*

PART IV

The Soul's Ascent

"He must increase, but I must decrease."
—St. John the Baptist, John 3:30

CHAPTER SIXTEEN

The Way Beckons

The Gospel of St. John, Chapter 3, states:

"For God so loved the world, that he gave his only begotten Son, that whosoever believeth in him should not perish, but have everlasting life. . . .

"He that believeth on him is not condemned: but he that believeth not is condemned already, because he hath not believed in the name of the only begotten Son of God.

"And this is the condemnation: That light is come into the world, and men loved darkness rather than light, because their deeds were evil.

"For every one that doeth evil hateth the light, neither cometh to the light lest his deeds should be reproved.

"But he that doeth truth cometh to the light, that his deeds may be made manifest, that they are wrought in God."

The soul's ascent can begin only after the discovery that happiness doesn't really come from things, from circumstances, or from other people. Once we accept this simple fact, and, according to our depth of clarity in the acceptance, cease lamenting that matters ought to be other than they are, we take full responsibility for our own happiness. We determine to work on ourselves, and stop trying to change the world and other people to our own liking.

An attitude of self-reliance is essential for spiritual development. Without inner strength, how can one know God, who is the source of all power in the universe? Self-reliance should, at the same time, be defined as reliance on the true Self (written with a capital "S")—that is to say, the divine Self behind our own definition of ourselves as this body and personality. The ego, indeed, is no more our true Self than other people are, and can no more give us happiness than they can. The ego, which (as Yogananda defined it) is merely the soul attached to the body, forever cheats us by giving us false expectations. Ego-satisfactions are always vicarious, and can never nourish the soul. To rely on God is to identify ourselves with that part of ourselves which endures forever. To believe in God, who is immanent in creation as the Christ consciousness, is to set foot on the pathway to everlasting life.

People misunderstand the above passage if they take it as encouraging passive dependence on divine grace. Dependence in itself is good, but it must take the form of dynamic self-offering. God is most pleased with courage even in the face of defeat. The true devotee is not one who cries, "Lord, please, I beg You: *Please* save me!" This is defeatism! A beggarly attitude, which many people consider a mark of humility, attracts only a trickle of divine grace. That is not to say that divine grace is ever withheld, but only that a begging attitude narrows the heart and limits its capacity for receptivity. We should stand lovingly before God, with the confidence a son has in his loving father. For what the Lord has to give us is our birthright in infinite bliss.

The ways of truth are subtle and not easy, at first,

to distinguish from some of the false trails of delusion that lead seemingly with promise, but only to vanish in a tangle of undergrowth, or curve back to rejoin the path at some earlier point.

Truth is absolute. In this world, however, all things are relative. Truths, therefore, when applied to human life, cannot but be relative also. They may be more true, or less so, depending on what they are related to. From a high level of insight, a truism may seem utterly fallacious. Nothing, on the other hand, can be absolutely false, if only because even great error is true also, in its own way, if only as a veritable delusion! An evening's entertainment, highlighted by drunken laughter, may be enjoyable to the participants, but with the morning's rude awakening and a hangover, or with the awareness that suddenly comes of the hollowness of the evening's laughter, the relative falseness of the revelry becomes painfully obvious. It is only in God, the Absolute, that truth passes entirely beyond relativity. Meanwhile, what mankind calls true must be understood as a *direction,* only. It leads out of relative ignorance toward relatively ever-deeper insight and understanding.

Ignorance, too, is a direction, not a static condition. There can be no such thing as *absolute* ignorance for the simple reason that absolute unconsciousness does not exist. Everything is a manifestation of consciousness.

Laziness, then—a form of spiritual ignorance— darkens the mind and induces ever-decreasing awareness. Human beings can "evolve" downward as well as upward, and can even take on again an animal body. Alas! some actually do so. Indeed, the ego can descend the ladder as far as it chooses, by ever-darker actions and attitudes. One of the ways of doing so is to refuse to act with a creative attitude. Merely to refrain from sinning is not, in itself, virtuous. It may be better to steal than to wait passively for riches to drop into one's lap—not, of course, that it is good in itself to steal, but at least a thief needs a certain ingenuity to be effective in what he does, whereas indolence only dulls the mind and deprives it increasingly of the ability for self-development.

Jesus, in referring here to the importance of belief, was speaking of *belief directed with energy!* Belief is not a careful nod of approval, while puffing thoughtfully on a pipe and saying something like, "Hmmm, yes, ye-e-es, that does appear to make sense." Such expressions of "belief" are typically followed by shrugs, then a comment like, "Let George do it!" Belief, however, as Jesus used the word here, means more than acceptance: It means *personal commitment* to whatever one accepts.

True belief is a hypothesis, which the scientist tests and either proves or disproves. True faith comes when a hypothesis has been proved valid. The belief needed for such definite results contains sufficient energy to commit theory to the test of experience. Of Thomas Edison it is said that he performed over 43,000 experiments before he found the right filament for the electric light bulb. His associates wanted to quit in discouragement after "only" twenty thousand experiments! Edison alone had the belief *and the energy* to continue on to success.

It was to *belief united with energy* that Jesus was

referring when he spoke of that belief which leads to "everlasting life."

This kind of belief is the secret of all spiritual success. Dogmatic belief may parade itself proudly, marching to the rhythm of an accepted pattern of thought, but it is as brittle as a tree limb through which the sap of life no longer flows. When strong winds of a new insight blow, the limb, instead of bending with them, resists rigidly, preferring time-sanctioned pronouncements to the risk involved in any practical test. When it is snapped off, it curses the wind, not itself, and mutters to Change itself, "You'll go to hell for your disbelief!"

The Bible tells us, *"Test the spirits, [to see] whether they are of God."* (I John 4:1) If we would know the truth, we must be willing to submit our most cherished beliefs to the challenge of doubt.

What Jesus offers us in this passage is not only the encouragement to seek everlasting life, but also the courage to test our beliefs and see where they lead. In addition, he gives us a clue as to the outcome of this process. For we are not alone on our voyage of discovery. The basic truths of human nature are as universal as the law of gravity. Belief in Truth and God lifts the mind in aspiration toward enlightenment. Doubt, on the contrary, depresses it, and makes a person fear the divine light. The test is based on the fact that one of these alternatives leads to what everyone really wants in life: perfect love and happiness, whereas the other leads to what nobody really wants, even if, by confused understanding, he feels himself attracted to them: hatred, fear, and unhappiness.

How shall we express belief in Christ? It is not necessary to be a Christian, or even to visualize Jesus as a person. What Jesus referred to here was the infinite Christ consciousness. Thus, anything that uplifts our consciousness toward Christ is, by his meaning, belief.

Interestingly, the process of testing can also be reversed: Instead of waiting to see what will uplift us, or what will cast us down, we can simply concentrate on the flow of energy in our own bodies, and control that flow. For if belief in Christ uplifts our consciousness, and if rejection lowers it, we can uplift or lower our energy and consciousness anyway, by the simple practice of redirecting the flow of our own energy in the spine.

It isn't always easy to find reinforcement outwardly for our belief in Christ, if we define that belief by such things as holy images. It is easier to practice seeing Christ, or God, everywhere: in the flowers, the meadows, in every kindly act. And it is easiest of all to uplift our consciousness, wherever we may be, by directing our energy to the Christ center between the eyebrows. Churches, temples, and altars of all kinds are limited as to location, but the Christ center is wherever we ourselves are. We can also breathe deeply with the thought of raising our energy in the body: In this case, the lungs act as magnets and draw the energy upward. Indeed, we can concentrate on the flow of energy itself, directing it up through the spine by an act of will. Most of the techniques contained in the yoga science are designed to assist in this process. What is more, by any insightful definition of yoga, Jesus Christ himself was a great yogi.

Seek by various means—by outer reminders, by an inner expansion of awareness and sympathy, and by the conscious direction of your own thoughts and energy—to manifest your belief in Christ. Don't let your belief be a sort of "New Year's resolution," intending more than it ever performs. Climb the mountain of awakening step by step. Every action, every thought, every feeling must be patiently attuned to the Christ within. To see all things not as separate realities in themselves, but as channels for God's love, is to make oneself a channel also for that love, and thereby to lift oneself into Christ's love.

It is not God who condemns us if we reject the light. We condemn ourselves by closing our eyes to it, thereby creating our own darkness. Whoever has belief enough to allow himself to be absorbed in that light will never perish, but will have everlasting life. More than anything else, Christ is Divine Love.

The proof of these truths is ever before us. We needn't wait for all the results to be in, as Edison had to do with his light filament, before we may state firmly, "Yes, now I know that this practice works!" For even our first tests already show us the way. Every time we turn away from the path of love and express hatred toward anyone; every time we criticize others unkindly; every time we desire to revenge ourselves on anyone; and every time we seek personal satisfaction at the expense of others, we reinforce the wall of egoism we've built around ourselves. Thus, we imprison ourselves and limit our ability to be happy. This wall of darkness is made of the "bricks" of our own thoughts.

Every time we open up our hearts to others,

however, and to God who dwells in their hearts, we shatter a few of those bricks and let in the sunlight of understanding.

Many results are immediate, and give us either instant punishment or instant reward: the subtle punishment of nagging self-doubt and unsettled feelings, perhaps, or the gratifying awareness of increased inner happiness.

The Bhagavad Gita encourages us, whatever our present station on the spiritual path, to grow upward and outward: upward, that is, in rising awareness; and outward in expansive sympathy for all. The Gita also urges us not to be discouraged if we don't find immediate self-transformation at all levels. A rock is seldom shattered by a single blow. We should proceed steadily, by natural degrees, and always joyfully. We should accept our own nature, for the time being, as it is, but seek to harmonize it ever more perfectly with our higher realities. As Krishna puts it in the twelfth Chapter:

Cling thou to Me!
Clasp Me with heart and mind! so shalt thou dwell
Surely with Me on high. But if thy thought
Droops from such height; if thou be'st weak to set
Body and soul upon Me constantly,
Despair not! give Me lower service! seek
To reach Me, worshiping with steadfast will;
And, if thou canst not worship steadfastly,
Work for Me, toil in works pleasing to Me!
For he that laboureth right for love of Me
Shall finally attain! But, if in this
Thy faint heart fails, bring Me thy failure!

Paramhansa Yogananda wrote concerning these lines that they are what make the precepts of the Bhagavad Gita "so sweet, sympathetic, and useful in healing the manifold sicknesses of suffering humanity."

Indeed, in all of God's Truth there is no room for any kind of negativity, and certainly none for judgment either of others, or of oneself. We are God's children. He has placed us all together in this School of Life that we might learn—from one another, as well as by our own inner reactions.

It takes time to grow in understanding. Not everyone by any means has reached the point in his spiritual evolution where he can offer his devotion one-pointedly to God. A St. Francis of Assisi or a St. Teresa of Avila is that rarest flower in the garden of earth: an almost-perfected being. Most people are obliged to struggle through varying degrees of spiritual confusion: laziness, indifference, dullness, negativity, doubt. How is the average person, enmeshed as he is in a web of restlessness and desires, to obey the Gita's commandment, "Cling thou to Me!"? or the Bible's, to love God with one's whole heart, mind, soul, and strength?

Both scriptures take into account that there are many grades in the school of life. Truth is absolute, but the pathway to it is winding and long. Those who, on their climb, find they have far yet to go to reach the summit may require something more immediately suited to their needs—a walking stick, perhaps, rather than a mountaineer's pick. For them, the teachings that are most helpful will relate to their present place on the mountain. The soul must have the freedom to advance according to its present abilities, and also the freedom to make its own mistakes. Without this freedom, it may never learn its lessons thoroughly.

Who can understand the evils of drinking so completely as one who has himself known the suffering and shame that attend alcoholism? No one, again, is so dedicated to healing the body as one who has, in the past, suffered physically. It seems unlikely, too, that compassion for those who are mentally unbalanced manifests so strongly in those who have not, in some previous existence, known some form of insanity themselves. What a person needs in his spiritual growth is not the judgment of others, but their encouragement. What he needs is practical guidance. He needs help!

Jesus, in the third chapter of the Gospel of St. John, said, *"For God sent not his Son into the world to condemn the world; but that the world through him might be saved."* And in the story of the woman who was taken in adultery, he told her, *"Neither do I condemn thee."*

It is we who condemn ourselves! For in our error we turn away from the light in apparent fear of God's judgment, though in fact our fear is of our own conscience! We close our eyes tightly against the "light" of self-recognition, perhaps laughing with abandon in the hope of convincing, not only others, but above all ourselves that we have done well. In fact, our very instinct to laugh indicates the greater wisdom of instinct than of self-justifying logic, for it demonstrates that our true nature never changes. Our true longing is for bliss, even if by our actions we demonstrate that we've chosen suffering!

God never wants us, His children, to suffer. He has

created us in His own bliss-image. When we fail to act in harmony with that image, we inevitably experience pain. It is only when we realize that the cause of all our suffering lies within ourselves, not in the world around us, that we feel the challenge to begin the task—arduous at first, then, as Paramhansa Yogananda put it, "effortlessly liberating"—of correcting the true cause of our pain and returning to the light, where our souls belong.

The Bhagavad Gita tells us not to be unduly upset over our imperfections, but to do what we can, with whatever good qualities we have to hand already, to climb toward God. He is eternally patient. "Rome," as the old saying goes, "was not built in a day." Especially helpful in the present context is a favorite saying of Paramhansa Yogananda's: "A saint is a sinner who never gave up."

Don't identify yourself with your mistakes. Above all, never tell yourself, "I live in darkness, therefore I *am* dark!" If your present nature impels you to reject the light, try this little experiment:

Turn bravely towards it, mentally, and gaze into it steadfastly. Having gazed a while, turn away again. By light we mean also joy, love, and understanding. As you turn away from that light, feel that you are spurning no mere dangling light bulb, but a state of consciousness. Compare now, as honestly as you can, the feeling you had when you turned in either direction.

For example, if you are tempted to explode with anger over someone else's behavior, then, instead of suppressing that "explosion," try deliberately to change its nature. If your urge is toward violence, direct your anger toward some constructive act; don't injure that person. Chop wood, knead bread (afterward you may want to throw it away, and not bake and eat it!), sing—anything, rather than reinforce your negativity by affirming it by outward action. Best of all, if you can manage it: Relax your heart's feelings, then expand them to include that other person's needs and realities. Expand your sympathy, until you find you can forgive and bless him mentally. Then reflect: Which of the two feelings has given you greater satisfaction: explosive anger, or calm forgiveness?

In explosion of any kind there is always a release of tension, which may in itself prove temporarily satisfying. Explosions, however, can cause suffering not only to others, but to oneself. They can also, however, be constructive—for example, they can build roads for carrying people quickly to their destinations. An explosion of energy for positive purposes bestows more than passing relief: It brings an expansive sense of inner power and spiritual joy.

Again—and do this especially when a measure of personal sacrifice is required: Share something of yours with someone else: money, perhaps, or an opportunity you've been coveting personally. Don't make a sacrifice greater than your own emotional readiness for it. Be realistic as to your actual, as opposed to your idealized, nature. You will soon find that with heartfelt generosity comes a deeper sense of fulfillment than you've ever known when you thought only of your own fulfillment!

When your feelings are deeply hurt by someone you love, ask yourself, "Will I gain anything by allowing myself to suffer *twice?* It's true that I've been hurt, but this hurt will only deepen if I allow myself to become bitter. Let me meet unkindness, instead, with love, even if for no other reason than this: that I am happier, when I love!"

No one can really hate the light, though he may temporarily identify himself with darkness and error: with anger, pride, and selfishness; or with hatred, and think of himself as angry and bitter by nature. The "theme song" of some people might be, virtually, "I love myself just the way I am!" Were their song instead, "I love my *true Self,* which is who I *really* am!" it would be a truth. What most people feel, however, is attachment to the way they presently define themselves: to contractive consciousness and sense-slavery. Even their suffering must, in their eyes, be an acceptable price for their sense-enjoyments.

How absurd! How could anyone possibly *prefer* bitter poison to delicious, wholesome food? No one could prefer suffering to joy. Who, indeed, would rather be mean-spirited than generous, once he'd experienced the difference between the two?

We live in an age of scientific experiment. So why not conduct these simple experiments on yourself?

Evil, as Jesus tells us in the above passage, hates the light. Yet no one can be evil forever. Everyone feels in his heart that he is a child of the light, not of darkness. Everyone believes himself intrinsically good, not evil. Were any person's nature dark to its core, he would rejoice wholeheartedly in his separation from light. Instead, there is no rejoicing. Darkness brings him suffering, which he is unable to banish by loud laughter flung riotously to the skies, or by the wheezing chuckles of unholy glee. There is no real happiness in error: There is only the pain of exile from that true state in which all of us belong. Our "condemnation" is not eternal, though it may seem so during times of suffering.

It is not possible to reach a mountaintop by a single leap. It must be attained step by step. Accept that, though there is satisfaction for the climber in every step upward, the journey to the peak will take time. It will be helpful, on the other hand, to take stock of your feelings every now and then. Are your spirits growing a little lighter? freer? happier? As your sense of inner fulfillment increases, your pace will quicken, until you find yourself fairly rushing toward the goal! At the top of the mountain you'll find a (literally!) breath-taking view spread out in all directions: range after range of shining peaks and slopes covered with fields that are colorful with wildflowers of joy.

At last you'll know that everything God ever wanted from you was the sweetness of your love. His own love has always been yours. What He wants, however, for your own true fulfillment, is *your* love. Everything you've ever sought was but a suggestion from your imagination, a hint of your soul's craving. God, forever, has been your sole reality.

CHAPTER SEVENTEEN

"Works" That Lead to Perfection

Outer "good works" and long-faced expressions of piety may impress people who mistake shadow for substance, and to whom shadow seems all the grander because it can be enlarged to any size one desires. True devotion, however, is of the heart. To make an outward display of it is to diminish it, as a shadow diminishes in size the farther the substance that produces it is removed from the light.

"I say unto you," Jesus Christ stated, *"That except your righteousness shall exceed the righteousness of the scribes and Pharisees, ye shall in no case enter into the kingdom of heaven."* (Matthew 5:20)

Jesus often scolded the priests of his time, who, though wearing the outer vestments of religion, lacked *inner,* spiritual righteousness. The words in this passage, however, hadn't that sting. He was implying that while it is good to be outwardly religious, for the true devotee it is not good enough, even if he is sincere. The "kingdom of heaven" to which he referred was the state of God-consciousness, not the beautiful astral heavens that most people visualize, where virtuous souls go after death.

We see an example of this "heaven" of divine union

263

in the parable of the mustard seed. The seed grew and became a mighty tree. This story, when read in its entirety, is clearly a metaphor for soul-expansion; no other explanation will suffice. Indeed, only the Gospel of St. Matthew presents this story as a metaphor for "the kingdom of heaven." Saints Mark and Luke explain it as a parable for "the kingdom of *God.*"

Jesus had to accommodate his teaching to the understanding of his times. And at that time, certainly, few could accept the staggering concept of cosmic consciousness. Even today, few are ready for such a possibility—even after the mind-expanding discoveries of advanced physics. Not all even of the disciples of Jesus could distinguish mentally between a heaven peopled by angelic beings and the infinite "heaven" of God-consciousness. (This conclusion cannot but be inferred from some of the questions that were put to Jesus.*)

Jesus in the above passage told his disciples that even righteousness, as ordinarily defined, is not enough for one of lofty spiritual aspiration. It may be pointed out also that, in the passage under consideration, he was not criticizing the priests, though he frequently did so in reply to their attempts to turn people against his teachings. Great souls naturally think in terms of principles, not of personalities. Jesus was not trying to disillusion people with their priesthood. What

---

* The "mother of Zebedee's children," for example, asked Jesus, "Grant that these my two sons may sit, the one on thy right hand, and the other on the left, in thy kingdom." Jesus, not wanting to burden her with an explanation for which she was not ready, replied simply, "You know not what you ask." (Matthew 20:21,22)

he wanted was to uplift their consciousness. His words were addressed to human nature generally, not to a particular set of individuals.

It is commonly assumed that religious institutions promote spirituality. Such, however, is not always the case. For human nature is self-centered and biased therefore against teachings that recommend giving up the ego. Even for those who dedicate themselves to the religious life it is seldom easy to abandon old ways of looking at things and old patterns of behavior. The ego, despite a sincere effort to transcend it, cannot but be a central point of reference until, after years of prayer and meditation, divine grace lifts one up to the state of superconsciousness.

The struggle against self-centeredness is universal, and delusion is nothing if not subtle! Just as one begins to think he is winning the battle against pride, for example, he is aghast to find himself becoming proud of his humility! And just when he feels a spirit of charity welling up within him, he ruefully perceives a desire— like a mouse sneaking furtively through the pantry— that others praise him for his charity.

What Jesus was really saying was not that imperfect goodness is evil, but only that normal human perceptions of virtue must be transcended. For even after virtue has been refined, it is still tied to ego-consciousness. As he put it elsewhere, *"There is none good but one, that is, God."* (Matthew 19:17)

Human goodness lacks intrinsic value, like clouds at sunset which, though beautiful, lose their radiance once the sun descends out of sight below the horizon. It is obviously good to be good! We should be grateful, then, if divine grace enables us to serve as channels of inspiration to others. We may even rejoice in the beauty of that inspiration. Delusion only raises its cobra's head when we turn our gaze back upon ourselves as channels for that inspiration, in forgetfulness of its divine source.

It might be helpful at this point to ponder a few of the ways in which religion can prevent, rather than assist, spiritual development. For, as Swami Sri Yukteswar (Paramhansa Yogananda's guru) said of religious institutions, they are like beehives, the purpose of which is to store honey. Religious institutions, similarly, can help people to husband the nectar of devotion. Association with other seekers on the path is important for the devotee, especially if he is a beginner. Living in association with worldly people, or in the absence of spiritual company, makes it difficult for the average person, caught as he is in the web of restlessness, to think of God.

Unfortunately, religious institutions themselves often stray from their spiritual calling, and dedicate themselves to making their "hive" larger, more important, and more magnificent than any other. Such dedication may be an act of devotion, but if too much energy is spent on what the modern sociologist might term "Hival Improvement," the quality of the nectar will diminish. Priests, clergymen, and other religionists often allow themselves to become so immersed in organizational activities that they forget the necessity for devotion. Years of institutional zeal may kill any hope of reviving the true spirit of religion, as one cannot light a fire with a damp matchstick. In this context a statement comes to mind, one that was made centuries ago by St. Odo of Cluny. "The floors of hell," he said, "are paved with the bald pates of clergymen!"

A spiritual group needs the inspiration of a living person. Mere rules and printed instructions are no substitutes for it. Without such inspiration, no matter how inspired a group was at its inception, time will draw it down into a mire of mediocrity. The real strength of every group is power emanating from its source. In the case of Christianity, that power derives ultimately from Jesus Christ. It also depends on people's devotional attunement with him. Finally, however, it depends on the living presence of at least one inspired individual. This person need not be the leader. Even the cook, or the gardener, if he or she is filled with love for God, can function as the actual inspiration for an entire community.

The living memory only of a saint can help to keep devotion alive through those disciples for whom that memory is still fresh. If the disciples themselves lose the immediacy of that memory, however, and assuming no one is left to carry forward the baton of inspiration, the group's devotion will wither in time like a plant without water.

That religious institutions should contain members of the "scribe and Pharisee" type is inevitable. Most people are satisfied with relative goodness, for their own aspiration soars no higher than the attainment after death of an existence in surroundings of astral beauty. Religious institutionalism is better, certainly, than blatant materialism. A problem religious institutions face, however, is the general tendency of every living thing toward either self-expansion or contraction. It is usually easier to maintain the spirituality of a small group than of a large one, provided that the group has someone of genuine charisma to inspire it. St. Teresa of Avila sought to combat spiritual mediocrity in her monasteries by limiting the number of their residents to eighteen.

As spiritual groups increase in size, they become not only organized, but institutionalized. Their leaders often reason that, since God is the Supreme Good, any increase in membership will benefit humanity itself. Once proselytizing zeal sets in like concrete, it is easy for one to be diverted from his spiritual goals. Mass conversion becomes a general ambition, and fervor for inner communion with God becomes increasingly viewed as, at best, a threat to group spirit.

To inspire thousands is no doubt better than to inspire only a handful, provided those thousands truly *are* inspired. The sheer effort involved in reaching them, however, cannot but affect one's own devotion. The attempt to satisfy mass expectations is one way of diluting high aspiration. In the very effort to transform those expectations into love for God, one's own devotion becomes compromised. The point is finally reached where worldly alternatives—the sale of "indulgences" in Martin Luther's day; the emotional rallies and "revivals" in our own—become acceptable as a proper means of attracting people to their "higher good."

Treading at first softly, then arrogantly, on the heels of such compromise comes the desire for worldly power, money, and fame. Justification for these ambitions is sought in the claim that power makes it possible to be more influential for good; that money makes it easier to achieve that end; and that fame can focus people's enthusiasm and make it possible to draw them to God.

Many religious leaders find this reasoning persuasive, indeed irresistible. Unfortunately, compromise always ends up compromising the compromisers. Power, money, and fame are snares set for the unwary by Delusion. No matter how cleverly one rationalizes these roundabout means to spiritual ends, they become ends, at last, in themselves. A zealous servant of God may feel that he is working for the Lord, but if his activities inspire no devotion in his own heart, how can they inspire it in the hearts of others? If once he recognizes his spiritual dryness, he should ask himself, "What am I really accomplishing?"

Often, even a service that began in a spirit of deep sincerity develops gradually into a tendency—reluctant at first, then accepted with a shrug as a regrettable necessity—to lie, cheat, and treat with ruthless indifference the needs of other people, whose well-being is perceived as being secondary in importance to the greater good. Resignation gradually develops toward destroying people's reputations for the sake of that "greater good." In extreme cases, even murder is countenanced—again, always, for the "greater good." In time, it becomes glaringly evident that the person they serve is not God, but the one we'll call "that other fellow."

When the "good" of an institution takes precedence

over normal human decency, Satan smiles, for he is well pleased!

Jesus in the above passage is saying, "Don't be satisfied with orthodox definitions of spirituality. Seek in God absolute, not relative, perfection. Don't court the praises of fools. Don't even seek verbal approval of your religious superiors. Seek it inwardly, from God." Indeed, only a few verses later Jesus states, *"Be ye therefore perfect, even as your Father which is in heaven is perfect."*

Christians often seek justification for their lackluster devotion and haphazard approach to spirituality in the words of St. Paul: *"For by grace are ye saved through faith, and that not of yourselves: it is the gift of God: Not of works, lest any man should boast."* (Ephesians 2:8,9) Those so-called Christians conveniently ignore St. Paul's sequel to that statement: *"For we are God's handiwork, created in Christ Jesus to devote ourselves to the good deeds for which God has designed us."* What Paul was really saying was that we should do everything with the awareness of God's guidance within. We should never allow ourselves to be driven by egoic desires.

How can our own righteousness exceed that of "the scribes and Pharisees"? Certainly not by striving to outshine them or anyone else by our religiosity. Comparisons, especially in this sense, are "odious." We cannot excel spiritually, either, by merely observing a set of outer religious rules. True righteousness is of the soul, invisible to human eyes although its *effects* usually are evident. Indeed, true righteousness is more often misunderstood and condemned by self-righteous people than appreciated by them.

We must consciously invite God into our lives: ask Him to use our hands, feet, and voices; to think His thoughts through us; to love through us; to inspire others in every way through our vibrations and example. Human righteousness must be offered onto the altar of Infinite awareness to be transformed into divine truth. For truth alone, Jesus said, can make one free.

To achieve transcendental freedom from egoic confinement requires far more than personal righteousness. It requires absolute, *impersonal* dedication to truth. Both St. Paul and Jesus Christ urged us to *live* in the Divine Presence; not only to pray, but to *commune* with God. Prayer is the practice of talking to the Lord; meditation is inner communion with Him.

Our will, then, must be directed toward conquering whatever resistance we have in ourselves to the flow of divine grace and to truth. Our restless thoughts, our likes and dislikes, our desires for worldly success—all these must be resolutely offered up in the silence to God's love.

Sri Krishna, in the seventh Chapter of the Bhagavad Gita, said:

Yet hard the wise Mahatma is to find,
That man who sayeth, 'All is Vasudev!'

This translation, in the poetic rendition of Sir Edwin Arnold, was often quoted by Paramhansa Yogananda. *Mahatma* means "great soul"; *Vasudev* is a name for the Lord. It is rare to find anyone so absorbed in the Infinite that wherever he turns his gaze he beholds only God. Generally speaking, it is not good to compare oneself with others, but if one must make that comparison let it be with the saints. Let it inspire us to become more like them!

God does not condemn people for sinning. As goodness is relative, so also is sinfulness. We must see the fact of relativity as an encouragement not to accept any limitation on our own spiritual growth. As Jesus said, *"The Father judgeth no man, but hath committed all judgment unto the Son."* (John 5:22) Judgment, in fact, comes not even from Christ, for Jesus stated also, *"God sent not his Son into the world to condemn the world; but that the world through him might be saved."* (John 3:17) It is we who judge ourselves—we, and the Christ who dwells at the center of our own being. We judge ourselves when we err. Jesus makes this point again two sentences later: *"Every one that doeth evil hateth the light, neither cometh to the light, lest his deeds should be reproved."* The Christ consciousness reproaches us silently when we err. We, unfortunately, in our infatuation with worldly things, create noise and confusion in the hope of silencing that soundless reprimand.

God awaits us eternally. It is impossible for anyone *not* to return to Him, eventually; it was for this destiny that we were all created. Even the slowest learner must come to realize, however late in his journey, that lasting happiness simply does not exist outside the Self.

Human consciousness, indeed, can be refined only gradually. It must be convinced to its core that the fulfillment it seeks really does lie in God alone. In stages along the way, the ego learns that true power lies in self-surrender, not in self-affirmation; that happiness comes from sharing with others, not from selfish gain; that far greater fulfillment can be found in loving them than in excluding anyone from one's sympathies.

If egoic individuality were intrinsic to human nature, Nature herself would dictate the wisdom of seizing everything one can for oneself. This advice has been actually propounded by a number of well-known (but unknowing!) philosophers, whose "love of wisdom" would be better described as love for their own conceits. Selfishness, however, is an offense against human nature. All of us are inextricably woven together, like threads running through the fabric of all life.

A seed grows slowly to become a tree. God doesn't expect us by the mere reading of scripture to become wise, any more than a schoolteacher expects children in his charge to absorb knowledge for which they are as yet unprepared. We have eternity in which to attain perfection.

We have also eternity, however, in which to suffer, if we so choose! The alternatives are simple: suffering on the one hand, joy on the other; turmoil on the one hand, peace on the other; darkness on the one hand, light on the other.

Francis Thompson's great spiritual poem, *The Hound of Heaven,* often quoted lovingly by Paramhansa Yogananda, describes God as saying to the soul, "All things forsake thee, who forsakest Me." Such must be the discovery, whether late or soon, of every human being. Fulfillment achieves permanence only when it is anchored in God.

How soon shall that fulfillment be achieved? That

is for each of us to decide. We may find it helpful, however, to bear in mind an attitude that Yogananda admired in America. As he put it: "Eventually? Eventually? Why not *now!* That is the spirit I like in this country!" Let us resolve *from now on* to live for God: to include Him in all that we do; to share with Him our every thought; to offer the fruit of our labors to Him alone. Thus may we too, someday, be in a position to declare, as the *"wise mahatma"* does: "All is *Vasudev!*"

CHAPTER EIGHTEEN

"Be Ye Therefore Perfect!"

Inner communion with God is the way to know Him. Paramhansa Yogananda and Jesus Christ emphasized it; so have many other masters. Indeed, Yogananda pointed out that inner communion should be a habitual attitude of mind, and not only a daily practice. "Seclusion," he told his students, "is the price of greatness." At the same time, every choice in life has its advantages and disadvantages. To be with God inwardly ought not to remove one's sympathies from other people. Even a hermit should keep his aura expanded, so to speak, to embrace humanity. This understanding comes naturally to one who seeks solitude as Jesus put it, *"in spirit and in truth."* (John 4:24)

To love God truly means also to love everyone in the recognition that He is equally in all. As Yogananda said, "Don't imagine you can win God's love without love for your fellowman. You cannot win Him if you are unkind to others."

The following passage offers powerful support for the exhortation to universal love. It forms part of the Sermon on the Mount, in Chapter 5 of the Gospel of St. Matthew, Verses 43–48:

"Ye have heard it said, Thou shalt love thy neighbor, and hate thine enemy. But I say unto you, Love your

enemies; bless them that curse you; do good to them that hate you; and pray for them that despitefully use you and persecute you; that ye may be the children of your Father who is in heaven: for He makes His sun to rise on the evil as well as on the good, and sends rain on both the just and the unjust. For if ye love them who love you, what reward have ye? Do not even the tax collectors the same?

"And if ye salute only your brethren, what do ye more than others? Do not even the publicans so?"

Jesus defines virtue as that which deepens our attunement with God. What is the reason we should love friend and enemy alike? Because God dwells equally in all. And how can we "bless them that curse" us? By giving love to all *impersonally*—not from egoic predilection, but with God's love. Jesus said we should see everyone, ourselves included, as children of our Father *"who is in heaven."** Our hearts' love should aspire toward union with God. Therefore the next words:

"Be ye therefore perfect, even as your Heavenly Father is perfect."

These verses are so inspiring for their message of universal kindness and love that one might easily overlook their deeper emphasis on divine attunement, as if he were telling us only to be virtuous in a human sense. What Jesus was saying was that perfection can be achieved, and expressed outwardly, only by God's grace. Personal effort can invite grace, but it cannot

---

* In the last chapter we saw that Jesus often used the term, "heaven," in reference to the state of God-consciousness. Popular fancy has always depicted heaven as an actual place, rather, where the Lord is seated majestically on a golden throne.

replace the need for it. Were it possible to become as perfect as God from our state of egoic confinement, it would imply the possibility of an infinite number of supreme godheads! Egoic "perfection" is a contradiction in terms. The ego is imperfect by the very fact that it makes us conscious of being separate from God.

Jesus made this meaning clear by admonishing us to live as "children" of God. It is only from God that the ability comes to love others purely. Attunement with Him brings realization of the oneness of all life. Everything in creation manifests the infinite Self.

In these few simple words, then, we find the essence of Christ's teaching: that we must seek perfection in God, live consciously by His love, visualize His presence in all, and share with them the love we receive inwardly from Him. Thus alone, with His grace, can we achieve all that we have ever sought in life.

The beauty of this teaching is that it encourages us to view divine consciousness as our fundamental reality and ultimate destiny. It does also emphasize, however, the magnitude of the task before us. Sri Krishna offered divine encouragement also, but added the same warning. In Chapter Seven of the Bhagavad Gita, he stated:

"Out of thousands, one strives for spiritual attainment. And out of those many blessed true seekers who strive assiduously to attain Me, one, perhaps, perceives Me as I am."

The spiritual challenge that every great master delivers to humanity is no mere exhortation to be moral: It is to become as perfect as God is! We are asked literally to expand our sense of selfhood to infinity.

Although the task is more than Herculean, it is one that showers treasures untold on all who sincerely attempt it: the sweetness of pure love; expanding happiness; deep inner peace; ever-growing wisdom; a soaring sense of freedom; and the awareness of divine support through every trial in life. Do other ways of life offer anything comparable?

In an earlier chapter we proposed an experiment based on the results *to oneself* of two different kinds of behavior: materialistic, and spiritual. Here let us propose another experiment, based on the results not to oneself, but to others. For although the scriptures tell us to judge no one, they also tell us to view reality as it is. Only with clear vision can we express true kindness.

To view with "kindly" approval, for example, deeds that cannot but harm their perpetrators would, in the long run, be *unkind.* To smile at drunkenness, for example, would be to encourage indulgence in it. We should be aware of the consequences of people's actions, not only that we may be of help to others, but for a more personal reason also. For awareness can spare us, too, great suffering by giving us clear understanding of how to behave.

Judgment implies condemnation. There is, however, no condemnation in being simply aware of people's faults and virtues, and of the effect these have on the people themselves.

Study the eyes, then, and the emotional states of people who are devoted to material pursuits. Then look at people who live by spiritual principles. Even the facial expressions, bodily gestures, and tone of voice say it all.

Worldly people betray inner restlessness in their every movement. Their awareness is centered more in the arms and shoulders than in the spine. Their fidgety glances reveal their restlessness; so also does the incessant movement of their hands and feet. A clouded mind is evident in a vacant expression and a habitual tendency to look downward. Disappointment is revealed in a harsh tone of voice, in jerky breathing, and in a forward stoop of the shoulders. Bitterness is evident when people defiantly square their shoulders.

Karmic complexities may allow an evildoer prosperity for a time, owing to good deeds he committed in the past. Prosperity, on the other hand, may be denied a virtuous person for a time, owing to misdeeds he committed in the past. "The mills of God grind slowly," as the poet Longfellow wrote. Karmic law may be delayed in its effects by "the thwarting cross-currents of ego," as Paramhansa Yogananda called them in *Autobiography of a Yogi.* A person's *thoughts,* however, usually show their outer effects much sooner.

Whatever the fortunes or setbacks in life for people who live by high principles, they radiate a constant inner serenity and contentment of spirit. Their gestures are peaceful, conveying a sense of inner harmony. Their voices are melodious. Their smiles, which begin at the eyes, include others. Their hand movements suggest an attitude of self-giving, not of self-protectiveness. Their walk is firm. Their spines are straight.

A clever actor may be able to mimic these characteristics outwardly, but he will never be able to conceal the actual vibrations he emanates. Spiritual people emanate vibrations of harmony. Materialistic people emanate vibrations of lust, greed, and disharmony. To a person of spiritual sensitivity, these vibrations are tangible; they can be felt in the heart, if one keeps his feelings open and calm.

To the worldly person, happiness reveals itself in outward excitement: in wild gestures, for example, and in dancing excitedly about the room. He may visualize monks and nuns, by contrast, as shrivel-faced, austere, and dour simply because he knows that meditation and prayer must have made them calm. In both cases, as it happens, the very opposite is true: It is monks and nuns who are happy, and worldly people who, because of their restlessness, find happiness elusive. As the Bhagavad Gita says, to the person without inner peace, happiness is not possible. Man's obsession with outer fulfillment brings him nothing but grief in the end. A spiritual life, on the other hand, sends the heart fairly dancing with *inner* joy.

To choose impersonally between these two ways of living should be very easy, for their consequences are so self-evident: happiness, on the one hand; unhappiness, on the other. Unfortunately, ego-involvement makes it difficult to be impersonal. Powerful urges, as Sigmund Freud (well known as the father of modern psychology) discovered, seethe in the subconscious and affect many, if not most, of our conscious processes.

Freud recommended that the conflict between conscious intention and subconscious urges be resolved by accepting that the urges define us as we really are. According to him, our intentions show us merely as we would like to be, or have been told we ought to be. Suppression therefore is harmful, he insisted, for it produces "complexes" that, in their extreme form, result in mental disease. In fact, the diseased mind, which abnormal psychology describes, was his point of departure in developing his ideas. To him, aberrations were the norm. They may be minimized, he said, but they can never be eliminated. The only solution Freud offered to the search for personal fulfillment was to accept one's lower nature frankly and honestly as one's reality, and to place on a shelf, so to speak, whatever idealized image one has formed of himself as a pleasant fiction.

The Bhagavad Gita warns also against suppression. Its warning, however, has a very different emphasis, for it teaches one to work *with* those subconscious urges and to refine and redirect them toward spiritual fulfillment.

To accept Freud's point of view is to conclude that evolution has deceived us woefully. For because of it we have inherited thin skins, which force us to keep warm by wearing clothes. Clad, consequently, we've "gotten above ourselves" to the extent of developing artificial mental attitudes as well: the notion, for instance, that we must go about "properly" dressed in public to protect an entirely false sense of modesty. This "hypocritical" attitude encourages us also to develop what it pleases us to consider "high ideals"—which in fact are nothing but mental "clothing" to hide our basic animality.

This was the bias of Western thinking long before Darwin and Freud were born. The Church proclaimed it in declaring the dogma that mankind is *inherently* sinful and can be redeemed only by Jesus Christ's atonement on the cross. According to Darwin's theory, man is little more than a precocious monkey. St. Thomas Aquinas, however, the foremost of Catholic theologians, anticipated Darwin by centuries with his famous definition, "Man is a rational animal." And man, because of his animal nature, is more likely to be irrational than rational. This aspect of human nature was long ago accepted by Christians, and attributed by them to the Devil and to "original sin."

Science, since Galileo's time, also prepared the way for the general acceptance of Darwin and Freud by side-stepping the whole issue of God, whose existence, it admitted, could not be proved.* From this confessed inability it proceeded to show proudly the many things it *had* proved, and concluded that God is "unnecessary" to the general scheme of things, and may safely be dismissed as non-existent.

The consequence of this cultural conditioning has been a deep-seated bias toward materialism and atheism.

Thus, modern thinking has turned the ancient *Vedic* declaration, *"Tat twam asi* (Thou art that)," on its head. In the *Vedic* view, as also in that of other great religions, man's inner conflicts will never be resolved except spiritually. Modern psychology, however, and especially Freudian psychology, takes quite the opposite stand: Not by spiritual aspiration, it insists, but only by liberating mankind from this "error" of aspiration, will fulfillment ever be achieved.

---

* The Sankhya teachings in Hinduism made this statement also: *"Ishwar ashiddha* (God is not proved)." The purpose of this statement, however, is not to deny God, but to point out that divine realization lies outside the limiting syllogisms of logic.

282

One has, however, only to look at the lives of people who accept this philosophy—in fact, to look at the cows and sheep, who, presumably, are more "grounded and self-honest" than we are, since they have none, or few, of the psychological "complexes" with which mankind is plagued—one has only, then, to look at such lives to see that the "solution" offered is fatally flawed. Many modern psychologists seek "answers" in what they, since Carl Jung, call the "unconscious," rather than in superconsciousness, which many mystics describe from their own experience. One waits in vain, however, for modern psychology to produce even one example of a radiant, mentally healthy human being. All that has been accomplished so far is that formerly disturbed people have developed a slightly less pronounced psychological limp.

It is a simple fact that the subconscious obstructs one's efforts to grow spiritually. It is *not* a fact that rejection of spiritual aspirations removes even a single obstruction to happiness. In the modern view, outer circumstances *pushed* us up the evolutional ladder without our conscious consent. A number of psychologists actually scoff at the notion that the direction of evolution is necessarily even *upward*.* To Christian theology, the soul's longing for God is a mark of divine

---

* A footnote in the author's book, *Out of the Labyrinth* (formerly titled, *Crises in Modern Thought—Solutions to the Problem of Meaninglessness*) reads: "James F. Crow [published] an article in *Scientific American* (the September 1959 issue). Rhetorically, Crow asked, 'Has man changed more in developing his brain than the elephant has by growing a trunk?'" Of course, if the sole criterion be survival, the answer to the question has to be, "No"—or, in the words of the popular song: "It ain't necessarily so."

grace. Theology rejects any claim, however, that this deep longing is innate in us.

Jesus Christ on the other hand, as we have seen already, said that high spiritual aspiration is part of our nature. *"Know ye not ye are gods?"* was the challenge he flung at his critics. We are the children of God, not the mere spawn of Satan. The accusations he leveled against the Pharisees—on one occasion he actually called them sons of Satan, and not, as they'd claimed, sons of Abraham—were in reference to their deluded understanding, and not to their spiritual potential.

It is our delusions that are the offspring of Satan. These delusions—the "devil" within us—are, as the word itself implies, false. Granted, man's subconscious urges rise to a conscious level in the form of physical desires, likes and dislikes, and of seemingly causeless emotions. They impede human progress not only spiritually, but in any direction one elects to take. The longing for God is in fact what the theologians have called it: a mark of grace.

Grace, however, is the soul's *recognition* of eternal realities—*smriti* (memory), as the Indian scriptures call it—even as the strings of a harp vibrate in sympathy with notes played on another instrument. We are not so much pushed upward from below by evolution as *pulled* up by the dim memory of who we are, in eternity.

Nevertheless, because our present awareness is of the body, our more present memories are physical also. Even the earnest spiritual seeker finds himself pitted in a life-and-death struggle against what mystics have called "the flesh."

The Bhagavad Gita says that even the wise can be tempted, until they are firmly anchored in God. Few people are even interested in seeking God. And of these few, rare indeed is the one who attains perfection.

Lest the seeker lose heart at the odds against him, it should be explained that most souls pass through successively spiritual planes on their way to final liberation. *"In my Father's house,"* Jesus Christ said, *"are many mansions."* (John 14:2) Few devotees even, on this plane of existence, rouse themselves enough to devote all their energies to seeking God. The earth is a grade school, so to speak, in God's vast universe. God's light on earth is dimmed by human ignorance, and is kept in constant turmoil by people's eagerness for self-glorification.

The Bhagavad Gita gives us more immediate consolation also, however. It tells us that God is pleased with any sincere effort to know Him. *"To one who offers even a flower or a leaf in My name,"* Krishna says, *"I Myself receive that offering."* Nor does the scripture remove from mankind the hope of attaining divine union while still one lives in a physical body. It merely poses the challenge: "If you want to know Me, don't delude yourself with thinking that the task is easy! The spiritual heights can be reached only by heroic dedication!" Not, be it noted, by mere belief, but by utter self-dedication.

There is another point to be considered here. For, raised as we've all been on democratic principles, we may imagine that anything accepted as truth by the majority must indeed, therefore, be true. Many religious organizations seek justification in the sheer numbers of their adherents. And people commonly think that priests and ministers speak for the founders of their religions simply because thousands, or millions, agree with them!

The Gita demolishes these false notions. Jesus Christ did so also, repeatedly. Consider how frequently Jesus offered spiritual teachings in the form of parables. He refrained from declaring them openly "to the multitudes" because, as he himself explained, his message was intended for those who had "ears to hear."

In every field of endeavor, it is necessary that certain knowledge be withheld from people who are not yet grounded in their understanding. It would be a waste of talent, for example, for a great pianist to devote himself to teaching scales to five-year-olds. It is far better that he keep his special knowledge for students who demonstrate a certain aptitude.

In the spiritual world also, great masters commonly reserve their deeper teachings for disciples who are competent to receive them. Were a master to give such teachings to lukewarm aspirants, he might only confuse their understanding. His more serious students, meanwhile, would not receive the attention they deserve.

Jesus told his disciples, "Cast not your pearls before swine." It wasn't that he wanted to *exclude* anyone from God's truth, but only that he knew that many people are ill prepared for it. Everyone determines, in this sense, what he himself will receive. What most people, including many religious people, want is ego-gratification. They want comforting advice like, "Don't try too hard; after all, you're only human! Don't be fanatical. God asks only that you be kind to others, truthful, and fair in your dealings with them, and that you remember Him occasionally." How many ministers of the Gospel are there who exhort their congregations, "Forsake everything for God!"?

Most people find the influence of mass consciousness difficult to resist. Even those who set out on their spiritual journey in a spirit of deep earnestness may lose heart when the tests become difficult, and may return to the life they once scorned as "worldly." Ignoring the sorrowful voice of their own conscience, and succumbing to spiritual cowardice, they conclude that worldly acceptance is preferable to worldly mockery and persecution. Proudly, now, they display to their erstwhile friends on the path the shiny new cars they've purchased, the beautiful clothing, the new homes. They preen themselves on their good standing in the world. Meanwhile, does the world care for them? Not at all! People's all-consuming interest is themselves.

Sri Krishna, in referring to the scarcity of deeply earnest seekers, wanted to help people to break the hypnosis of mass opinion. To live truly in God, he implied, one must be willing to stand alone, to be ridiculed by uncomprehending friends and family members, and persecuted by worldly people (who, after all, are only spiritual children). As Jesus cried out from the cross: "Father, forgive them, for they know not what they do."

To know God, we must realize that, even as in physical death we leave everything behind, so with the death of the ego we leave creation itself behind. Nothing remains—not even *nothingness!* (This is to suggest how utterly beyond human comprehension is that Ultimate State!)

Ah! but in that "tangible nothingness" is attained oneness with all that Is!

What God asks of us is the willingness to enter the divine "kingdom" all alone—approved of by none but Him. Wonder of wonders, then: Approval suddenly rings out from every "particle" of divine light in creation!

CHAPTER NINETEEN

Restlessness vs. God-Centeredness

This reading is from the Gospel of St. Luke, Chapter 10, Verses 38–42:

"Now it came to pass, as they went, that he entered into a certain village: and a certain woman named Martha received him into her house. And she had a sister called Mary, which also sat at Jesus' feet, and heard his word.

"But Martha was cumbered about much serving, and came to him, and said, Lord, dost thou not care that my sister hath left me to serve alone? Bid her therefore that she help me.

"And Jesus answered and said unto her, Martha, Martha, thou art careful and troubled about many things: But one thing is needful: and Mary hath chosen that good part, which shall not be taken away from her."

This story is usually repeated to contrast the two paths to God: the outer one, of service, and the inner one, of prayer and meditation. In Western monasticism, these two ways are epitomized in the religious orders: those devoted to "good works" such as teaching, healing, and feeding the poor, and those designed primarily for a life of prayer and contemplation. In India, the inner way is usually given the greater emphasis, but the path of action, or *karma yoga,* also has numerous adherents.

Both paths are spiritually valid. Indeed, each usually needs the other, for balance. Jesus in this passage, however, was not even saying that Martha's activity was spiritually valid. Instead, he scolded her for her lack of spiritual focus.

Could his meaning possibly have been that service itself is lower in God's eyes than a life of silence and prayer? Of course not! Many times during his mission, in fact, he praised service as highly as he did prayer and meditation. *"God is a Spirit,"* he said, emphasizing the latter, *"and they that worship Him must worship Him in spirit and in truth"* (John 4:24); but he said also: *"Verily I say unto you, Inasmuch as ye have done it unto one of the least of these my brethren* [served them, in other words] *ye have done it unto me."* (Matthew 25:40)

Worldly minded Christians commonly seek to justify their entanglement in material interests by saying, "Well, we 'Marthas' of the world are needed, too." Worldly minded Hindus, like their Western counterparts, often try to excuse their materialistic tendencies by pointing to the example of Arjuna, whom Krishna urged to "fight" in the righteous war at Kurukshetra. Both groups—superficial Christians and superficial Hindus alike—miss the truth those scriptures were propounding. For whereas both outer service and inner communion are paths to God, activity alone, with an only nominally spiritual aim, is not the path of karma yoga; it is not, in itself, a spiritual service. Jesus was not scolding Martha for serving him, but for her restlessness. Nor was he comparing the relative merits of service and meditation. What he said was, "Mary's is the *only* way." His words were a rebuke, not a qualified compliment. He was telling Martha that she was too much centered in her work. She should have been thinking of God even in the midst of physical activity. Thus would her activity have been transformed into a path to God.

Martha's error was one into which devotees often fall. In her own opinion, no doubt, she was serving God, but Jesus said to her, "If you allow your mind to become wholly engrossed in your work, how can that work be spiritual? You are not with God. What you are serving is your own restlessness!"

Martha's mind was filled with thoughts of all those dishes steaming on the stove, of endless dicing and slicing and sifting and spicing to produce a feast for their honored guests. The needs of work, however, should not have become her excuse for spiritual absent-mindedness. Had her work been offered up mentally to God, the meal itself, in fact, would have turned out better than it could have, produced in agitation of mind.

The consciousness with which a thing is done infuses into the product itself the vibrations of that consciousness. This is true especially in the case of food preparation, for what one eats permeates the body, and is not something merely felt with the hands or appreciated with the eyes. The concern Jesus expressed to Martha, however, was not so much for the vibrations she was putting into the food as for Martha herself. He was saying, "Deepen your attunement with my spirit."

Needless to say, Martha did reap spiritual benefits from her work, as anyone does who works for God, however superficially. She was depriving herself only of the deeper blessings that might have been hers had she been centered more within. "Martha consciousness," then, is an error not of commission, but of omission. Martha was serving the Master outwardly, but not in her heart. She accepted that Jesus was a great spiritual teacher, but she was not attuned to his soul vibrations.

On another occasion, Jesus explained the importance of drawing upon the spiritual *consciousness* of a true master. *"He that receiveth a prophet,"* he said, *"in the name of a prophet shall receive a prophet's reward; and he that receiveth a righteous man in the name of a righteous man shall receive a righteous man's reward."* (Matthew 10:41)

To be a prophet means to be united in consciousness with God. A person who lives a merely righteous life may not even believe in God, necessarily. To receive a prophet's reward means to attract those blessings which result, finally, in becoming a prophet oneself. To receive a righteous man's reward means to acquire merely good karma: a fortunate and happy life on earth, and a long residence in heaven, perhaps, after death. By good karma alone, however, it is not possible to be freed from all karmic bondage. "Chains, though of gold," it has been wisely said, "still bind."

To receive a prophet, then, "in the name of a prophet" means to attune oneself with the prophet's spirit. Outward service to him should be performed with awareness of the grace flowing through him.

That same flow continues on to others through his disciples. Jesus, after describing those who would receive a prophet's reward, went on to say, *"Believe me, anyone who gives even a drink of water to one of these little ones, only in the name of a disciple* [that is, with the thought that he is my disciple], *will by no means lose his reward."* (Matthew 10:42)

As an interesting aside here, Paramhansa Yogananda included in the meaning of the word *prophet* those disciples of a great master who, even if they are not yet liberated, are highly advanced spiritually. In conversation with the author, he once remarked, "Judas had some bad karma, as a result of which he fell, spiritually. But he was also a prophet." The author expressed surprise at this astonishing description of the greatness of Judas. Yogananda then, with a typically Indian head-gesture of affirmation, replied, "Oh, yes! He had to be, to be one of the disciples."

He continued, "Judas was spiritually liberated in this century, in India. I knew him there personally. Jesus appeared in vision to a great master, and asked him to give his disciple liberation."

The author, fascinated, then inquired, "What was Judas like in this life?"

"Very withdrawn in himself," the Master replied. "He still showed traces of his old attachment to money—not in the sense of desiring it personally, but as a means of helping others. His brother disciples teased him about it. The guru, however, reproached them quietly. 'Don't,' he said."

Martha is an example of the ordinary devotee, who serves God nominally but whose mind is elsewhere. Superficial service of this kind is thrust at God, so to speak, without pausing, first, to intuit whether He really wants it or not! It is a presumption, not a loving offering. Had Martha been thinking lovingly of God as she worked, Jesus would certainly have approved, not disapproved, of her activity. He might even have sent Mary to the kitchen to help her. Indeed, he may have done so anyway; the Bible doesn't tell us he did not, and we know from other accounts of his concern for other people's needs. What he wanted of Martha was that she work with devotion and non-attachment, and not with busy fretfulness and the anxiety that he scold her sister.

To serve God with the right attitude is purifying. It opens the heart to divine love, and enables that love to flow out to others, changing their lives.

Jesus, here, was actually offering three teachings in one. The first concerned non-attachment while serving. The second underscored the need, while serving, for keeping the mind focused on God. And the third emphasized the supreme importance of inner communion.

Without non-attachment one may still acquire good karma, but one will not attain inner freedom. If the mind is not on God, even the good karma one acquires will be less. And without inner communion, it is not possible to experience God as a reality, or, ultimately, to realize Him.

Jesus' reproach to Martha was not for her service, as such; and his praise of Mary was not for the choice she'd made not to serve. "Mary's part," as he termed it, alludes to the true goal of the spiritual path. Without developing the awareness of God's presence, service itself may be described as merely a "good karmic investment." Nor is that "good investment" as beneficial, outwardly, as people like to think. Jesus once said to Judas, "The poor you have with you always." The world is never greatly improved, whether socially or in any other way, by serving it with a worldly attitude. What is needed is that people's consciousness be uplifted.

"Mary's part," then, deserves special treatment, which it will receive in the next chapter. Meanwhile, let us bear in mind that living for God means remaining *aware* of His presence, especially in the heart. What counts is not the wearing of long robes, the bellowing of loud chants, and the decorous waving of sticks of incense. The important thing is the devotion, love, and concentration we offer up in the stillness of our own hearts.

The Bhagavad Gita expounds these themes also. Action, it says, must be undertaken first in a *spirit* of service, and not restlessly or for personal gain. Ego-motivated action is not karma *yoga.* Rather, it is merely karma. It doesn't lead to union with God, but only to continued involvement in delusion.

Stanza forty-nine of the Second Chapter of the Gita states:

"Actions performed under the influence of desire are greatly inferior to those which are guided by wisdom.

Happiness eludes people when they act from motives of self-interest. Seek shelter, therefore, in the equanimity of wisdom."

Action is guided by wisdom when it is kept centered in calmness, and in that calmness, offered to God. The highest action stems not even from the thinking mind. This level of "actionless activity," however, is not possible without high spiritual realization.

It is important to understand that the Gita, too, is not warning against activity itself. Indeed, its entire dialogue is a call to act, but in an uplifted state of mind. The Gita even states that God cannot be realized by mere renunciation of activity. Its warning, then, is the same as that which Jesus gave to Martha. It is a warning against *ego-involved* activity.

Self-interest leads to attachment. Attachment stirs up restless winds of eager anticipation. If one's effort ends in failure, there ensue driving rains of disappointment, anger, and discouragement. But if, on the other hand, they end in success, there ensue blinding snow flurries of excitement, which are equally disturbing to mental equilibrium.

"Why, O mind, wanderest thou? Go in thy inner home!" These words from a devotional chant by Paramhansa Yogananda offer the ultimate solution to all human seeking. The satisfaction of a desire brings rest to the mind only temporarily. Lasting release comes through non-attachment to satisfaction itself. This doesn't mean that the end of all striving is an attitude of indifference, but rather that true soul-joy is attained only in transcending mere emotional satisfaction.

Rather than renounce activity, then, we should

renounce personal motives. Desirelessly we should serve God with love, enthusiastically. The conclusive argument against desire-motivated activity is that it is self-defeating! People who act from self-interest do so from a desire for happiness, but any fulfillment they glimpse is but fleeting. Like snowflakes on a warm day, the fulfillment of desire melts within minutes to form shapeless puddles of unhappiness.

Look at the "snapshots" that memory holds in the mind: those, first, of little children. How fairly bursting they are with energy and enthusiasm, dancing about and laughing gaily! How suddenly their enthusiasm dissolves, then, into wails of tears and disappointment! The dualities of this world are more evident in them, for their feelings have not yet been reined in by adversity. Instead, they are like the balls they love to bounce on the pavement: up and down, ceaselessly up and down.

Then observe those same children as they grow older. On reaching adolescence, they start to spin threads of ambition for the future and weave them into colorful tapestries that depict their dreams of success. "Someday," they assure themselves, "I'll have a good job, be rich, and be loved by a beautiful wife or a dashing husband. We'll live in a lovely home and raise wonderful children. Oh, how everybody will envy us!" At seventeen, the future seems to stretch out before them like a verdant meadow, blanketed with fragrant, colorful flowers of fulfillment.

Then see those same people at twenty-five. Don't their eyes already betray a slightly driven look—a hint of inner tension? Their voices are beginning to have a slight edge; their gaze, a suggestion of dogged determination to beat life at its own game. Life already is becoming more of a struggle than they expected. "Well," they console themselves, "I still have my dreams intact."

How, then, do we find them at forty? Many, alas, have already grown irascible in the face of life's disappointments!

Look at the final snapshots in that photo album. People at the age of sixty, seventy, seventy-five, and older: How do you find them? The race is finished for them; their energy is spent. How pathetically little there is to show for all those years of struggle and pain!

A survey was once made of people in their late thirties and early forties. The question was put to them: "What was the happiest day of your life?" Many discounted their later years of supposed "success," and replied sadly, "The day of my high-school prom!" Years of strenuous effort had brought them no happiness. All they could do was look back nostalgically to a time, years earlier, before their dream ship of hope had crashed on the hard rocks of reality. One wonders: Did nostalgia itself supply a sweetness that was, perhaps, absent on the actual occasion?

Waves surging on the sea are wrinkled with many ripples. Every wave of desire, similarly, cresting to fulfillment, is wrinkled with little ripples of further, not fully formed desires. Fulfillment conditions the mind to seek further and still further fulfillment. In this respect, desires are like the nine-headed Hydra of Greek mythology, whose heads grew out again as often as they were stricken off. Hercules discovered the solution to the problem: Quickly he cauterized each stump the moment he'd lopped off the head. His method suggests how we ourselves might handle desires: We should prevent them from growing again by "cauterizing" them at the root. As Paramhansa Yogananda said, "The best way to rid yourself of desire is to catch it at that moment when it first appears in the mind."

Modern "wisdom," by contrast, plumbs the subconscious for clues to human motivation. It encourages people to raise to the surface whatever reeking denizen they find in those murky depths. "Don't suppress your desires," it says. "Bring them into the open. Gaze at them; only then, release them. That way, you'll free yourself of them." How often, ask yourself, has this system worked for you? Not often, surely. In fact, only when the desire itself was quite superficial.

Another school of thought is more valid in the sense that it doesn't actually ask for trouble. Its method, however, helps only those who have already achieved some measure of mental detachment. This method demands an attitude of impartiality. "Watch your thoughts and desires," it teaches. "If you gaze at them calmly, they will shrivel and disappear."

The first suggestion, that of plumbing the subconscious, might be described as the "primal scream" approach. The attempt to rid oneself of harmful emotions by giving them free rein results in only temporary relief. That relief is followed, almost as soon as the "purgative" screams have died away, by an exuberant resurgence. It seems an attractive therapy, for people do tend to prefer the way of least resistance. What soon becomes evident, however, is that it has lent added strength to those "complexes" by affirming them.

As for dispassionate self-observation, this may be effective in the peaceful atmosphere of a Buddhist monastery where few distractions exist. For busy modern people, however, caught up as they are in a swirl of intense activity, to watch one's thoughts "impartially" is not only impossible, but, potentially at least, disastrous. Self-observation needs to be practiced from a center of deep, inner calmness, and preferably in a superconscious state. Otherwise. it isn't one's problems that shrivel and disappear: It is one's own peace of mind! Worse still, one may lose faith in one's own ability to do anything at all to improve oneself. For the problems, once they are held close to the eyes, loom larger than ever.

Neither self-indulgence nor self-preoccupation brings Self-liberation. Rather, both practices imprison the mind in the ego. In the process, they shut out a world of opportunities for self-development and deepening understanding. Self-centered people try to create a "self-support system" by wrapping themselves in a blanket of indifference to everything and everyone but themselves. They find themselves at last, however, stranded and alone in a hostile universe. (Such, at least, is their perception of things.)

It is those who give selflessly of themselves who attain happiness. Their sympathy for others expands their awareness. It is in self-expansion that happiness is found. Action without personal motive, guided by equanimity, brings not only inner stillness, but a deep sense of joy.

To return, then, to the story of Martha: The need

for God-centeredness during activity is clear. But there remains an important question: *How?*

Those steaming pots in the kitchen were the challenge Martha faced. What if the rice burned, the vegetables got over-cooked, the stew boiled over and created a mess on the stove? Martha could not have dismissed these concerns by merely closing her eyes and denying their existence, while affirming, "Peace! Be still!"

Inner attunement must be adapted to outer necessities. The devotee must strengthen, and not relinquish, his grip on reality. He can do that by accepting it calmly, not by rejecting it, nor by seizing on it desperately as something that *"has* to be done!" The best way to strengthen one's "grip" on reality is not with tension, but by mentally sharing all that one does with God.

Consider an example: People often find themselves at work chatting with others. Why not, then, talk inwardly with God? Why not sing to Him? If outward singing is not feasible, then why not sing inwardly? Repeat mentally, "I am Thine, Lord! Be Thou mine!" Other word-formulae will do as well; choose one that you find inspiring. This practice is known in India as *japa.* It holds an honored place in Christian mystical tradition as well.

Yogananda once had a vision of St. Francis of Assisi in which the saint gave him this beautiful poem, which he called, simply, "God! God! God!":

From the depths of slumber,
As I ascend the spiral stairways of wakefulness,
I will whisper:

God! God! God!
Thou art the food, and when I break my fast
Of nightly separation from Thee,
I will taste Thee, and mentally say,

God! God! God!
No matter where I go, the spotlight of my mind
Will ever keep turning on Thee;
And in the battle din of activity, my silent war-cry
    will be:

God! God! God!
When boisterous storms of trials shriek,
And when worries howl at me,
I will drown their noises by loudly chanting

God! God! God!
When my mind weaves dreams
With threads of memories,
On that magic cloth will I emboss:

God! God! God!
Every night, in time of deepest sleep,
My peace dreams and calls, Joy! Joy! Joy!
And my joy comes singing evermore:

God! God! God!
In waking, eating, working, dreaming, sleeping,
Serving, meditating, chanting, divinely loving,
My soul will constantly hum, unheard by any:
God! God! God!

That single word, "God," can be repeated endlessly.
Alternatively, you may like to repeat (or to sing mentally) the entire poem.* Repetition will make it much
easier to keep God's presence in mind.

* The author wrote a melody for it years ago. It is available from
the publisher.

Yogananda made a further interesting remark on this subject, "Once I was working so hard," he said, "that I was afraid of forgetting God. Then all at once I realized that, in the very thought, I was remembering Him!"

Remembrance of God must be practiced *consciously and deliberately.* Activity is not so much a time for *receiving* energy as for *giving* it. God-remembrance must be charged with energy. Only thus can we offset the energy demanded of us by our work. Gradually, putting intense energy into everything we do, our minds become conditioned to the upliftment needed for raising our consciousness, later, in meditation.

These two paths then, meditation and service, must work together. "When they are balanced," Yogananda said, "then meditation helps your work, and work helps your meditation."

Pause every now and then, when your work allows it, and momentarily be aware of God's inner presence. Breathe deeply several times. As you inhale, affirm "I"; as you exhale, affirm "AM." Thus: "I (in) . . . AM! (out)." Or, alternatively, breathe in and out with the affirmation, "God (in) . . . IS! (out)." or, "Joy! . . . Joy! (both in and out)." When resuming your work, concentrate on the energy-flow itself. Remember, divine energy is the true power behind everything you do, physically.

Then continue to sing in your heart, "I am Thine! Thou art mine! I am Thine! Be Thou mine!" If words are not feasible—for example, if words are needed in your work—concentrate on the energy in your heart *chakra,* then uplift that energy to the Christ center between the eyebrows. Whatever energy you feel in these chakras, offer it up to God in joyful devotion.

Your work, when performed in the right spirit, becomes itself a kind of meditation. "Mary's part" in the Biblical story was not so very different from what Martha's might have been, had Martha been acting consciously for God.

One final thought: When singing or talking mentally to God, address Him, or Her, in the second person. Think "You" (or "Thou"), not "He" or "She." When you feel the flow of inner energy, share that flow with the Divine Beloved. No one in any case can do anything by his power alone. We are all parts of the Infinite! Feel, then, that you and God are working together; that, together, you are directing energy through your mind and body.

"The greater the will," Paramhansa Yogananda used to say, "the greater the flow of energy." Direct energy with will power and joy. See yourself as playing, dancing, and working with God: hand in hand together through all activity.

CHAPTER TWENTY

The "One Thing Needful"

"The deeper the self-realization of a man, the more he influences the whole universe by his subtle spiritual vibrations, and the less he himself is affected by the phenomenal flux."—Swami Sri Yukteswar, in *Autobiography of a Yogi*

In the last chapter we saw that Jesus scolded Martha for being too much centered in her work rather than in God. Her sister Mary had been sitting quietly at his feet. *"But one thing is needful,"* he said, *"and Mary hath chosen that good part, which shall not be taken away from her."*

For one who is sincerely seeking God, the important thing is to develop an ever-deepening awareness of God's presence—not during meditation only, but in every activity. Work engaged in for God's sake, but without the thought of God, is good karma, but it cannot lift the soul out of karmic involvement altogether into cosmic freedom.

What counts most is the intention behind a deed. In the story of Martha and Mary, it wasn't what Martha was *doing* that Jesus criticized, but her consciousness while doing it. Mary's "better part" lay in her silent attunement to Christ, not in the fact that she was seated before him instead of working in the kitchen.

There is an anecdote from the lives of three shepherd children in Fatima, Portugal, who in 1917 were blessed with visions of the Virgin Mary. In one of the visitations the Madonna showed them a vision of hell which affected them deeply. The reactions of the two younger children, Jacinta and her older brother Francesco, were particularly noteworthy. Jacinta expressed deep compassion for the suffering of sinners. Francesco's love expressed itself as a deep desire to console God for the suffering that people's sins caused Him, and by their indifference to His love.

In these responses we see "in a nutshell" two of the attitudes of a true devotee: a longing to bring souls out of darkness and sin into the light of God, and an all-absorbing love for God alone. Both attitudes are dear to Him. Many great masters, however, including Krishna, Jesus, and Yogananda have said that most pleasing of all to God is a combination of these attitudes. For outer service to God is above all blessed when the inspiration for it is centered in silent communion with Him in the heart.

Mary's worship combined both of these ways. Her outer service was evident in the fact that she was participating actively in Christ's mission. And her inner communion was clear from the fact of her sitting quietly at his feet, and from the praise Jesus bestowed on her for doing so.

Mary's soul was attuned to the vibrations of his divine love. Martha, though serving him outwardly, differed greatly from Jacinta in her mental restlessness and lack of focus.

The important point here is that, while it is right

and good to work for God and to offer up to Him all that we do, the more divinely attuned we are during our activity the more closely we are drawn, by means of it, to God. Meditation is necessary also. Mental botheration while working for God brings us no inner peace, which alone can lift the soul up to higher consciousness.

Action performed from a center of deep inner stillness is more beneficial, even outwardly, than action performed for its own sake. This point is of immense practical value. For people imagine, as Martha did, that to do anything well requires total immersion in one's work. Few realize that everything they do is an outward expression of their consciousness.

Consider music. No matter what music it is, its full effect goes deeper than sound. Figuratively speaking, it is a crystallization of thought and awareness: first of all, of the composer's consciousness, then that of the conductor standing before his orchestra, and finally that of the musicians as they play. Subtly conveyed to the audience are conscious attitudes, whether affirmative or life-negating, expansive or contractive, kindly or self-involved. We are in contact, as we listen, with the consciousness of all who bring the music to us.

Can anyone feel peaceful under the frenzied beat of "rock 'n' roll" music? Surely not—unless he is able to detach himself from sound altogether! And can anyone honestly claim that peaceful music—Handel's "Largo," for example—makes him seethe with restlessness? Only if his emotions are so violent that he cannot tolerate calmness! The most gloriously uplifting music, moreover, always conveys something of a lower consciousness also, if the musicians who play it are weighed down by worldly concerns.

A composition containing no overtly spiritual theme may for all that be inspiring, if the composer's *feelings* were uplifted as he wrote it. Music written to express human love, for example, sometimes affects people on a soul level also, if the composer felt inspired by pure love.

On the other hand, if a composer tries to express exalted love but has never experienced anything like it himself, his work will be bombastic and uninspiring.

To the "Marthas" of this world, Mary's silent absorption in the vibrations emanated by Jesus may seem useless and non-productive. In fact, however, spiritual silence is the key to the highest creativity. As a line from a song of the author's puts it: "Without silence, what is song?" And a stanza of another one says:

> Out of the silence came the song of creation!
> Out of the darkness came the light.
> Out of the darkness, out of the silence,
> Thunders the Cosmic Sound, Amen!
> Out of the darkness, out of the silence,
> Thunders the Cosmic Sound, AUM!

The vibrations of music are conveyed primarily through melody, rhythm, and harmony, of which the most effective for evoking specific feelings is melody. Music itself, even when it is meant only to be danced to or to entertain, is one of the best means of transmitting consciousness. Everything one does, however, communicates vibrations, and does so to a greater or lesser degree depending on the energy with which one does it. The colors, lines, shading, and texture an artist uses are all vehicles for his consciousness, even if he is only reproducing a street scene. If his heart is disturbed, however, his most delicate shading will in some way be disturbed also. And if he is inwardly at peace, his every shading will convey a sense of harmony. One senses these vibrations intuitively, when the heart's feelings are concentrated and calm.

Probably it would not be possible to analyze all the reasons why a work evokes feeling, for apart from outer signs everything in the universe is composed of vibrations of energy. Matter expresses them, but can never define them. An exact replica of a great painting never conveys the full impact of the original. Certain works evoke deep feeling; others awaken some feeling at least, and still others—the majority—convey little more than a sort of mental fuzziness, reminiscent of the saying of Jesus, *"Let the dead bury their dead."* A sensitive person may enjoy music on a record player in his home, but if he hears that same music played by live musicians he is almost sure to recognize in it a greater vibrancy and power, even if the musicians are less gifted than the recording artists.

Many people have had the experience of being in a "happy" house. This feeling may be experienced there even before the house is lived in. The consciousness of the architect, of the workmen, and the anticipations of the prospective residents cannot but affect the whole outcome. Human beings live, far more than most of them realize, in an electro-magnetic universe, not in a solid, material one. We are constantly surrounded by vibrations of energy and consciousness: a known fact now, since the discoveries of modern science, though the vibrations being discussed here are subtler than the radio and television waves with which we are all familiar.

We are also influenced by beings in the astral universe. Disorder and confusion on the material plane appeal to lower astral entities. Material beauty and serenity attract the blessings of saints and angels.

Mary then, in this account, anticipated not only the devotion demonstrated centuries later by Francesco of Fatima, whose one desire was to comfort God, but also the devotion of Jacinta, whose greatest desire was to serve God *through* others.

Martha's service, it must be understood, was by no means wrong in itself. It was merely, considering her spiritual potential, inadequate. Jesus reprimanded her because she had that potential. She might have received greater blessings had she served him with inner peace. Even if she lost touch with inner peace as she worked, if she'd continued thinking *about* God Jesus would have been able gradually to draw her closer to divine consciousness. He was saying, "Be more God-conscious; see His presence in everything you do." His praise of Mary was for her God-centeredness.

In the third chapter of the Bhagavad Gita, Krishna says, *"By the path of right action alone, Janaka and others attained perfection."*

Janaka was a royal sage in ancient India who achieved divine union by his inward spiritual focus in the midst of intense outer activity. He would not have achieved that exalted state had his consciousness been extroverted also. Instead, he demonstrated a perfect

310

balance between inwardness and outwardness, and showed thereby that work done for God is soul-liberating when performed both diligently and with love for God.

Janaka was born spiritually great. A lesser person could not have attained perfection by work alone. Meditation is necessary for most people as a means of centering themselves in the Self. But so also is outward activity for God necessary. One who only meditates, unless he does so superconsciously, is in danger of sinking into a mire of indolence, which to him may seem a peaceful lake, but which is more likely to be, or to become in time, a stagnant pond. Outer activity helps by lifting one's meditative peace to a state of dynamic inner calmness.

Jesus was saying, however, that, of the two activities, inner communion—that "good part" played by Mary—is the more important. It is sad how far in this respect the followers of Jesus have departed from his teaching. His recommendation of the "one thing needful" has been all but forgotten, even in monasteries, where most monks and nuns think of ecstatic meditation as a blessing that God may bestow by special favor, but that no one can attract by his own efforts. Present-day spiritual directors don't urge their charges to consider communion with God as a state to be sought and confidently expected.

A certain abbot in the Tenth Century was once asked, "What should one do if he is lifted into an ecstatic state, and the bell sounds the hour of communal worship? Should he remain where he is, or go join the others?"

The abbot responded: "He should remain in that state to which God has called him. The purpose of worship, whether private or communal, is to bring one to inner communion with God." To paraphrase his response, the abbot was saying, "If by some miracle a banquet should appear before you, don't wait instead to be served your daily gruel!"

Considering the answer Jesus gave to Martha, that abbot's reply was in perfect keeping with the scriptures. Since that time, however, there has been a polar shift in orthodox thinking. The same question was posed relatively recently by another monk, and the answer he received was a direct contradiction of that earlier one. "The blessings God gives you," his abbot replied, "will be yours to enjoy in heaven. As long, however, as you still live here on earth, your first duty is to obey the rule of our monastic order." This reply has been cited frequently as representing the Church's position on this and on all similar matters.

This attitude calls to mind a story about Kaiser Wilhelm of Germany, who complimented a soldier for delaying his obedience to a direct imperial command until he'd first checked with his superior officer. The Church, similarly, views its prelates and ministers as captains and lieutenants in God's army. According to its attitude, God's will is passed down through church "officers" to mankind. This is the world's way of thinking. It suggests a reason why Paramhansa Yogananda used the term *Self-Realization* in naming his organization.

Paramhansa Yogananda was sent to the West to remind Christians of what Christ originally taught them, just as Jesus was sent, according to his own words, *"to fulfill the law and the prophets"* of Judaism. The essence of Jesus Christ's teachings included meditation practice. Yogananda declared that it was by the will of Jesus himself that he was sent to the West, to revitalize Christianity by re-emphasizing the importance of meditation. Inner communion with God is the essence of both these religions, and was recognized as such by spiritually minded Jews and early Christians alike.

Inner communion was central especially to the teachings of the Gnostics. The Gnostic emphasis on inwardness gave the Church ample reason to discredit their teachings, though its leaders were not lax in searching out other reasons as well, for the Gnostics' emphasis on inner guidance went against the Church's efforts to centralize its authority. In the estimation of Church officials, the Gnostics posed a serious threat to their hegemony.

That was a time in history when most people had little or no intellectual training, and lacked the mental refinement necessary for recognizing potholes on the pathway of theology. Intellectual definitions can help to clear a way through the jungle of human ideation, but they limit human thought by encouraging a tendency to consider concepts more important than experience. A carefully phrased dogma may, in fact, make a superconscious experience intellectually acceptable, but it cannot replace the experience itself.

The Church considered it necessary to control the dissemination of Christ's teachings lest false doctrines dilute biblical revelation as defined by its theologians.

Even today, the Church claims that the time of revelation is past, and that any teaching since the New Testament must fit into the structure theology has erected since then. In effect, dogmatists have placed the teachings of Jesus Christ in mothballs.

There is an urgent need today for a spiritual renaissance. The spirit of Christianity, not merely the form, needs revitalizing. This rebirth could not emerge from a tradition that for two thousand years has committed itself to defining Truth intellectually. Patterns of belief are the hardest of all habits to change. Rebirth had to come from outside established tradition, and free of the hypnosis of Church influence. The natural source for this renaissance was India, where religious freedom has always been cherished—even as political freedoms have come to be cherished in the West. It is not that Truth ever changes: People simply need to learn to perceive it more broadly, now that they are faced with new self-awareness and increasing knowledge of the universe.

A notable feature of the teachings of both Paramhansa Yogananda and Jesus Christ, apart from the fresh insights they brought to the world, was their unswerving loyalty to their own traditions—a loyalty Yogananda expressed equally to the teachings of Christ. Jesus Christ was by no means the firebrand revolutionary certain writers have claimed. His statement, *"I came not to send peace, but a sword,"* (Matthew 10:34) was not an inflammatory call to arms, but a reference to the "sword" of discrimination, essential for slicing through the chains of outward attachment.

It is the saints who have always been the true custodians of religion. They alone are qualified to declare Truth authoritatively, on the basis of personal experience. Needless to say, there are gradations of spiritual experience even among saints, until full enlightenment is attained. For wisdom is not static; it is ever-expansive.

"Is there any end to evolution?" someone once asked Paramhansa Yogananda.

"No end," the Master replied. "You go on until you achieve endlessness."

To return, then, to Church dogmas and to Mary's "good part": If a shopkeeper whose one ambition in life is to grow rich says to you, "Well, we 'Marthas' of the world are needed also," ask him, "Who taught you that?" If he replies, "Why, the Bible, of course," then ask, "What makes you think you've understood that teaching?" He will have to answer either (with staunch ignorance), "Jesus spoke clearly for all people to understand,"—in which case you might ask him why Jesus so often said, "He that hath ears to hear, let him hear"?—or he will answer, "The Church is my instructor in these matters," in which case ask him, "*Who* in your church, specifically, is your instructor?" He will probably answer, vaguely, "I read it in some publication," or, "Everyone is in agreement."

Can wisdom be institutionalized? We have seen that it cannot. If, on the other hand, a true sage tells you something you've never heard before, ponder his statement for its possible truth; don't analyze it for its inherent fallacies—if, that is to say, you want to *grow* in understanding. A spiritual truth is more easily recognized by the heart than by the intellect. The intellect is more inclined to spurn any new idea that hasn't been formatted for its mental "filing system." No matter what your intellect tells you, trust the calm, impersonal feeling of your heart. For such feeling is the secret of intuitive understanding. Be at least open to what the sage tells you, and don't depend proudly on your intellect as the supreme arbiter.

The Church protects its back by making people saints only after they are dead. But since it is God who actually makes people saints, the safest course, if you want true spiritual guidance, is to go to a wise, and living, teacher. Intuitive soul-guidance will lead you to such a person.

In India, as we have already seen, the problem of true guidance is usually resolved not by scholarly committees, but by saints. The Indian scriptures themselves encourage people to seek personal contact with God, and not to rely on teachers who speak from books or from hearsay instead of from direct experience. Needless to say, not all the "guidance" one receives even in meditation is based on true insight. Subconscious "inspiration" may masquerade as superconscious experience. The difference between these two lies largely in the intensity of awareness that accompanies them. Indian tradition acknowledges that imperfection is endemic in this world, and that it will never be eradicated by suppression. Instead, in recognition of the fact that the Truth is beyond most people's comprehension, India's teaching is that Truth must be given the freedom to express itself in its own way. For no one can force Truth to "behave itself," like a household pet! The sages of India have always considered it their primary task to inspire people to seek God. In divine contact alone, they say, can wisdom be attained. No "board of elders" can ensure against an upsurge of ignorance, especially since the elders themselves are often ignorant also.

In India, in fact, teachings that are not compatible with proved reality generally end up being disregarded without recourse to flurries of "crisis management" or to emotional calls for religious war. For it is not definitions that matter, but only direct experience. Modern science, comparably, has managed to discipline itself fairly well without bureaucratic control. In India, an occasional word of caution from a saint usually suffices, when correction is needed. Self-proclaimed prophets may rave about hierarchies of angels and archangels as though these were what religion is all about, but the public usually manages eventually to separate the outrageous from the reasonable for the simple reason that God resides in all hearts.

The Apostles, including St. Paul (whom fundamentalists erroneously enlist in their support), were true Gnostics, for they believed in verification by personal experience. Other teachers came after them who, while claiming "gnosis" (personal insight) as their authority, made statements that would be unacceptable to any true saint. Some of those teachers stated, for example, that all worldly enjoyment is evil. The Church quite rightly rejected this and similarly absurd statements, as any discriminating man or woman would even without prompting from the clergy. Unfortunately, the errors of the false Gnostics stiffened the Church in its denunciation of Gnosticism as a whole.

Thus, the Gnostics ended up being anathematized. The theologians denouncing them, however, based their "wisdom" on a perceived need for institutional control. "Universal truth," as they understood it, meant virtually any statement that strengthened the Church's authority. Often they overlooked deeper teachings, or else twisted them to support their premise of hierarchic centralization. And the Christians in their charge were told to seek spiritual guidance only from Church representatives.

Truth, however, has no obligation to endorse official policies, no matter who formulated them. Truth simply IS. Thus, error entered the official teachings, including a diminishing emphasis on meditation, or *inner* communion. Instead of personal contact with God, congregational worship and Eucharistic communion were given increasing importance. It is of course true that many people have found outer worship inspiring. The question is, to what depth have they been inspired? People can only receive to the extent that they are receptive. If their minds are not calm, divine insights will fly over their heads like migrating birds. For grace never descends by divine whim, touching the good and the bad indiscriminately. A hoodlum might attend Church regularly, but if he hasn't renounced violence his attendance will bring him few benefits.

It was, as we've stated already, to remind Christians of their forgotten heritage that Paramhansa Yogananda was sent to the West. His mission was initiated by Christ's will, "to inspire a return," Yogananda used to say, "to the original Christianity of Christ in the Bible and the original teachings of Krishna in the Bhagavad Gita."

In the Gospel of St. John, Chapter 4, the woman of Samaria said to Jesus, *"Sir, I perceive that thou art a prophet. Our fathers worshiped in this mountain; and ye say, that in Jerusalem is the place where man ought to worship."*

Jesus answered her, *"Woman, believe me, the hour cometh, when ye shall neither in this mountain, nor yet at Jerusalem, worship the Father. . . . [T]he hour cometh, and now is, when the true worshipers shall worship the Father in spirit and in truth: for the Father seeketh such to worship him. God is a spirit: and they that worship him must worship him in spirit and in truth."*

Later in the same chapter he said: *"Say not ye, There are yet four months, and then cometh the harvest? behold, I say unto you, Lift up your eyes, and look on the fields; for they are white already to harvest."*

He was telling the woman,* "Don't look to outward observances for your salvation. And don't look for salvation in the distant future: Seek it here and now, in yourself."

---

* Paramhansa Yogananda explained that this account, which begins, *"And he must needs go to Samaria,"* contains a hidden meaning. The woman was a fallen disciple of his from past incarnations. It was in the hope of rescuing her that he was inspired to pass by way of Samaria. First, however, she needed to show herself spiritually ready. Thus, to test her, he said, *"Go, call your husband."* She passed the test by answering truthfully, *"I have no husband,"* thus confessing her sexual weakness in the fact that she'd had several, and that she wasn't married to the man she was living with now. Her truthfulness showed that she was mentally ready to be guided by him.

Interestingly also, his advice to *"lift up your eyes"* has an entirely yogic significance, for gazing upward in concentration at the point between the eyebrows is an ancient practice for attaining ecstasy.

Christ's statement concerning Mary has broad implications. For the more we are calm and at rest in our own center, the more we succeed at anything we attempt. The contrast between outer restlessness and inner calmness has been emphasized repeatedly in this book, and needs frequent reiteration. The Bhagavad Gita, in the 56th stanza of Chapter Two, states:

"He who is not shaken by anxiety during times of sorrow, nor elated during times of happiness; who is free from egoic desires and their attendant fear and anger: Such an one is of steady discrimination."

Worldly people are tossed up and down endlessly on rising and falling waves of pleasure and pain, success and failure, happiness and sorrow, fulfillment and disappointment. Whatever understanding they gain of life's deeper purpose is like brief glimpses of the ocean's surface from a succession of cresting waves.

People tend to avoid deeper issues, considering them abstract and theoretical. Preoccupation with pleasures and with subsequent pain leaves them little energy to do much thinking at all! When experiencing pain, they surrender to it, or cast about urgently for some pleasure to distract them. And when experiencing pleasure, they forget how invariably their past pleasures have crashed like waves and become troughs of disappointment.

Unreflective minds actually welcome emotional extremes. They imagine it would be impossible, without these, to experience intense happiness. The American poetess Edna St. Vincent Millay wrote:

I burn my candle at both ends;
   It will not last the night.
But O my foes, and ah, my friends,
   It gives a lovely light!

Is the light of dissipation really as beautiful as her lines suggest? Far from it! Extremists confuse happiness with excitement, and intensity with mere tension. They imagine they've found peace, when all they've done is become emotionally exhausted. Even their pleasures are simply synonyms for confusion!

Only when the recollection of past suffering weighs too heavily upon their hopes for the future do they begin to long for a better way of life.

The Bhagavad Gita teaches that the secret of true happiness is inner tranquillity: not the delusive peace of spent emotions, but the deep calmness attained when one has transcended his emotions.

Non-attachment does not imply indifference; nor does calmness imply aloofness. Rather, both enable people to expand their awareness. This expansion may be compared to a river opening out onto a vast ocean, whose depths are not affected by the activity at its surface.

Life's tests would prove instructive, not painful—they might even prove inspiring!—if we could only broaden our self-identity! The stability of a rowboat is threatened by relatively small waves, but an ocean liner moves unperturbed through high seas. The broader our spiritual base, the less affected we are by outer hardships. Steady discrimination gives us a sense of proportion, and reveals all things in relation to a universal reality.

The non-attachment referred to by the Gita in this passage, and the calm inwardness which Jesus praised in Mary, should not be confused with apathy. Such is the popular, but erroneous, caricature of stoicism. True non-attachment is achieved not by dulling one's sensibilities, but only by deepening one's Self-awareness. Perfect Self-realization is the fruit of daily, deep meditation. With self-expansion comes a universal identity, which replaces the all-separating delusion of ego-consciousness.

In the silence of inner communion, the soul rises above its identification with petty human nature and its turbulent passions, to soar through radiant light into infinite freedom and eternal bliss.

CHAPTER TWENTY-ONE

The Inner Way
of Pilgrimage

Everything in existence is both alive and conscious. The very atoms express these aspects of reality at least latently—and perhaps even more than latently.

Freeman Dyson, the well-known physicist, stated, "Atoms in the laboratory . . . [behave] like active agents rather than inert substances. They make unpredictable choices between alternative possibilities according to the laws of quantum mechanics. It appears that mind, as manifested by the capacity to make choices, is to some extent inherent in every atom."

God is not separate from His creation. Far from being "Wholly Other," as theologians have described Him, He is different from us and from all things only in His and our contrasting degrees of awareness. God's awareness is absolute. Man's is imprisoned in a little body and ego—like the moon's reflection in a teacup. Awareness in the lower animals—to continue the analogy—might be compared to the moon reflected on a pinhead. Even the rocks have a certain degree of awareness, albeit very dim—like moonlight weakly reflected in a thick, dark carpet, but not like the complete lack of reflection in a darkling abyss.

Physicists cannot predict absolutely the movement

of atoms, for even these, to a degree incomprehensible to science, are self-directed. Divine consciousness exists at the center of every particle in existence: "center everywhere," as Paramhansa Yogananda put it; "circumference nowhere."

What science can see is only the husk of reality, so to speak, not its living seed. Therefore scientists speak so matter-of-factly of life itself, as though everything were basically inert. They see everything in the universe as observers, from outside. Their concern is with effects, not with living causes. The rules of science cannot help them to bridge the gap between their own awareness and consciousness in anything else. To them, the awareness even of those near and dear to them should be considered an effect. If a scientist intuits his own wife's feelings, but doesn't actually see them expressed, for example in a pleased smile or a frown of displeasure, he feels it necessary to exclude that intuition rigidly from his reasoned understanding of the event. His scientific training has taught him that intuition is subjective, and therefore unacceptable as a phenomenon.

A person with some degree of spiritual awareness, on the other hand, if education has not filled him with doubts induced by scientific dogma, easily bridges the identity-gap with others. For his awareness of the life in himself binds him in empathy to life everywhere.

Take moonlight as an example. It shines everywhere impersonally. No "bottomless abyss" can negate it. If one concentrates on moonlight itself instead of on its reflection in the little teacup of his ego, he knows that the light is the reality of which those reflections are only parts of its countless appearances.

Everything, to the materialist, is a lifeless husk. He views the living seed within in relation to that husk, and judges it commonplace—a mere object. Even a work of genius is something he appreciates for its skillful execution more than for the inspiration that gave it birth. To a person who is spiritually inclined, on the contrary, even the husk is a manifestation of its inner germ of life.

Divine worship is therefore, and quite naturally, inward as well as outward. To one whose view is inward, all things are sacred. All life is, in this sense, a pilgrimage, and everything in existence a holy shrine where resides the Lord Himself.

Without meditation, however, it is not easy to experience inspiration even in a holy shrine—what to speak of in a mere rock. For to see God everywhere, and not merely to affirm that He is omnipresent, one must be aware of Him first within oneself.

It is important, therefore, to worship God first in the temple of one's own body, and to become conscious of Him as a living reality. Without reverence, the most sacred shrine on earth cannot inspire love for God.

Jesus Christ said, *"Destroy this temple, and in three days I will raise it up."* His critics thought he was referring to the temple at Jerusalem, where he was at the time. They pointed out that it had taken forty-six years for that temple to be constructed. How did he think he could do the same job in three days? The Bible concludes, *"But he spake of the temple of his body."* (John 2:19,21)

Jesus was not saying that the magnificent temple at Jerusalem did not deserve people's veneration. All he said was that the supreme pilgrimage is within, not without.

On other occasions also he placed supreme importance on this inward pilgrimage, without thereby denying the value of outer pilgrimage also. We have already considered two of those occasions. The first was when the woman of Samaria said to him: *"Our fathers worshiped in this mountain; and ye say, that in Jerusalem is the place where men ought to worship."* Jesus answered, *"Woman, believe me, the hour cometh, when ye shall neither in this mountain, nor yet at Jerusalem, worship the Father. . . . The hour cometh, and now is, when the true worshipers shall worship the Father in spirit and in truth: for the Father seeketh such to worship him. God is a Spirit: and they that worship him must worship him in spirit and in truth."* (John 4:20–24)

To worship God "in spirit and in truth" means to commune with Him in inner silence. The meaning of this passage is unequivocal: We should worship God above all in ourselves, and outwardly only to express the devotion we feel in our hearts.

In Luke 17:21 Jesus said also, *"Neither shall they say, Lo here! or, lo there! for, behold, the kingdom of God is within you."* It is surprising, indeed, considering how outward most people are in the practice of his teachings, to consider the austerity with which Jesus himself directed their attention inward to the soul. Consider also his famous words, *"When thou prayest, enter into thy closet, and when thou hast shut thy door, pray to thy*

Father which is in secret; and thy Father which seeth in secret shall reward thee openly." (Matthew 6:6)

At the same time, he didn't *oppose* outer worship or outward pilgrimage in general. That famous occasion when he washed his disciples' feet demonstrated perfectly his belief that one's love for God should be expressed outwardly also. And he approved of communal worship, indicating that endorsement by saying, *"For where two or three are gathered together in my name, there am I in the midst of them."* (Matthew 18:20) The austerity with which he counseled inwardness, then, was intended rather to correct an excessive outwardness in people than to denounce outer worship and pilgrimage altogether.

Every religion teaches that in certain places on earth there are holy vibrations. God is equally present everywhere, but His *manifestations* are not all equal. A rock is different from a plant. God's blissful consciousness, too, is manifested *variously* everywhere. In some places, the divine vibrations are particularly potent, owing to the fact that divine miracles have been performed there, or that spiritual masters have lived there. Paramhansa Yogananda, to strengthen this awareness in his disciples, told them one day, "I have meditated in every place on these grounds at Mt. Washington."

The uplifting vibrations of certain places are due also to the fact that devout pilgrims for centuries have worshiped in them. When a place becomes impregnated with spiritual power, its vibrations linger on for centuries. Jesus met the woman of Samaria at Jacob's well, an ancient site still venerated in his day. Indeed, the benefit of going on pilgrimage to holy places, such as the Holy Land, is not because of their rich history, but for the fact that divine blessings can be experienced when visiting them. Their very soil is impregnated with a higher consciousness.

The Holy Land itself is an example of such a place. So also is India. To meditate in the Himalayas, especially, and even to visit them with a reverent attitude, is to be affected with their vibrations of inner freedom. The shrines also at Lourdes in France, and at Tarakeshwar in Bengal, continue to this day to produce healing miracles.

Yet the reply Jesus gave to the woman of Samaria was a universal teaching: *"Believe me, the hour cometh when ye shall neither in this mountain, nor yet at Jerusalem, worship the Father."* Outward pilgrimage, he was saying, without corresponding *inner* communion with God, is of little benefit. The important thing is above all our *inner* relationship with the Lord.

When visiting holy places, we should tune in sensitively to their vibrations, with a deeply prayerful attitude. If our hearts' feelings are uplifted calmly to receive the divine blessings, the benefits we gain will be enduring.

Above all, however, what Jesus recommended was the "pilgrimage" to our own divine Source, within. Wherever we are, physically, we should worship the Father "in spirit and in truth," making a portable altar of our hearts. Outward pilgrimage is a good way of reinforcing and deepening our attunement with God, but the true altar of Spirit is a heart purified of attachments and desires, and uplifted to His love. To worship God "in spirit" means, in deep meditation, to rise above body-consciousness. Otherwise, what is pilgrimage? Most people consider it a way of getting divine blessings without bothering to be worthy of receiving them. To worship God "in truth" means to go beyond mere intellectual concepts, and beyond imaginary subconscious "inspirations"; it means to persist in meditation until God raises us to ecstatic communion with Him.

The validity of superconscious experience can be tested and verified by all sincere devotees. It has transforming power over every aspect of life. Divine experience, unlike the shadowy images that arise from the subconscious, and unlike the brief peace experienced in holy places, leaves no one that it touches ever the same again.

Jesus here, then, is saying, "If you want to be the kind of worshiper whom God Himself seeks, set aside some time every day for superconscious divine contact in meditation. Enter into the silence of inner communion." This "holy of holies" can only be symbolized, externally. Its reality is the sanctuary of the heart. On that altar we should keep always lit the sacred lamp of our devotion.

True pilgrimage, then, like true worship, is primarily inward. It is perhaps not so difficult to visualize the body as a *place* of worship, for in meditation one is, outwardly, motionless like a temple. Pilgrimage, however, implies moving from one place to another. An unmoving body gives no impression of movement at all. The Bhagavad Gita says that outer motionlessness during meditation is important. In the 6th Chapter, the 10th Stanza, in the poetic rendition of Sir Edwin Arnold, the scripture states:

Sequestered should he sit,
Steadfastly meditating, solitary,
His thoughts controlled, his passions laid away,
From every craving for possessions freed.

Stillness, yes. But *pilgrimage?* Pilgrimage to sacred shrines is a symbol of the inner, spiritual quest. As a symbol, however, it seems lacking in that one feature: movement. Yet, strange to relate, there is definite movement during meditation. The movement is not outward. It takes place *within* the body.

To begin with, for understanding this truth, it would help to know something of the vastness of our inner universe. Man's physical size is more or less midway between that of the largest body in the universe and the smallest. Small as we seem to be, physically, we are vast compared to the atoms. The space in our bodies is comparably vast also. A veritable universe shines within us like a galaxy seen from outer space, its subtle lights scintillating from every atom in our bodies. The very space between those atoms is as vast, relatively speaking, as that between the far-spread stars. Alternatively, we may say with perfect truth that nothing—neither the outer nor the inner universe—exists at all except as a figment of thought in the stillness of Absolute Consciousness.

Within the vastness of our inner space—real to us, as long as our consciousness moves outwardly with the Cosmic Vibration—there exists a solar system, which is centered in our egos. There is an inner as well as an outer astronomy, and an inner and an outer astrology. In ancient times, both were the same science, though nowadays there are many who belittle astrology as a pseudo science. They do so partly because the uses to which they put it are trivial, and partly because astrologers themselves have only a superficial understanding of their own science. That astrology *is* a science, however, has been averred by the wise for thousands of years. Even the view of modern science is changing: not its view of astrology itself—this, it has yet to give serious consideration—but of the universe. Science has discovered it to be a vast electromagnetic field, in its intricacy subtly inter-connecting all material phenomena. The claims of astrology, when viewed in light of these new discoveries, are by no means "pagan." Indeed, they are reasonable. And they are also scientific in the true sense, for many of them have already been tested empirically and found to work.

The Book of Genesis (1:14) tells us, *"And God said, Let there be lights in the firmament of the heavens ... and let them be for signs."* There are "planets" and "constellations" in our inner universe comparable to the electromagnetic vortices of planetary and stellar bodies in outer space. And there are movements of energy in the body comparable to the movement of sun, moon, and planets through the zodiac.

This is not the place for a lengthy discussion of astrology. It will facilitate understanding of our theme, however, to point out that a pathway exists which the bodily energy follows, both in its normal function and in its ascent toward enlightenment. This journey is our inner pilgrimage. This way of pilgrimage takes us through the spine.

The meditator should begin by understanding that his spine is not composed merely of gristle and bone: It is a subtle passageway for the flow of the life-energy. The spine even physically is the route by which energy passes between the brain and the body. The human will—both consciously and subconsciously—sends energy to the body through the nerves in the spine, commanding movement, tension—even the breath. The body's energy seems endowed with very little power, for its effect on material instruments is minimal. The deeper one's spiritual realization, however, the more he realizes that mastery over this energy gives one control over everything in the universe by simple command of the will. Thus did God make His creation. Man himself, in harmony with divine will, is godlike in power as well. In this sense, miracles as such do not exist. Certain people there are who simply understand and are aware of certain aspects of truth, of which most people are ignorant.

Conscious awareness of the body's energy brings one to the source of *all* energy. To tap this source is to gain command of matter itself. Even today, though 400 have passed years since the times of Galileo and Newton, we stand barely at the dawn of scientific discovery. Yet man has already found that, the greater his command over the *atomic source* of matter, the greater his command over matter itself.

Thus, the inner pilgrimage is very real. It is *movement,* not stasis. Only at the end of the journey is absolute stillness attained. This journey is subtle, however. As it is not easy for a wrestler to thread a needle, because of his thick fingers, so one who is accustomed to "wrestling" outwardly with matter may not yet have acquired the subtle awareness needed to master the finer energies of the body. On outward pilgrimage, it may sometimes be necessary to heave heavy rocks aside, if there has been a rockslide. On the inner pilgrimage, similarly, it may be necessary to heave aside the "blocks" of restlessness, or to blow aside with a puff of yogic breath the mental cobwebs that obscure one's path.

Outwardly, we belong to the whole universe. The most distant star exerts some influence upon us, and affects our energy and consciousness, and, through them, our lives. Certain groupings of stars, or constellations, bear the same names even today. The particular influence of each of them was anciently described. The constellations along the zodiacal path, which commonly are called *signs,* gain additional energy in the way they affect us as the sun, moon, and planets move across them. Astrology is by no means a modern fad, but had its origins far in the past, in an age that, according to the Hindu scriptures, was spiritually more highly advanced than our own. The science, as anciently known, was based on variations of magnetic influence in the universe, and on people's individual reactions to those influences.

Superstition has blurred the picture, for people like to think of the universe as focused personally upon them, with malicious or benevolent intent. Influences do exist, however; they vary according to innumerable factors. To human beings, it should be explained, those influences are utterly neutral. It is people's response to them individually that makes them personally significant, just as one person finds expansive inspiration in a moonrise, whereas another feels only, in the same moonrise, a sense of sadness. The astrological influences begin affecting us from the moment of our birth. How we respond to them is still subject to our free will. We can alter the way we respond, or even reject certain influences altogether. Still, the influences themselves begin to work on us from the moment we come onto the stage of life and take our first breath.

Breath sets into motion an inner "astrology." For the breath is intimately connected with the movement of energy in the spine. In meditation, it is relatively easy, by inner awareness, to sense the energy in the spine flowing upward and downward: upward with inhalation, downward with exhalation. Indeed, this energy-flow is the actual *cause* of respiration. Without it, the body itself would be unable to respond to the need for oxygen.

The spine is also the pathway to spiritual awakening. Not fancifully has every civilization described heaven as situated above us, and hell as below. The higher our center of energy in the spine, the happier we feel. And the lower that center, the more we are depressed. Even the words we commonly use to describe those two states reflect this truth. We speak of feeling high or low, "up" or "down," elated or depressed. In moments of exhilaration, we inhale automatically. With a sudden accession of grief, we automatically sigh. Habitually happy people have a stronger inhalation. And people who are chronically morose have a stronger exhalation.

Again, happy people tend more to look upward, to sit up straight, and to square their shoulders, whereas people who are unhappy tend to look downward, to stand and sit slumped forward, and let their shoulders droop. The inner pilgrimage of awakening is a process of raising one's energy and consciousness through the subtle astral channel of the spine to the brain. This end is accomplished by controlling the breath, deliberately bringing the energy upward and downward in the spine in conjunction with the breath. The spine is thereby magnetized, the energy of the body drawn within, enabling it to raise one's entire awareness toward soul-consciousness within, and to free one from the outer influences of the universe.

There are subtle centers of energy in the spine that correspond to the neural plexuses through which nerves carry energy to and from the spine and the parts of the body. From the lowest plexus, the coccyx, nerves pass to the legs. From the next plexus above that, the sacral, nerves pass to higher portions such as the sex organs. From the lumbar plexus located opposite the navel they pass to the digestive organs. From the dorsal plexus, opposite the heart, they nourish the heart and lungs. From the cervical plexus, opposite the throat, they affect the vocal cords, throat, and neck. And from the medulla oblongata they reach the brain. At the medulla, indeed, they divide and become the two currents of energy in the spine, taking the energy upward and downward with the breath. The medulla oblongata is, indeed, intimately connected with the heart and lungs.

Each of the subtle energy centers above (*chakras*, they are called in Sanskrit) corresponds to the outer universe and its constellations, twelve of which are along the zodiac. The inner world mirrors the outer, in a sense. The twelve zodiacal signs, as they are called, represent in combination the whole nature of man. By bringing these inner correspondences into balance, we achieve our eternally allotted task: self-perfection. With soul-awakening, the energy ceases its upward and downward flow, and rises in outer breathlessness through the center of the spine to the brain. There, perfect inner union is achieved at last. This union carries the consciousness beyond delusion's veils to union with God and with all creation.

At the end of every outward pilgrimage there is usually a temple or some other shrine where movement ends (ideally, at least!) in meditative stillness. The same may be said of the soul's pilgrimage within. The upward journey of energy and consciousness in the spine ends in the perfect stillness of Self-realization.

To become conscious of the inner energies of the body, it is necessary, first, to withdraw the mind from its identification with the world of the senses. This withdrawal is accomplished by first sitting upright and motionless, the spine straight, the gaze directed upward with half-closed eyes (indicative of the superconscious state, halfway between consciousness and subconsciousness), the mind focused at the point between the eyebrows. When the body is still, awareness awakens of the subtle flow of energy in it.

How long ought one to sit in meditation? A good rule is to meditate as long as one can do so *with enjoyment,* or with keen interest and alert attention. Never sit for long hours merely to test your endurance. And don't sit long, if in doing so you meditate absent-mindedly. Far more important than the duration of a meditation is its intensity. Absent-mindedness, and what Paramhansa Yogananda called "lackluster devotion," are the greatest barriers to spiritual progress. Even five minutes of deep meditation would be preferable to sitting a whole hour "in the silence," if all one did during that hour was watch the clock!

In fact, a good practice is to sit as if your time for sitting were indeed only five minutes. From the very moment you assume your meditative posture, enter immediately into your spiritual practices. Resolutely set aside all attachment to restlessness. Refuse to move even a muscle. Discipline your body, mind, and emotions, that you may offer them all up to God. Concentrate your whole being on your upward flow of aspiration.

Isn't an hour little enough time out of one day to give to God? What if He were to forget you for one second? It would be impossible for Him to do so, of course, for you are an inextricable part of Him, but were it possible you would cease to exist!

Think how many hours you give to sleep at night. The commonly recommended norm is eight hours, though in fact it is easy to get by on less. Another eight hours, more or less, are given to work. This leaves another eight hours for eating, talking, shopping, traveling, and relaxation. Out of this third segment, can you not set aside one or two hours for God? Again, out of the hours you spend in subconscious sleep, can't you devote one or two of them to the much deeper rest of superconsciousness?

The sincere seeker should make it a practice to meditate at least one-and-a-half hours every day: better still would be the same amount of time *twice* a day. This recommendation, however, is for those especially who are well established in meditation. Beginners would generally do well to meditate less, and to discipline themselves rather to intense absorption in their meditative efforts. Only with inner absorption will they find long meditation beneficial.

✳ In any case, let your taste for meditation grow naturally. Never force it. The more deeply you experience joy in the soul, the more you will want to meditate long hours without urging from anyone. Once you can meditate deeply, remember this: the longer, the better. For the mind is like a glass of water, clouded by the particles of restlessness that float in it. It takes time for the clouded water to become clear, as the particles in it settle to the bottom. ✳

There is a peculiar notion nowadays, due especially to propaganda in a few churches, that meditation is addictive! People have actually compared meditation to the taking of hallucinogenic drugs! Deep meditation is, indeed, *far more* enjoyable than any drug. To confuse soul-joy with consciousness-altering drugs, however, or with self-hypnosis, is absurd. Meditation is the way *out* of bondage, not into it!

One wonders how such misconceptions develop. Perhaps they begin owing to the fact that meditation induces a temporary withdrawal from the senses. If all people know is their sensory impressions, they may assume that any withdrawal from those impressions is like drug addiction. And yet, this is what everyone does, in sleep! Of course, restless minds are uncomfortable in the presence of people who are calm. Worldly consciousness often finds calmness irritating.

The truth, in any case, is that meditation, by calming the mind and silencing the ego's demands, actually makes it possible at last to tune in to reality at every level. Unlike hallucinogenic or subconscious experiences, moreover, meditation actually increases a person's *authority* over the outer world. It demonstrates thereby that the superconscious state puts one in touch with a *higher* reality.

Even the novice finds, after meditation, that he can relate better to other people, and is more able to understand and help them. Meditation even intensifies sensory enjoyment! After deep meditation, the world seems filled with wonder and delight. Colors appear more beautiful; music, more exquisite. On return to outward awareness, one feels far more refreshed than after a long, deep sleep. Even the food one eats tastes more delicious! All things seem vibrant with joy, and thrilling because manifestations of your own self.

As far as "practical" life is concerned, the mind of someone who meditates regularly gains increased clarity and power of concentration. Problems that, for most people, require days or months for solution are solved easily, often in mere minutes.

The first step toward divine union is to spend a little time every day alone with God—"sequestered," as the Gita puts it, one's thoughts controlled, one's passions stilled. Yogananda would often say, "Seclusion is the price of greatness." This is inward pilgrimage: the "straight and narrow" path to liberation. Here we find the hidden meaning of the words of John the Baptist, quoted from Esaias: *"Make straight the way of the Lord."* (John 1:23)

The spine is the true highway of pilgrimage. It is the way to your own liberation. Keep it straight always, even during activity. Strive to direct the energy of your body to the brain. As an aid in this direction, mentally chant always to God.

CHAPTER TWENTY-TWO

The Inner Kingdom

There is the inner spiritual pilgrimage, of which outward pilgrimage is a symbol. And there is also the inner universe, which in many ways is like the outer one. Paramhansa Yogananda once said, surprisingly, that the sun is a symbol of the spiritual eye in the forehead. His statement suggests persuasively that the outer universe, too, is but a symbol of the inner one, rather than the reverse; that astrology is a symbol of the inner movements of energy around the spine, rather than the other way around; and that the planets and constellations are symbols of more real (or at least more immediate) mental and spiritual characteristics in oneself.

Usually, symbols represent phenomena that are larger and more enduring than themselves. A candle may symbolize the sun, but no one would think of the sun as symbolic of a candle. Size, however, is an illusion. And permanence is better gauged not in terms of earth years, but of eternity. Thus, Mount Carmel has long been for Christians a symbol of everyone's spiritual climb toward perfection; Mount Meru, for Hindus, is a symbol of the challenge to divine attainment; and the river Jordan, for Jews and Christians alike, is a symbol for baptism not only into their respective faiths, but (for those with deeper understanding) into the stream of energy in the spine. What can be perceived inwardly by everyone under the right conditions—the spiritual eye, for example—is no less objective or permanent than anything perceived outwardly through the senses. Universal truths are manifested as perfectly in the atom as in a galaxy. The greatest, regardless of its apparent size, is that which manifests reality *to the greatest degree.* The closer a sage or yogi comes to realizing the source of his own being, the greater his mastery over all manifested existence. He realizes space and time themselves to be only figments of the cosmic dream, their apparent reality a mere imposition on the mind by the Cosmic Dreamer. To know one's Self to its ultimate depth is to realize God.

When Jesus Christ said that the kingdom of God is within, his meaning was more literal than even mystics as a rule imagine. For every human being is a veritable kingdom in himself. His soul, acting through the ego— which is, by Paramhansa Yogananda's definition, "the soul identified with the body"—reigns supreme, and the multifarious qualities of his personality are the citizenry, each one with its distinct personality. Thus, every human being is made up of a multitude of traits, both positive and negative: hope, aspiration, faith, nobility, generosity, discrimination, and self-control on the one hand; and on the other hand, disturbers of the inner peace such as selfishness, rebelliousness, restlessness, greed, lust, avarice, envy, jealousy, and the whole gamut of what the ancient Greeks called *hoi polloi,* the people, or—more aptly in this case—the rabble. The aristocrats of this populace are the noble qualities—an aristocracy of merit, not of power. These better-class society members nourish the well-being of the entire "body politic." The lower social element, composed of ignoble qualities, detract from that well-being and disrupt the kingdom's harmony and happiness.

As the citizens of a kingdom play their own roles—butcher, baker, candlestick maker (or, in more up-to-date terms, physicist, computer programmer, engineer)—so our mental citizens keep themselves busy with a variety of self-supporting tasks. Some of them try conscientiously, with approval from the ego, to contribute to the kingdom's over-all welfare. They engage in a wholesome give-and-take of energy with other kingdoms. Others, though accepted by the ego, work only in their own interest. An example is the psychological trait of self-pity, when the ego mutters to itself, "I deserve better treatment than this! Do people think I'm a *nobody?*" Citizens like these deplete the royal coffers of energy by constantly pleading for support and sympathy. Still others—though perhaps only with reluctant consent from the ego—are predators by nature. Lacking peace themselves, they do all they can to spread discord and disharmony among others—as when the ego seeks, out of sheer meanness, to hurt others, though it knows that, later on, it will suffer negative consequences in terms of anger-created tension and remorse.

It is not unusual to see someone, kind and loving under certain circumstances, be fiercely competitive, even vindictive under others. Certain Nazi rulers in Germany of World War II were sensitive lovers of art.

Yet they rapaciously stole art treasures from other nations.

There is no man so evil that he lacks utterly the touch of divine yearning in his soul. For everyone's only reality, though he bury it deeply in the sand of delusion, is God.

The ego, reigning as king in our inner kingdom, is our sense of personal reality. If this "I" is weak-willed and vacillating, the kingdom will be kept constantly disrupted, reflecting the citizens' growing self-involvement and self-will. Disunity and conflict can deprive a kingdom of the energy it needs for accomplishing anything worthwhile. Poverty-consciousness develops, and failure-consciousness, and health-destroying attitudes such as fear, doubt, anxiety, and despair.

It may be difficult to imagine one's personality traits as separate individuals. After all, they are projections of the same, one ego. In fact, it is the ego that assumes all their roles, like an actor upon a stage. Each role, however, represents a commitment on the ego's part to that particular trait. In the same way, the one divine Self plays the roles of every ego in the universe, yet each becomes so immersed in his role that he forgets his own infinite identity. We dream the attitudes that our egos assume. Each one of them, like the ego itself, is only imaginary: a role played for a time, then abandoned.

Consider the single trait: envy. Envy, like all the others, has no visible features; it is expressionless, and abstract. Soon enough, however, it can be visibly etched on a countenance, the very lines of which reveal emotional upheavals, past and present, that envy has caused. The eyes gaze with a slight squint under droop-ing lids; the mouth turns habitually downward, while its corners twitch upward nervously from time to time out of a wish to seem forgiving. The glance tends to be oblique rather than direct. And the sufferer often develops a nervous habit of keeping his chin lowered toward the chest, as if determined to protect his self-worth from others in their want of appreciation for him.

So completely may an emotion enforce its personal-ity, even briefly, that one who is normally cheerful may, during a bout of depression, be hardly recognizable to his close friends.

A friend of the author's once went to a train station to meet his wife, who was a strikingly beautiful woman. He'd last seen her only two weeks earlier; it would seem almost impossible for him not to recognize her after so short a time, yet so it proved. The woman had been passing through an emotional crisis. The man watched the passengers descend from the train, but didn't see her among them. Thinking the crowd must have hidden her, he went to the waiting room to see if she was there. A woman stood alone in the center of the room; she seemed a stranger. He paused, then hesi-tantly uttered her name as though asking a question. She looked up: It was his own wife!

We are not our personalities. The soul never changes, but our personalities undergo constant muta-tion according to the way we've reacted to inner and outer circumstances. A personality trait that we may once have laughed off lightly as "not really me" may become indelibly stamped on our features, in time, as

the trait hardens into a fixed habit. The sweet inno-
cence shining in a child's face may be transformed in
old age into vicious intolerance and cynicism, if that
life was lived unwisely.

There is a story of an artist who, to paint a portrait
of Jesus Christ, used for his model a pure-eyed, beautiful young man. Years later, he needed a live model for
a painting of Judas, and found someone who displayed
all the characteristics he imagined in that greatest of
history's villains: pride, deceitfulness, meanness of
spirit, personal ambition. To his astonishment, the
model turned out to be the same one he had chosen,
years earlier, for his painting of Jesus Christ!

The citizens of a kingdom can be inspired to live
together in productive harmony if the king sets them
an example of justice both firm and kind, inspired by
magnetic aspiration toward high ideals. The same may
be said of our inner kingdoms. When our egos, acting
on behalf of the soul, are uplifted by noble aspiration,
they inspire all our mental citizens with a desire for
upliftment also. The need seldom arises, then, to police
them: Their virtue increases of its own accord as the
energy and consciousness in the body flow toward the
brain. Even energy that has been wasted in "slum-
ming"—reveling, that is to say, among the "flesh pots"
of sense pleasure—reforms itself happily. Forsaking
low pursuits, it recognizes that all the fulfillment it ever
craved is to be found in self-giving, not in self-absorp-
tion.

Such, indeed, is the message in the great scriptural
epic, *The Mahabharata,* of which the Bhagavad Gita
forms a part. This epic is an allegory of the soul's fall

from grace and its eventual return to God. Such also is the theme of two great poems in the English language: *Paradise Lost* and *Paradise Regained,* by John Milton.

The first chapter of the Bhagavad Gita outlines the opposing forces within man. It describes them as armies: the good, or spiritual, and the bad, or self-seeking. These armies are ranged against one another on the eve of their conflict. The ensuing war of Kurukshetra takes place in both time and eternity, for every divine aspirant must face this inner struggle not once only, but forever, until his soul achieves final victory. Only when all the energy that we have devoted to ungodly pursuits is re-channeled in aspiration toward God can we achieve what all of us have been seeking for eons of time.

Man's energy for accomplishment even in a worldly sense is frustrated by "the thwarting cross-currents of ego," as Paramhansa Yogananda called them. Only to the degree that these currents become untangled and directed upward to the brain do they become strong, because focused at last. The personality then shines with spiritual power.

As a person meditates deeply, he finds his inner energy increasing. Gradually he becomes aware of that energy as a light radiating particularly from the chakras, or spinal plexuses, and outward around the entire body as an aura of light, and as a halo about the head. This light shines with a variety of colors depending on a person's state of consciousness. The brighter the light, the more spiritually refined the consciousness.

In the first chapter of Revelation—this Book of the

Bible, Paramhansa Yogananda said, is filled with deep yoga teachings—St. John describes his vision of the spiritualized astral body: *"His head and his hairs were white like wool, as white as snow; and his eyes were as a flame of fire; and his feet like unto fine brass."* (1:14,15) John's description of a dimmer light in the feet increasing in brilliance as the energy rises toward the head indicated, Yogananda said, the upward direction of the divine energy in the body. Many Bible passages corroborate this teaching of an inward wakening of energy, as a person's inner psychological conflicts yield to self-integration, and as the struggle between worldly desire and soul-longing becomes resolved in divine devotion.

"Thou hast been in Eden the garden of God," wrote the prophet Ezekiel, *"thou wast upon the holy mountain of God; thou hast walked up and down in the midst of the stones of fire."* (Ezekiel 28:13,14) The "stones of fire" refer to the spinal chakras. To "walk up and down" the mountain signifies the yoga technique of bringing energy up and down the spine, magnetizing it and thereby opening the subtle spinal passageway to the brain. This technique is known today as Kriya Yoga— specifically, the Kriya Yoga of Lahiri Mahasaya, who for the first time in this age brought it back to the world. At the beginning of one's Kriya Yoga practice, the energy is circulated through outer channels in the spine, known as the *ida* and *pingala,* which correspond to the sympathetic nervous system in the physical body.

In the Old Testament, the prophet Zechariah was given a vision: *"And [the angel] said unto me, What seest thou? And I said, I have looked, and behold a candlestick all of gold* [the channel within the spine, known in yoga teachings as the *sushumna*], *with a bowl upon the top of it* [the *sahasrara,* or "thousand-rayed lotus," a subtle light emanating from the brain], *and his seven lamps* [the seven chakras] *thereon. . . . And two olive trees by it* [the *ida* and *pingala* channels], *one upon the right side of the bowl, and the other upon the left side thereof."* (Zechariah 4: 2,3)

The Hindu scriptures, to which the teachings of yoga are integral, liken the body to an upturned tree. The spine is the trunk; the hair, the roots; and the nerves spreading outward from the spine, the branches. This is the true "tree of life," through the trunk of which flows the "sap," or energy, of divine awakening.

The Bhagavad Gita states, *"The wise speak of an eternal ashvatta tree, with its roots above and its branches below."* (15:1) Although the physical spine, like the body, is ephemeral, the *principle* behind its manifestation is, as the Gita says here, eternal.

The Book of Genesis, referring to this "tree of life," states, *"And the Lord God planted a garden eastward in Eden. . . . And the tree of life also in the midst of the garden, and the tree of knowledge of good and evil."* (Genesis 2:8,9) The story of Adam and Eve is an allegory; it describes how the first human beings dissipated the power of the tree, whose treasure had been bestowed upon them. They were persuaded by the "serpent" of delusion to view it as a tree of the "knowledge of good and evil": that is to say, of duality and delusion. Adam and Eve ate the fruit of this tree, and found it pleasing to their senses.

Paramhansa Yogananda explained that the sin of

those first human beings was to choose enjoyment of
the outward creative energy over the bliss to which
God had invited them: the flow with the "sap" of
divine energy in the spine. The "tree of life" was
described as growing "in the midst of the garden," for
the spine runs through the center of the body. Adam
and Eve were souls that, evolving upward from lower
animal forms, had attained a level of spiritual development that fitted them for a more refined physical vehi-
cle for the expression of their consciousness. The
human body has a sensitive nervous system which
facilitates higher spiritual evolution. The memory of
past sex indulgence lingered, however, in the subconscious of Adam and Eve. Their creative urge might
have produced "children" of a subtler kind: intense
inner joy, wisdom, and spiritual love, had it been
directed toward the brain. Soul-union between Adam
and Eve could have manifested limitless divine powers
of accomplishment; outward "children," born of their
united consciousness, would have been possible: great
works of art, inspired musical compositions, innovative
ideas, scientific inventions, and other works that
would have benefited all humankind. The "children" of
the creative impulse, when it is directed inward and
upward in a perfect unity of feeling and reason, is capable of producing great wonders. Above all, it helps very
much toward divine realization.

Adam and Eve might, Paramhansa Yogananda said,
have produced even human children, without recourse
to sexual reproduction, had their energy been united
lovingly in the spiritual eye. Thus, they might have created families also by inviting spiritual souls to dwell

with them for their continued soul-evolution. This method of procreation is the norm among highly evolved beings in the astral world, where souls descending from the subtler, causal region for rebirth in the astral world are invited by couples to dwell with them. Adam and Eve, however, influenced by delusive memories, chose the familiar, physical course of procreation. Thus, divinely produced progeny became for them, and for their descendants ever thereafter, an impossibility.

Other sensory enjoyments (the fruits of those lesser "trees in the garden" that stood not at the center) would not have blinded them with delusion. The author recalls one day asking his guru for help in overcoming the liking for good food. Paramhansa Yogananda, with a gentle but dismissive smile, replied, "Don't worry about those little things. When ecstasy comes, *everything* goes!" The sex nerves are unlike other senses, however, in that they are more directly connected with the spine, the "tree of life" at the center of the garden. The two main nerve channels, *ida* and *pingala,* join together at the base of the spine, generating a powerful energy. An outward flow at this point drains away energy that might otherwise rise to the brain.

That the tree of life is not itself evil, however, is emphasized in Revelation: *"He that hath an ear, let him hear. . . . To him that overcometh will I give to eat of the tree of life, which is in the midst of the paradise of God."* (Revelation 2:7) And again: *"Blessed are they that do his commandments, that they may have right to the tree of life, and may enter in through the gates into the city."*

351

(Revelation 22:14) "Gates," here, incidentally, refers to the spinal chakras.

Another reference to the chakras as "gates" is in Proverbs 8:34: *"Blessed is the man that heareth me, watching daily at my gates, waiting at the posts of my doors. For whoso findeth me findeth life."*

The energy at the base of the spine flows naturally outward with the body's creation. Hence the human inclination from birth is toward outwardness. The gaze, which at first is turned naturally inward, shifts gradually outward in focus on the surrounding world.

A friend of the author's relates a fascinating story. Two friends of his, a married couple, had a son. Some time later, the wife gave birth to a second one. The older boy kept insisting, "I want to speak to my baby brother, alone." Concerned that his request might be motivated by sibling jealousy, they agreed reluctantly but stood quietly outside the door, and listened.

When the older child thought he was alone, he leaned close to his baby brother and whispered, "Please help me. What was it like there? I'm beginning to forget!"

Even in outwardness, a child's increasing involvement with the world needn't enmesh him in duality, provided he keep his energy moving upward by expressing joyful enthusiasm for life, generosity toward others, and non-attachment. With these attitudes he can retain an awareness of the inner kingdom and increase his inborn spirituality. Most children, however, exposed as they are from birth to sensory stimuli and to grown-ups who are steeped in outwardness, forget their inner kingdom and become, in effect, "absentee landlords."

Thus when, in the natural course of events, the reproductive organs develop and stimulate the sex instinct, the child is swept away in a roiling white water of impulses from which, for lack of any prior training, he is helpless to extricate himself. The desire for sexual pleasure, the fruits of the "tree of life," seizes him. The tree becomes then, for him, not a tree of wisdom, but the tree of "the knowledge of good and evil"—of duality. Even his outer fascination with sex emphasizes his absorption in duality: boy seeks girl; girl attracts boy. Each sees in his or her complement a promise of fulfillment that can, in fact, be achieved only when the mind is turned inward, toward union with God.

The force of energy generated by the union of *ida* and *pingala* at the base of the spine produces a spiral magnetic field, in the same way electricity does when flowing through a wire. Thus, the downward-moving force is fittingly described in the Bible as a coiled serpent. In Genesis we read, *"Now the serpent was more subtle than any beast of the field which the Lord God had made."* (Genesis 3:1) Other ancient scriptures also, especially the Indian, describe this energy as serpent-like. In the yoga teachings the name for this energy is *kundalini*. When kundalini's course is upward, there occurs in meditation a spiral movement which often causes the whole upper body to rotate.

II Kings, 2:11 describes Elijah as being taken *"up by a whirlwind into heaven."* The "whirlwind" here described is a reference to the awakened kundalini.

In Numbers 21:8,9, we read, *"And the Lord said unto Moses, Make thee a fiery serpent, and set it upon a pole; and it shall come to pass, that every one that is bitten, when he looketh upon it shall live. And Moses made a serpent of brass, and put it upon a pole, and it came to pass, that if a serpent had bitten any man, when he beheld the serpent of brass, he lived."* Here described are two kinds of serpent-energy: the downward-moving kundalini, which draws the mind toward sensual pleasures; and the brilliant light of upward movement in the spine, described here as "setting the fiery . . . serpent of brass upon a pole." The awakened kundalini alone can bring healing to the "poison-bite" of delusion.

Jesus was referring to this kundalini awakening when he said: *"And as Moses lifted up the serpent in the wilderness, even so must the son of man be lifted up."* (John 3:14) The son of man, as Jesus uses the expression here, signifies not himself as a man, but man's physical body as distinct from the soul. Physical consciousness, in other words, must be "lifted up" in meditation, with kundalini.

Revelation 22:1 states: *"And he showed me a pure river of water of life, clear as crystal, proceeding out of the throne of God and of the Lamb."* Here, "the lamb" refers to the indwelling Christ consciousness. The "pure river of water of life" is the "sap" flowing through "the tree of life."

Revelation continues in the next verse: *"In the midst of the street of it, and on either side of the river, was there the tree of life, which bare twelve manner of fruits, and yielded her fruit every month: and the leaves of the tree were for the healing of the nations."* These words refer to the six chakras in the spine (the seventh is located at the top of the head). The six become twelve by polarity as energy rotates upward and downward in the spine through the *ida* and *pingala* nerve channels.

As energy rises through the spine to the head, it is focused in the spiritual eye midway between the eyebrows. Physiologically speaking, stimulation of this section of the frontal lobe of the brain induces intuitive, superconscious awareness. Therefore Revelation 22:4,5 states: *"And they shall see his face; **and his name shall be in their foreheads**. And there shall be no night there, and they need no candle, neither light of the sun; for the Lord God given them light: and they shall reign for ever and ever."*

Jesus said, in Matthew 6:22, *"If thine eye be single, thy whole body shall be full of light."**

The place of divine vision in the forehead is described in scripture as "east" in the body: *Kedem* in the Hebrew, meaning, "That which lies before." Thus, when Genesis says, *"And the Lord God planted a garden eastward in Eden; and there he put the man whom he had formed,"* (2:8) the inner meaning is that at the time of the first man's creation he had spiritual awareness. He fell from that high state owing to his misuse of the body's energy. "Eastward in Eden" signifies that the

---

* This translation appears in the standard King James version. Most modern translators, unable to make sense of the image of a "single" eye, have changed "single" to "sound." Some of them have even "gone the extra mile" by making the "eye" plural, thus: "If your eyes are sound." The Lamsa edition improves matters by saying, "If your eye be clear." All of these versions, however, miss the metaphysical meaning of "single," which is supported by universal ancient tradition, with its legends of a "third eye."

natural focus of his attention—his native "habitat," so to speak—was in the spiritual eye.

Thus, in Ezekiel's vision (Ezekiel 43:1,2) we read: *"Afterward he brought me to the gate, even the gate that looketh toward the east: And, behold, the glory of the God of Israel came from the way of the east: and his voice was like a noise of many waters: and the earth shined with his glory."*

This "voice of many waters" signifies, as we have already seen, the mighty Vibration of God, AUM, or Amen. As Revelation 3:14 states: *"These things saith the Amen, the faithful and true witness, the beginning of the creation of God."* Paramhansa Yogananda explained that it is AUM which John called "the faithful and true witness," for the cosmic sound heard in meditation makes one aware that he is in touch with Infinite Bliss, whence cosmic creation was manifested.

Revelation 14:2 states also, *"And I heard a voice from heaven, as the voice of many waters, and as the voice of a great thunder: and I heard the voice of harpers harping with their harps."* The "voice of harpers," incidentally, is the sound produced by the third chakra, *manipur* in Sanskrit, the lumbar plexus. This sound is generated when energy is concentrated there. The sound is like that of a plucked string instrument. From this fact the Christian tradition arose of angels playing on their harps. AUM is the bridge to cosmic consciousness. Thus, Revelation 3:20 states: *"Behold, I stand at the door, and knock: if any man shall hear **my voice** [the Amen], and open the door, I will come in to him, and will sup with him, and he with me."*

Psalm 81 states, *"Thou calledst in trouble, and I delivered thee; I answered **in the place of thunder.**"*

And Job 37:5 states, *"God thundereth marvelously with his voice; great things doeth he, which cannot be comprehended."*

Jesus underscored the eternal nature of these truths in the words, quoted already in this book: *"Say not ye, There are yet four months, and then cometh harvest? Behold, I say unto you, Lift up your eyes, and look on the fields; for they are white already to harvest."* (John 4:35) People look to the future for earthly fulfillment, but God lives in the Eternal Now. The counsel to "look up" is found in many spiritual teachings, for the eyes, when turned upward, focus also the mind at the point between the eyebrows, the spiritual eye. Hence the words of the psalmist: *"I will **lift up mine eyes** unto the hills, from whence cometh my help. My help cometh from the Lord, who made heaven and earth."* (Psalm 121)

It would be timely, here, to reiterate the immortal words of Jesus: *"The kingdom of God cometh not with observation: Neither shall they say, Lo here! or, Lo there! for, behold, the kingdom of God is within you."* (Luke 17:20,21) Through the practice of yoga-meditation, and by spiritual living, we can discover for ourselves the little-known inner kingdom of God.

Students interested in this subject will find it helpful to study also the first three chapters of the Book of Revelation, which contain a detailed, though veiled, presentation of these teachings.

Deeper truths are not for people whose minds are engrossed in worldly desires. As Jesus said repeatedly, *"He who hath ears to hear, let him hear."* Nevertheless, they are stated—or, rather, very subtly *under*-stated—in both the Old and the New Testaments of the Bible and in many other scriptures as well, particularly in those of India.

Yoga is a science, discovered in ancient times, carefully preserved since then, and developed by sages through millennia of tradition. Its goal is to help one work *with* the subtle nature of the body. Many spiritual aspirants, unaware of the inner aspect of their own bodies, imagine that the only thing needed is heartfelt aspiration, through love for God and through prayer and contemplation. Even if a person's love for God is intense, however, the illustration of a bent hose explains the problem every aspirant faces.

For the stronger the flow of water through a hose, the more important it is that the hose be kept straight. One that is only slightly bent may straighten itself out if the flow of water is gentle, but if the hose is bent sharply and the flow of water is strong, serious damage to the hose may result. For this reason many saints, unfamiliar with the subtle spinal channels, have, when subjected to powerful rising currents of inner energy, been known to suffer severe illness, and considerable physical pain.

These teachings have persisted in the West since Biblical times, as saints made their own discoveries and spoke of them to others. The ancient Hesychasts, a school of Eastern Orthodox mystics, counseled breathing in and out with the prayer: "Lord Jesus Christ [on inhalation] have mercy upon us [on exhalation]." Certain of the traditions taught that with inhalation there would be a sensation of rising energy in the spine, and with exhalation, of descending energy. One tradition described bringing a *cool* current upward through the spine with the breath, and a *warm* current downward, as happens, in fact, with the practice of Kriya Yoga.

St. Teresa of Avila described her ecstatic experiences as resembling "the upward shot of a bullet through a gun"—an acceptable account of kundalini awakening. She also stated, from experience, that the seat of the soul is at the top of the head (the *sahasrara*).

These teachings, however, would require a deeper and detailed study, and lie outside the scope of the present work.

Sri Krishna in the Bhagavad Gita, referring to Raja Yoga (which blends the main paths of yoga with the practice of meditation), tells his disciple Arjuna, *"The yogi is greater than the ascetic, greater even than the followers of the paths of wisdom* [Gyana Yoga] *or of action* [Karma Yoga]. *Be thou, O Arjuna, a yogi!"*

CHAPTER TWENTY-THREE

How Devotees Fall

We saw in the last chapter how Adam and Eve fell spiritually owing to their misuse of the creative force. The misuse was not, as far as we know, excessive, but only downward in the direction it took: toward sexual union instead of upward to the brain and spiritual union. Had the energy been directed upward, the result would have been a high kind of creativity. Indeed, many creative people, especially in the arts, discover for themselves that the clarity and energy necessary for refined self-expression require at least sexual moderation.

This is not an easy teaching for most people to accept. For although negativity is often associated with sexuality—feelings of guilt and self-reproach, for example, or self-righteous criticism and judgment, and, in addition, the problems that commonly occur in marriage around sex—few would be able to contemplate with disinterest the complete relinquishment of this activity. If sex were no longer important, half the energy expended on it would have to be rechanneled: an enormous challenge to people's inventiveness!

Humor apart, however, judgment of others not only harms them—except in rare cases where a person responds courageously by reaffirming his own inner freedom—but attracts to oneself, by karmic law, the very thing one judges.

The creative force is related to creativity of all kinds. It is natural, therefore, that creative people should have strongly sexual, or at least romantic, leanings. These leanings can be rechanneled, but they cannot be suppressed. People with only weak sexual desires often criticize those in whom this tendency is strong, but they themselves usually have little creativity of any kind. There is no magnetism in the negative quality of merely not wanting something.

Paramhansa Yogananda once, to encourage his monks in mental self-control, held up the example of one of them who was seldom if ever troubled by temptation. A newcomer to the ashram life—and not exactly (shall we say?) a product of higher education—rejoined with a jeering laugh, "Gee, Sir, he ain't even got the *energy* to be tempted!" The Master, instead of rebuking him as one might have expected, replied with a chuckle, "That's true!"

People, however, for whom creative refinement is important discover for themselves the importance to such refinement of mental and spiritual clarity, and therefore the importance of sexual self-control. Failure in this respect never produces truly great works, though sometimes it succeeds in gaining a certain artistic notoriety.

Jesus Christ said, *"There are eunuchs who were born this way from their mother's womb; and there are eunuchs who were made eunuchs by men; and there are eunuchs who made themselves eunuchs for the sake of the kingdom of heaven."* (Matthew 19:12)

In Romania, which was the author's home during the first thirteen years of his life, a religious sect centered in Bucharest had what they believed was a solution to the challenge of temptation. The men of this sect worked—they may still do so—at driving horse-drawn carriages for tourists in the park. It was their practice to marry and have children, then after several years to be castrated. Yogananda strongly disapproved of this practice. "It robs a man of his energy," he declared. "Don't even think of it as a solution!" In fact, one seldom or never hears of *"castrati"* who became saints.

The way to God is never contrary to Nature. It works in cooperation with it, always, although in certain respects it also emphasizes little-known aspects of natural law.

It is quite possible to fall spiritually without reaffirming the first couple's Original Sin. If a person's consciousness moves downward in the spine, it draws from the surrounding universe thoughts and emotions reflective of that lowered consciousness. As Paramhansa Yogananda stated, "Thoughts are universally and not individually rooted." We live in a conscious, not a materially inert, universe.

In the last chapter we discussed the inner, mental kingdom. The "citizenry" of this kingdom, we saw, are of many types. In the same way that concentration in the spiritual eye leads to enlightenment, so energy that is focused in the lower chakras draws one's consciousness downward to materialism. The upper-class "citizens" of this kingdom live in the better "neighborhoods" of the upper chakras in the spine and brain. The lower classes, comprising ignoble thoughts and sensual qualities, crowd together in the "slums," or lower chakras.

The image of "crowding together" in these centers is apt, for materialistic attitudes are as numerous as wavelets on a choppy sea. Noble thoughts, on the other hand, and the qualities of self-control they inspire, are like the slow swells on a calm sea. Error cancels itself out to a great extent with its restlessness and vacillation. The desire to be rich is opposed by a tendency to spend more than one's income. The enjoyment of having one's own home and garden is opposed by a desire to travel. Conflicting tendencies chase one another like kittens pursuing a ball of yarn. Sincere commitment to virtue, however, is single-minded. Becoming reinforced by divine grace, it becomes all-powerful.

The Bhagavad Gita is not trying to discourage the devotee with this statement: *"The forces on our side* [those of delusion] *are innumerable, whereas their forces* [those of soul-aspiration] *are few."* (Chapter 1:10) What looks like strength to the worldly man challenged by spiritual promptings—that is, the sheer quantity of his worldly tendencies—is in fact his greatest weakness.

In the *Mahabharata,* Krishna gives Duryodhana (representing material desire) and Arjuna (symbolizing the aspiring devotee) an important choice: Krishna's army, on the one hand, consisting of a million soldiers, or Krishna himself alone, as a non-combatant. The choice is first offered to Arjuna, who answers: Krishna! even under the conditions stated. For he declares that, wherever the Lord is, there victory is assured. Duryodhana is well satisfied to have Krishna's million soldiers fighting on his own side.

It is Arjuna, of course, who wins in the end.

It must be mentioned, however, that lower psychological characteristics such as greed, selfishness, anger, and pride are not without a certain magnetism of their own. The mind, dwelling on them, is drawn downward. Concentration on any chakra creates a vortex of energy, which *is* its magnetism. By concentration on the lower three chakras (the coccyx, sacral, and lumbar), lower energies are attracted. Some call those energies demons, for they are in fact conscious. Others think of them as merely negative psychological traits. In any case they are real to us, and are not so easily dismissed. Regardless of their first impetus, moreover, reinforcement comes to them from outside one's self. The satanic force is that aspect of infinite consciousness which responds to lower kinds of magnetism in mankind, and increases their strength.

Other people's thoughts make up part of this outside influence. The author lived for some time on a street in San Francisco that was unusually quiet. The noise level at noon was not much higher than at three in the morning. Yet during the early morning hours, when most people were asleep, there was significantly less restlessness in the air.

Another example springs to mind: In German Switzerland many years ago, one of the author's traveling companions asked him a question regarding some simple point of Italian grammar. The author was studying Italian at the time, and ought to have had the answer ready. The group were surrounded at the time, however, by a whole populace thinking in German. He couldn't answer, but said, "Wait till we reach Lugano, in the Italian part of Switzerland. There I'm sure I'll find it easy to answer you." And so it proved.

The question is far more even than one of telepathy. If people feel anger, pride, or hatred, it means those emotions were already in existence. *"That which has no existence,"* the Bhagavad Gita states, *"can never come into being."* Tides of thought and emotion pass about us like radio waves. They affect us if we tune in to them and place ourselves on their wavelength.

Moreover, the more we develop spiritually, the greater the challenge we offer to the lower forces. The subconscious will not cede victory to superconsciousness without a struggle. By offering opposition, rather, it attracts reinforcements. For the forces of Satan actively oppose man's spiritual efforts. When those forces observe a saint slipping out of the net of delusion, they gather for battle. (This, however, is another subject. We include it here lest some readers think it is being ignored. The subject will be treated later, but lies outside the limits of our present chapter.)

A point may be added here, lest the reader who has some knowledge of these matters be confused by the fact that certain yoga techniques actually require one to focus on the lower chakras. These techniques are intended to uplift the energy from those chakras; therefore they teach concentration simultaneously on the spiritual eye. This is a spiritually beneficial practice, not a harmful one.

The Bhagavad Gita describes in the following words the downward road leading to a spiritual fall: *"If one ponders on sense objects, there springs up attraction to them. From attraction grows desire. Desire, impatient for fulfillment, flames to anger. From anger there arises infatuation (the delusion that one object alone is worth clinging to, to the exclusion of all others). From infatuation ensues forgetfulness of the higher Self. From forgetfulness of the Self follows degeneration of the discriminative faculty. And when discrimination is lost, there follows the annihilation of one's spiritual life."* (Chapter 2:61–63)

A notorious example of someone who fell spiritually was Judas Iscariot, who betrayed Jesus Christ and brought about his crucifixion. It was not only the fact of that betrayal, but also that Judas fell from such a height, that makes his example so appalling. For Judas was, as we all know, one of the twelve apostles. Necessarily, therefore, he was a great soul. Yet the seeds of that betrayal were evident already long before the tragedy he caused.

The following episode occurred less than a week before the Crucifixion. It reveals, however, an attitude that must have been festering in Judas for a long time:

"Mary took an earthenware jar containing pure and expensive oil of spikenard, and anointed the feet of Jesus, then wiped his feet with her hair: and the house was filled with the fragrance of the perfume.

"And Judas Iscariot, one of his disciples, who was about to betray him, said,

"Why was not this oil sold for three hundred pennies, and given to the poor?

"He said this, not because he cared for the poor; but because he was a thief, and the purse was with him, and he carried whatever was put into it.

"Jesus then said, Leave her alone; she has kept it for the day of my burial.

"For the poor you have always with you, but me you have not always." (John 12:3–7)

Let us reconstruct the story of Judas's downfall from what is known about him. The above story mentions his dishonesty with respect to money. Would a thieving tendency suffice to account for his betrayal? It seems most unlikely. Indeed, had Judas been a thief from the beginning it seems very unlikely that Jesus would have chosen him as an apostle.

Much more probably, Judas's personality was already tainted by a far more insidious fault: pride. "Pride," as we've all heard, "goes before a fall." Pride is also, frequently, the last defect to go. The ego assumes too easily to itself the power acquired in meditation, and only unwillingly gives to God alone the credit for this power. No sincere disciple—and surely Judas was sincere at least in the beginning—would have presumed to correct his spiritual teacher, least of all in spiritual matters! Judas, in his obvious spirit of rivalry, revealed a pride that must have entered him long before his act of betrayal. He actually implied that he, himself, was the wiser of the two!

Whence could such a delusion have arisen? For Judas was no buffoon, preening himself on a merely imaginary excellence. His pride must have been based on some actual ability.

From what we can gather, Judas was highly intelligent. He was also, according to tradition, personable, handsome, and magnetic. Many of his fellow-followers, so one imagines, considered him the Master's foremost disciple. Indeed, anyone as susceptible as Judas was to the delusion of pride would hardly have kept his gifts a blushful secret!

Still, on what possible grounds could this exalted disciple have ended up so deluded that he betrayed Jesus *to his very death?* That he was being critical of Jesus in the above passage, not of Mary, is clear. For although Mary was anointing the Master's feet, it was with the consent of Jesus. She continued doing so, moreover, until (as the Bible tells us) "the house was filled with the fragrance of the perfume."

This is a vitally important point. For the attitudes that led up to Judas's supreme act of betrayal had—and continue to have—grave consequences for Christianity through all succeeding centuries.

Great historic events have a way of repeating themselves, like musical motifs. Only a major shift in mass consciousness succeeds, sometimes, in changing that pattern. Thus, with the betrayal of Jesus Christ a direction was established that has continued in Christianity up to the present day. Jesus was crucified once, but the living spirit of his teachings has been betrayed—indeed, crucified!—ever since, for reasons very similar to those which motivated Judas.

Although the intellect of Judas was clouded, surely only a fool would have imagined himself equal in wisdom to Jesus Christ. What tortuous reasoning could have led Judas to the conclusion that he himself knew better, even if that "wisdom" was in worldly matters? For him as a disciple, this was a fatal assumption, for in his pride he saw more importance in worldly than in spiritual values.

Conceited as he was in the thought of his practicality, Judas followed the descent into delusion that was outlined by Krishna in the Bhagavad Gita. His thinking must have gone something like this: First, he dwelt on the thought of practicality itself, and on the need for it in his master's mission. Next, he allowed attachment to this concept to grow until it became for him all-important. One imagines him thinking, "I know the Master is a great soul, and I believe in him deeply. He could even be our people's salvation. But what a way for him to fulfill his destiny! It is totally inappropriate.

"Who will listen to him, sleeping casually as he does on the ground, mixing with the lower classes (who lack any social standing or influence!), and scorning the need for the approval of the religious leaders of our day? Is it possible that he is actually indifferent to his glorious mission? He tells us to be unconcerned for the morrow. Is *this* the right attitude for a great man, empowered by God with a great mission? The Master laughs—good heavens! like a child. He sings. He tells quaint little parables. And he talks as though we all lived in eternity instead of here, in measurable time, on solid earth.

"I do believe in him. Still, let's face it, the man's head is in the clouds! How can anybody so unworldly understand how to get his teachings out to people on the scale they deserve? The sad truth is that, great though he surely is, Jesus is not a practical man!"

Perhaps Judas never dared to voice even to himself the logical corollary to this line of reasoning: "Jesus may be wise spiritually, but he lacks *my own* down-to-earth, practical common sense!" It seems very probable

369

that Judas was in fact practical. Otherwise he would not have been given responsibility for the finances of the group.

He must have tried to persuade the Master to tailor his "public image" to fit the mentality of "responsible" members of society: persons in positions of power, like the Pharisees. Oh, he would never have urged Jesus to adopt their materialism. He would only have urged him to respect them, and to make his teachings more "accessible." We can imagine him saying (or at least thinking), "After all, acceptance by important people would guarantee the success that our mission deserves."

Instead, Jesus denounced priestly hypocrisy. "How could he be so lacking in tact?" Judas must have marveled; "so blind to every accepted principle for achieving worldly success?"

Indeed, Jesus scoffed at worldly success.

Brooding, as Judas must have done, on the Master's indifference to "public relations" as people speak of it today, he must have identified himself ever more deeply with those who, to his way of thinking, needed to be "won over." From this growing identification with them, it would have been only a step to desiring money, for it is on wealth, ultimately, that worldly power rests.

The Gospel states plainly that Judas was a thief. Dishonesty, however, must have developed in him only gradually. One imagines him mentally justifying even his dishonesty by some rationalization such as, "Jesus *deserves* to lose his money! Maybe only this will convince him that wealth does, in fact, count for something in this world."

On the other hand, Judas Iscariot could not have

offered this rationale to anyone else, no matter how much he nourished it in himself. Anyone as anxious as he was for worldly acceptance would have conjured up only reasons that, in his opinion, would be acceptable to worldly people. Thus, as we've seen, he spoke of selling the oil and giving the proceeds to the poor. Doesn't this very argument point to the next step in his downfall, as Krishna outlined the process: anger? *("Desire, impatient for fulfillment, flames to anger.")*

Judas's arrogance; his disdain for the Master's lack of practicality (a quality so exaggeratedly important to himself); his inability to convince Jesus of the need for being more "down to earth": all of these, as the Bible hints openly, stirred him to anger. Thus one sees how the need for self-justification led him beyond anger to that final act of betrayal.

His betrayal of Jesus Christ set into motion also a mass karma that has not yet been expiated, for it has continued ever since then to influence Christian history and thinking. *"From anger there arises infatuation. From infatuation ensues forgetfulness of the higher Self. From forgetfulness of the Self follows degeneration of the discriminative faculty."* Judas, persuaded by the pride he indulged in his own practicality, and incited by a natural tendency toward arrogance, became angry first at the Master's "obtuseness," then so infatuated with his own "rightness" that he lost all ability to discriminate between truth and error.

In how many similar ways since then have Christian leaders disguised their infidelity to their supposed beliefs! They belittle as impractical and unrealistic— indeed, as hardly more than a pious pretension—a life of total, heartful devotion, though it was this life that Jesus himself recommended. Churchmen today often declare with great conviction that the proper preoccupation of people in religion is with social problems—much like Judas's complaint that the expensive oil should have been sold to benefit the poor. Man's highest duty, theologians themselves insist, is to love his fellowman. Love for God, they say, must be, and can only be, expressed by loving humanity first. For who, they ask rhetorically, can love God for Himself alone? The Bible itself, they point out, says He cannot even be seen.* Surely, they conclude, one can only love what is visible—that is to say, other people.

The natural corollary to this insistence on love for humanity as the supreme virtue is stated almost as frequently, though usually by people outside any church because its emphasis on the ego smacks of heresy. This is the psychological approach, of which the primary concern is self-development. In order to love others—so goes this claim—one must above all love oneself.

The author was invited to be one of several speakers at a large convention, years ago. The theme of the event was self-fulfillment. Hundreds (exclusive, however, of the author) joined in chanting fervently, "I love myself *just the way I am!*"

As a matter of fact, the subtle motivation behind people's zeal for human betterment is almost always a desire for acceptance. Zeal of this kind, having no inner relationship with God, often needs to find in social service compensation for its own lack of devotion.

---

* *"No man hath seen God at any time."* (John 1:18) See Chapter Eight for a commentary on this verse.

Judas fell so deeply into the delusion of money-attachment as the corollary of worldly acceptance that he was capable, as if in a dream, of accepting silver from the chief rabbi for his betrayal of Jesus.

Lest anyone doubt the terrible power of delusion to draw people into actions that are diametrically opposed to everything they most deeply believe, the fate of Judas must stand forever as a salutary, even a terrifying, lesson. No one, no matter how brilliant, is safe from delusion until he is established in God-consciousness. Jesus placed the strongest emphasis on inner communion with God. It is God alone who can save us, through our inner communion with Him.

The downward road described by Krishna is inevitable if one is not calmly centered in the Self within. One's mental balance is upset by attraction to things, persons, and ideas. It is followed by a desire for them. Soon one finds oneself sliding down a slope of anger and infatuation into a quagmire of delusion. Desire for imaginary pleasures, or—as was the case with Judas—for imaginary gain, leaves one floundering helplessly at last in a bog of spiritual confusion.

Three great delusions are recognized in the Indian scriptures, and are implied also in the Jewish and the Christian: sex, wine, and money. These three promise much, but deliver nothing.

Sexual indulgence is one of the great delusions because it promises supreme joy while draining away the very energy one needs for experiencing joy. The exhilaration often felt after a sexual encounter is no less transitory than any other emotion, and is as tied as all of them are to their natural, opposite consequences.

The peace felt, moreover, is merely a pleasant preliminary to exhaustion. What can remain of true value is
that feeling which is offered up in love from the heart
to the spiritual eye.

Wine—an example, only, of intoxicants of all
kinds—is one of the supreme delusions because it
promises escape from pain, but dulls the mind to both
pain and pleasure, and creates only a disturbance in
both mind and body. What can remain of true value is
a feeling of detachment from those disturbances, and a
determination to seek stimulation, not in wine, but in
divine joy.

And money is a major delusion because the enjoyments it suggests are only hinted at—like the misty
effect photographers try to create around portraits of
young women to enhance their beauty. Money, similarly cloud-like, suggests to the imagination many fulfillments, but in consequence only bewilders the mind.
Money's promise is like lottery ticket advertisements,
which bedazzle one with glossy brochures offering fan-
tastic acquisitions and exciting adventures. Apart from
the fact that a person's chances of winning a lottery are
minimal, even those who do win become notoriously,
in most cases, bitterly disillusioned.

Money is sought for its own sake, as a rule, rather
than in order to meet a specific need. When desire is
tied to something actual, like a new coat or a car, it can
be brought into somewhat realistic focus, but money in
itself is purely a delusion. Held in the hand, it is nothing. What it represents to the mind, however, are endless opportunities. The more vague and undefined they
are, the more the imagination puffs them up with

absurd longings, the thought of which lifts one emotionally until he finds himself soaring in a basket under a balloon of dreams, marveling at the ever-expanding, because ever-receding, scenery below. Reality is finally lost sight of altogether. And then, very often—the crash!

Judas, raised high by the delusion of money, met his death literally at last in the crash of remorse and horror at what he'd done.

A survey was made in America years ago. People in a wide variety of income brackets were asked the question: "Are you satisfied with your present level of income?" The typical answer was, "Well, I *would* be, if I had just ten percent more." Thus does the delusion of money lead one onward, like the fabled carrot on a stick tied to the donkey's head. What can remain of true value is the realization that money represents not things, but energy, and that energy increases as it is given, not hoarded; expanded, not shrunk and enclosed in a box of selfishness.

Such is delusion's power to bewilder reason itself that many people react to any analysis of their own pet delusions with total and indignant rejection. The problem with all delusion, finally, is that it become habitual, and as such protects itself ferociously from exposure, like a mother bear protecting her cubs.

Many pitfalls await the seeker on the spiritual path. Krishna described them succinctly, for the pattern of all of them is the same. One of those pitfalls—not the one into which Judas fell, but one that he alluded to in attempting to justify himself—is that of doing good works for their own sake, rather than out of devotion to the only *true* good, which is God. Many religious believers hide a dread of divine love, all-absorbing as they know it must be, behind good works. For divine love is the greatest challenge the ego can ever face. Good works are their means of, at least hopefully, placating God. The truth, however, is that good works, too, often constitute a kind of outward involvement that leads to forgetfulness of God.

Judas suggested that the precious oil of spikenard be sold and given to the poor. Jesus, however, replied, "The poor you have always with you, but me you have not always." Judas meant his words to sound virtuous, but Jesus Christ, ignoring his attachment to money (which to him was self-evident), responded to a more important and universal issue. Judas Iscariot was, or seemed to be, pleading for social upliftment over soul-communion with God. To Jesus Christ, however, mankind's relationship with God is the most important issue there is.

Jesus certainly was not indifferent to human suffering, including poverty, which so many endure. His entire life was a veritable beacon-light of compassion. Several modern writers have gone so far as to describe him as a social activist. Others, expanding on that theme, have called him (absurdly) a firebrand revolutionary! (In this way, invariably, do people project their own characteristics onto others!)

Social upliftment was very important to Jesus, certainly. His highest mission, however, was to awaken people to the divine truth within them. As for revolutionary zeal, the only "uprising" he encouraged was to urge people to "revolutionize" their inner, spiritual outlook. Jesus Christ came on earth to inspire people to seek union with God. *"My kingdom,"* he said, *"is not of this world."* (John 18:36) Constantly he urged them to seek God-consciousness.

Thus, when he told Judas, "The poor you have always with you," his meaning was that injustice will never be eradicated so long as God is ignored. All suffering springs from trying to live without God. The eradication of earthly sorrows depends above all on eradicating our indifference to the Lord, and only secondarily—though not insignificantly—on hard work. Poverty cannot be alleviated except temporarily by gifts of money, the chief reason being that charity fails to attack the problem at its roots. Moreover, charity can have negative consequences as well. Often it merely increases people's poverty-consciousness, making them passive. Only by standing firmly on one's own two feet does one acquire the magnetism to attract success in life. As for giving in charity, this is certainly a good thing to do, but it must be done selectively. Often, unfortunately, while paying lip-service to justice, charity only increases injustice in this world by encouraging people in their weaknesses, not in their strengths. Indeed—and this may sound cynical, but it is the truth—social charity on a grand scale is often proffered merely to *encourage* weak-willed dependence. Self-reliance is the last thing the vote-hungry politician desires in the people he governs.

Inequities will continue in this world, if only because people are attached to self-gratification, and because some of them are cunning enough, and others foolish enough, to make it appear that profits can be reaped from empty promises, effortlessly on one's own part. "Social injustice," Jesus implied, "is inevitable as long as people choose to cling to delusion. The world's problems will be solved only by increased awareness of the only reality, that is to say, God."

His statement, "Me you have not always," was not only a reference to his impending death, but to Christ's presence in every soul. His statement is relevant even today. For what he said was, "Never take for granted any blessing you receive."

"Me you have not always." Yet God is with us eternally! It is we who are inconstant. The important thing is to establish constancy in our love for Him. Whatever we feel of His presence in our souls, we should hold on to determinedly. To give gifts of money may be good, but it can enslave others and also oneself. To give others joy and uplifted awareness, however, can enable them to solve their own problems permanently.

If a person seeks God sincerely, he must at least sometimes experience an upliftment of Spirit. How easy it is, at such times, to imagine that this state of blessedness will be his forever! For the divine presence, when we sense it, seems eternally right and natural, for our souls came from God. Patanjali, the ancient sage of India, defined such experiences as a "remembering." Alas, our memory begins to diminish the moment we return from meditation to ego-consciousness. We must strive always to deepen our attunement with God, by daily meditation and constant practice of His presence, until the ego vanishes from our awareness altogether.

Service to mankind is not, as such, the highest calling, though it can be a path to God if it is truly the Lord one is serving through others. Service with devotion is also, of course, a means of channeling God's love to others and, therefore, of purifying the heart. God's call in our souls, however, is to reverse the direction of our energy-flow from matter identification to infinite freedom in Spirit. Everything we do should have God's love for its focus. Anything less is idolatry.

What practical service, indeed, can the unskilled devotee offer to the decrepit, the ill, or the needy compared to that which is competently offered by doctors, nurses, and charitable institutions? Outward efficiency is not the deeper issue where spiritual service is concerned. The truly poor are not in any case those who have no money, but those who haven't God. The unique gift of the true devotee is the grace he receives to channel God's love and grace to others.

To serve in this way, one must do as Mary did, not as Judas urged: offer the fragrance of devotion at the feet of the Lord. In silent inner communion, attunement deepens gradually, and one becomes an ever-clearer channel for God's love. Thus, the true devotee plays a vital role in banishing spiritual poverty from the world. He also helps to free the world of those attitudes which attract material poverty. Through meditation, one's outer service, too, can be perfected. Most importantly, in divine union the soul knows infinite bliss. Every soul, once it becomes enlightened, uplifts the entire world in ways that could not be equalled even by millions of people dedicated to social betterment.

Why do devotees seek God? Because it is their eternal nature to do so.

Why, then, do devotees fall? This question deserves

another: Would it be in the fitness of things for a treasure so infinitely valuable to be discovered easily? The important thing to remember is this: No spiritual fall is ever permanent. No eternal hell awaits the sinner, with Jean-Paul Sartre's depressing message blazoned over the entrance: "No Exit!" We are not sinners: We are sons of God! Our ultimate destiny, though we postpone it indefinitely by our own choice, is union with Him.

CHAPTER TWENTY-FOUR

How Devotees Can Rise Again

In the last chapter we considered how devotees fall. In this one let us consider the opposite question: how devotees can rise again, after a fall. For no fall is permanent, though a spiritual one is more to be dreaded than any plunge down a precipice, from which one recovers after dying only once. Whether a fall is dramatic or only a slip depends on one's attitude, primarily: especially one's courage and devotion. God wants nothing but our good. We ourselves, however, falling into delusion, may reject His love.

"God will never abandon you," Paramhansa Yogananda said. "but if you tell yourself all is lost, it will be so at least for this lifetime." The question to be addressed here then is: How can a fallen devotee stop falling further and turn his steps back toward God? The answer is simple, though not always easy to follow: Gaze not at darkness, but at the light.

There is an inspiring passage in the Book of Isaiah: *"The people that walked in darkness have seen a great light: they that dwell in the land of the shadow of death, upon them hath the light shined."* (9:2) The Gospel of St. Matthew quotes this passage with a slight change of wording:* *"The people who sat in darkness have seen a great light; and for those who sat in the region and shadow of death light has dawned."* (Matthew 4:16)

What is needed by one who has gone astray is not to give in to despair, but to ask himself honestly, "What can I do now?" There is no point in cowering before God's wrath, which in any case is entirely imaginary. Still less point is there in railing angrily at oneself. Mistakes do occur in life, after all. Instead of raging against oneself, one's remorse should redirect energy toward a solution. And the solution is implied here by Isaiah: Focus on the light.

Krishna described the downward path into delusion. Let us reconsider his words from an opposite point of view. What he said was:

"If one ponders on sense objects, there springs up attraction to them. From attraction grows desire. Desire [impatient for fulfillment] *flames to anger. From anger there arises infatuation* [the delusion that one object, or set of objects, alone is worth clinging to, to the exclusion of all others]. *From infatuation ensues forgetfulness of the higher Self. From forgetfulness of the Self follows degeneration of the discriminative faculty. And when discrimination is lost, there follows the annihilation of one's spiritual life."* (Chapter 2:62–63)

"Annihilation" is the end result of concentrating on sense objects. Viewing this stern warning from that end, we find a hint as to how lost ground can be

---

* These quotations have been taken from two translations of the Bible: the first, from the King James edition, and the second, from The New Oxford Annotated Bible. The choice was based on purely poetic considerations. No essential difference of meaning exists among the various translations the author consulted.

regained. For by concentrating on the light, on higher truth, and on images that bring truth to mind, attraction to the light will grow again.

Yogananda used to say that darkness cannot be driven out of a room with a stick. "Turn on the light, and the darkness will vanish as though it had never been!" If affirming darkness develops attraction to it, then the same may be said of focusing on the light. For awareness grows by what it feeds on. Bad moods are self-perpetuating. Lust only increases with indulgence—rationalizations to the contrary notwithstanding! A number of "self-help" systems counsel the "purging" of anger by hurling mud at a wall. Hurling anything in anger, however, only affirms anger. Any focus on negative attitudes only strengthens them.

To judge others for their sins, also, affirms sin itself—not only in others' minds, but in one's own. Karmic law rules that whatever one judges in another he must experience himself, someday.

It is a mistake even to affirm good attitudes with a negative emphasis. To tell oneself, for instance, "I am *not* weak!" or, "I am *not* a sinner!" only emphasizes what one is trying to overcome. The consciousness of error cannot be willed out of existence. Thus, if a young man sees a voluptuous maiden, or if a maiden sees a beautiful young man; or if the mind is seized by any other object of attraction, it is difficult to stop thinking about it, but one can gradually *redirect* one's energy. Try, under such circumstances, to focus the mind—to do so even fiercely!—on the light.

Yogananda, after saying that darkness cannot be driven out of a room with a stick but can be banished by turning on the light, advised, "Don't try to drive the darkness out of your mind, either. Instead, turn toward the light."

What ought one to do if he finds himself sinking into the quicksand of delusion? First, he must refuse to accept that downward direction as his reality. For nothing, anywhere, is ever static.

One looks at a baby and thinks, "What a little dear!" Few can easily visualize that baby as a future adult. A mother may still behold her baby even in the grown man or woman. The author once bought a greeting card for his mother, to her huge delight, depicting a muscular man with a barrel chest, a large chin which sported a three-day stubble, and smoking a large cigar. He was wearing little shorts, like a boy's, and holding a toy balloon straining upward on a string. Smiling shyly, he was saying, "Happy birthday, Mother, from your little boy!"

In Romania it was once common for males to be given the name "Baby" at baptism. To be called that must have been intensely embarrassing for the grown man, who possibly stood six feet tall, and spoke in a deep voice!

Fallen devotees often define themselves similarly, by their present condition. They see themselves in static terms. Human reality, however, changes constantly. Absoluteness is reached only in the state of freedom in God. No fall into delusion is a full stop, no thudding crash to the ground. Rather, it is only a *directional movement* of thought and energy. Whatever stage one reaches in his downward descent—even that last stage, which Krishna named "annihilation of one's spiritual life"—is still only a movement, and can eventually be reversed.

Conceivably, the fall might continue indefinitely; it might even reach the low level of a germ. Krishna was not referring to soul-destruction in his allusion to annihilating one's spiritual life. Elsewhere in the Bhagavad Gita he said that annihilation of that sort is impossible. Nor can spiritual aspiration be totally annihilated, once it awakens in the heart. For aspiration, too, is a desire, and as such follows the law of karma. Once its energy has been set in motion, it must, sooner or later, attain its natural end. The desire for God, then, once awakened, continues forever until it attains fulfillment. Krishna was speaking of a *relative,* not an absolute darkness.

Once a sincere longing for God appears in the heart, even if one falls spiritually thereafter, his salvation is assured—soon, moreover, relatively speaking. To tell oneself, "I am weak! I am no good! I am evil!" is perhaps the greatest wrong one can inflict on oneself, for it may delay salvation for incarnations.

No negativity, however, can cancel out that final destiny. No eternal damnation awaits the fallen soul. "Annihilation of one's spiritual life" is not a crash. It causes suffering, surely, but it cannot destroy the soul.

When meditating, concentrate on the chakra specifically related to the delusion you want to combat, and from that chakra try to draw the energy upward. The lower three chakras govern material desires. Sexuality, for example, governs, and is governed by, energy in the second chakra: the sacral or *swadisthan.* A technique yogis use is to take whatever stimulation one feels in the sex organs, and withdraw it to that chakra. Then direct it up the spine toward the brain and the spiritual eye in the forehead.

Energy in any of the three lowest chakras focuses the mind on worldly desires, and is also directed toward those chakras by desire. Stimulation of the uppermost of these chakras, the lumbar or *manipur* opposite the navel, can magnetize and uplift energy from the chakras below it. To raise the energy above the *manipur,* thus ceasing to identify it with material consciousness altogether, one must concentrate simultaneously at the spiritual eye. It is helpful while practicing this technique to chant AUM mentally at the point between the eyebrows. Thus, the lower energies will be raised and spiritualized.

Focus on the third chakra, moreover, has a special virtue. It stimulates the consciousness of self-control. This is the practice, often ridiculed in the West, of "contemplating one's navel." In fact, one's concentration should be on the chakra in the spine *behind* the navel, not on the navel itself. The gaze should be directed toward the *ajna* chakra between the eyebrows, the location of the spiritual eye, to uplift the energy toward spiritual awareness.

The pivotal chakra for the ascending and descending energy in the spine lies opposite the heart. This is the dorsal or *anahat* center. The meditating yogi may feel intense devotion if his feelings are focused here. Stimulation of this chakra, however, though it can take the mind soaring up in divine awareness, can also take it downward in the case of one who is still susceptible to worldly emotions and desires. For the heart's feelings are central to both devotion and delusion. The energy here, as a focus for meditation, should be directed upward to the spiritual eye.

One of the most widely accepted methods, especially among Christians, for cleansing the heart of sin has been the practice of confession. *"Ego ti absolvo,"* the priestly formula of absolution, is believed to release the penitent from sin. Psychologically, some people may find confession, even in public, helpful. If they have a tendency to conceal their weaknesses, especially from themselves, such self-honesty may provide them with a measure of release. The danger of confessing to someone one knows is that, once one's weaknesses are known to him or her, that person may hold them over one's head in moments of anger, and thereby discourage him, perhaps making him weaker still. It is better to confess to someone wiser than oneself, whom one can trust. It may be helpful also, if one feels so inclined, to confess one's weaknesses to a stranger or to strangers, especially if (one thinks here of the group, Alcoholics Anonymous) he or they are trying sincerely to conquer the same weakness. Best of all, however, offer your problems and weaknesses up to God. He alone will never misunderstand you. It is His grace alone, moreover, that purifies the soul in the end.

Energetic effort is always necessary. The pull of delusion is very strong: stronger than most people realize. Victory is achieved by living consciously in the thought of God, by practicing His presence, by meditating daily and deeply, and by offering oneself up unceasingly as a channel for His love and joy.

Implicit in Krishna's warning is a note of hope. For

by concentrating on God-reminding objects and on spiritual ideals instead of on sense objects, one feels increasingly attracted to them. From attraction develops a desire to live better. This desire grows gradually over time to become an intense yearning for God. Divine yearning flames to the opposite of anger: impatience with anything that might hold one back spiritually. From impatience with delusion arises absorption in divine consciousness. From this superconscious absorption ensues forgetfulness of the senses. And from forgetfulness of them arises indifference to worldly attitudes and behavior. Estrangement from outward consciousness ends in the annihilation of all one's delusions!

Such is the ascending path. The opposite one, to which the ignorant are drawn like water swirling down a drain, sweeps them into spiritual confusion. The upward path leads to eternal freedom. The fundamental difference between the two paths is that matter-attraction, unlike the upward pull of Spirit, is one-directional. Material objects, that is to say, are not themselves aware of the affection people lavish on them! Love alone that is given to God is fully requited.

The secret of fulfillment is, as Krishna hints in this passage, to reverse the direction of attraction from the sensory world to the inner, intuitively perceived realm of the Spirit.

The Gita's warning describes varying stages on the descent into darkness. At whatever point one finds oneself on the long slide, he can redirect his movement upward. He must remind himself always that a continued slide into further delusion will never bring the fulfillment he craves.

The easiest stage at which to stop and turn back is the first. If any special sense object appeals to you, broaden your perception of it to include the whole world. Next, offer that perception up to God. Thus, initial sensory attraction can actually feed the fires of devotion, instead of robbing them of their fuel.

Restless frustration, ending in anger, can be redirected upward, at first, by deep breathing and by vigorous exercise. Next, to expand your sense of identity, be of service to others. Finally, direct your consciousness of self upward in meditation, to God.

Infatuation, which is the next stage after anger, is more difficult to rise from. The downward flow can be at least resisted here, however, as long as you retain some memory of your higher Self. Once you lose even this memory, however, the only hope left for you is to see in yourself, rather than in the world, the cause of the sufferings you endure as a consequence of your fall. For suffering, from then on, cannot be avoided.

What can you do if you feel already attracted to spiritual darkness and to its attendant evils? The advice to "concentrate on the light" may arrive too late to be of practical use: You may find you cannot even visualize the light, and if you can, you will probably consider it unattractive. As Jesus Christ put it:

"Every one that doeth evil hateth the light, neither cometh to the light, lest his deeds should be reproved.

"But he that doeth truth cometh to the light, that his deeds may be made manifest, that they are wrought in God." (John 3:20,21)

If the light of virtue, whether some specific virtue or simply goodness in general, fails to attract you, concentrate on the inevitable consequences of evil. Krishna, in the above passage, mentions only the final consequence of a fall: "annihilation of one's spiritual life." This, for the sincere devotee, would be the greatest loss imaginable, but for the worldly person, steeped as he is in materialism, the threat offers no new or special danger. Even so, if he is not already so blinded by delusion that he cannot contemplate any longer the direction his folly is taking him, he should give serious thought to the fact that the downward road leads to inescapable suffering.

Darkness may seem attractive and the light, hateful. One cannot actually desire suffering, however—except, conceivably, as an abstraction. By concentrating on the consequences of action, however, good as well as bad, one can summon up the courage to direct his efforts toward the good, and toward wisdom.

Thus, if you don't contemplate the sordid "beauty" of darkness, but contemplate rather the suffering that comes from living in it, you will have the first tool you need for redemption. If by "pondering on sense objects" you feel attracted to them, then by pondering on the ultimate consequences of indulging in sense pleasures you will gradually find them repulsive.

It is relatively easy to rise above all attraction and repulsion, if you relax the feelings in your heart. With inner relaxation, it will be possible to redirect your concentration upward to the light.

Disillusionment with material pleasure is an important incentive to spiritual dedication. Another, and much stronger, incentive however is devotional love. Disillusionment by itself leaves one embittered by "the injustice of it all," even though it was oneself who set the karmic law into motion in the first place. Love, then, is what lifts the soul out of ego-consciousness, into contemplation of, and ultimate absorption in, Infinity.

CHAPTER TWENTY-FIVE

The Eternal Present

We have been discussing the spiritual path: how to move forward on it; how to avoid slipping back; how to regain lost ground if one does slip back. It is not only theoretically interesting, but of immense importance to realize that no path actually exists except in our own perception. As long as "here" and "now" relate to a "there" and a "then," they are unfixed and temporary. Space and time are mists sectioned off by mind-made beginnings and endings. Beyond them, so Paramhansa Yogananda said, lies endlessness.

The illusion of space and time is produced by movements of thought in divine consciousness. It is by movement, or vibration, that cosmic creation is manifested. Without movement, Absolute Consciousness alone would remain. Movement actually *produces* the space within which it vibrates. Without movement, the relativities of past, present, and future could not exist. The universe itself is finite in time and space; modern physics in fact declares it so. What scientists have not addressed is the further phenomenon, that the universe is as large and as long-lasting as consciousness makes it. That is how scientists can state that, outside the universe, literally *nothing* exists—to which fact the yogi might add a whimsical paradox: "There is nothing there for it not to exist in!" The essence of everything *is* consciousness.

Thus, Paramhansa Yogananda, in his poem *Samadhi,* stated: "Present, past, future: no more for me, but ever-present, all-flowing I, I, everywhere!" Even that word, "everywhere," is only a figure of speech, for both time and space are *here* and *now.* Therefore he said, "Don't ask yourself fretfully, 'When will I have God?' Say, rather, 'I have Him! I am with Him *now!* He is my very own!'"

Jesus Christ declared, *"Before Abraham was, I am."* (John 8:58) His combination in a single sentence of the past tense with the present emphasizes the timeless-ness of truth.

Chapter 24 of St. Matthew presents a lengthy state-ment by Jesus that seems at first prophetic, but that is seen on further thought to be mystical, not literal. He states: *"Then shall all the tribes of the earth . . . see the Son of man coming in the clouds of heaven with power and great glory."* Three verses later he announces, *"Verily I say unto you,* **This generation shall not pass,** *till all these things be fulfilled."*

To place a literal construction on these words is self-defeating. Jesus would have to appear on an infi-nite number of clouds: For example, were he visible over Assisi, Italy, he would have to appear *separately* over Perugia, a mere thirty kilometers away. To be clearly visible in places in between, he would need to manifest on other clouds as well. And if he addressed the populace, those at one location would see him face on while others relatively nearby would see him turned away from them. What a confusion!—and over one

393

tiny spot, only, on earth. What about the whole planet? Seldom does literal interpretation of scripture offer so much to bewilder the mind.

The only way this passage can be accepted literally is to imagine it describing some far-off future, and one, therefore, lacking in solid reality, like a dream in which inconsistency acquires a logic of its own, and common sense seems sublimely inconsequential.

Jesus, however, was describing a time when many who were then present would still be alive. *"This generation shall not pass,"* he said, *"till all these things be fulfilled."* Since then, numerous generations have passed, but nothing has occurred even remotely suggestive of that event, if his description of it is taken literally. Was he simply wrong, then? He must have been, if this was his meaning. Yet he showed perfection in his dedication to the truth. Only his followers, in limited numbers, have been willing to separate their spiritual expectations from common sense. Many naive Christians even today await the Second Coming as an act on the stage of history. Meanwhile, Jesus has been seen inwardly over nearly two thousand years in many places on earth by *individuals* (but never by crowds) blessed with deep faith in him.

The Second Coming is an *inner* event; as such it has occurred repeatedly already. The expression, "the clouds of heaven," refers not to earthly skies, but to the astral nimbus that is often seen in visions. "The son of man" in this passage means that Jesus was promising to appear in human form as distinct from his manifestation as the infinite Christ consciousness.

That a Second Coming may also occur outwardly is

not precluded here, though it would not—*could* not—in this case be a simultaneous manifestation to "all the tribes of the earth." An appearance everywhere on earth could only be to individuals here and there who were rapt in ecstasy—or else, if outward, then as a new incarnation.

In another passage, quoted earlier, Jesus offered the following analogy: *"Say not ye, There are yet four months, and then cometh harvest? behold, I say unto you, Lift up your eyes, and look on the fields; for they are white already to harvest."* (John 4:35)

Divine experiences are outside of time and space. Seemingly distant, at least in time, their truth is ever present beneath the surface restlessness of life. Paramhansa Yogananda used to say that time is like a motion picture film. It can be turned backward or forward at will by the projectionist, whose sense of time is unrelated to the episodes on the film. This simile is inexact, of course; similes always are. For if we think of God as the projectionist, time doesn't pass for Him as the film turns. In God, no time exists; there is only *now*. No space exists; there is only *here*.

If these truths seem abstract, they gain practical usefulness when we realize that our need, in seeking God, is to rise above the consciousness of time and space. There is no necessity for us to travel here or there—to visit this holy saint or that sacred shrine—in order to realize God. If time is required to know Him, it is only because we live under the hypnosis of time. If we think it important to visit some saint, it is because we don't see that the saint, if he is indeed a master, is consciously with us even now. As a saint in modern

India said, in response to an invitation from America, "I am there already!" This is not to denigrate the very real value of pilgrimage, especially to living saints, or the need for patiently awaiting a divine response to prayer. The point is mentioned only to help readers to rise mentally above the delusion that there is anything new awaiting them at a distance, or in the future. All that we need is, with combined concentration and love, to puff away the mist of delusion that encloses our perception of reality. Time, to our minds, seems simply a matter of fact. For us, then, time has to pass for our consciousness to change. In our love for God, however—and there is no way to know Him but by love—we should tell ourselves constantly, "I have Him already!" Never can we, to even the slightest degree, be closer to Him than we are right now. He is our very Self.

Thus, whenever we find ourselves beset by trials and feel pulled downward in spirit, we should remind ourselves firmly that this suffering cannot last forever, though it may seem like forever at the time.

A man once was driving his car to go skiing. Arriving at the snow line, he applied the brakes, but didn't realize that the tires were bald. The car skidded on a patch of ice and rammed into the side of a large bus. Though barely scratching the bus, the car was put out of commission permanently. The man, intent on continuing his trip to the snow, entered the bus. As he did so, a passenger exclaimed commiseratingly, "What a pity! You've totaled your car!" The man, however, dispassionate by nature, was viewing the incident as an abstract event, simply, about which he'd obviously need to do *something,* but not immediately. Surprised at the emotion in the passenger's remark, he replied with a smile, "Whatever the case, I'd be happy again in another week. Why waste that time in feeling sorry for myself? I'm happy right now!"

Wisdom helps to smooth out the cresting and crashing waves of success and disappointment, victory and defeat, pleasure and pain. For with wisdom comes the recognition that every reaction is followed by its inherent opposite, even as night follows day. When delight wells up within you, tell yourself firmly, "It won't last. I refuse to let my happiness be conditioned by anything outward." Why let yourself be a slave to circumstance? When sorrow comes your way, similarly, tell yourself, "This inconvenience is temporary. Eventually it will yield to its opposite satisfaction."

This doesn't mean one should live without joy, or be indifferent to grief and the seeming injustices of life. Joy should, however, be directed inward, to its source in the Self. Thus, pleasure can actually feed the inner joy. If, on the other hand, one gives in to pleasure, his delight in it will diminish gradually, for its sustaining energy will be drained away from its source. Happiness is a *projection,* from within, onto the things we think we enjoy. As light dims with distance, so also does joy when it is directed outward from the Self.

Both happiness and grief should be turned inward—not toward the ego, but toward soul-perception. There, they feed the fountain of inner joy by reminding us how temporary all emotional states are.

A final point needs to be made here: Nothing can be gained by numbing oneself to pleasure and pain.

Numbness is a kind of suicide. When we deaden the capacity for feeling, we lose the capacity for love.

The path to God can be exquisitely painful sometimes, as pleasure and sorrow change into an awareness that everything in life is illusory. One then sees how easy it is for all that to be caught up in things that are unreal. Soon, however, pleasure and pain turn to joy in the realization: "If all this really is a dream, I can wake up from it!"

Once the oppositional states of pain and pleasure resolve themselves into the timeless *here* and *now*, there bursts upon the soul an oceanic joy. The realization dawns that joy has been with us always, subtly hiding beneath every emotion, thought, and action. Everything we ever sought, every fulfillment we are now struggling to attain, is already with us at the core of our awareness, though it will never be found at the rim.

How can we attain perfect freedom? Above all, we must meditate regularly to establish contact with superconsciousness. As long as we identify ourselves with our present and lesser wakefulness, we will be unable to withdraw altogether from our periphery, but will remain tied to the senses and to outwardness. Our egos must be purified until, gazing at the world, we no longer intrude upon it our egoic awareness. We then see everything as a manifestation of the one, eternal Self.

Attachment to time and space must be whittled away gradually, until love bestows on us the power to demolish it in a single, brilliant explosion.

The place to begin our whittling is at the edges of our awareness. Distance in time as well as space surrounds places and events with an attractive halo. Grass looks greener, as we know, at a distance. Noisome insects no longer disturb our enjoyment of the scene. Breezes do not chill the skin. Rutted pastures seem to invite us to take a pleasant stroll. The past, similarly, assumes a dreamlike quality that bears little resemblance to actual experience. And the future suggests a shining contrast to the gray present.

The ray of aspiration awakened by thoughts of the future may at times be somewhat dim and uncertain, but the past gives us something actual to ponder. Nostalgia plays a central role in many people's lives. They may read tales of knighthood in the Middle Ages, and fancy that those times were nobler and more brightly colorful than the pedestrian present. Absent from today's awareness is the brutishness of those days: the meanness of uncultured peasants; the cruelty of many glittering so-called nobles; the unpaved and muddy roads; the menace of unlit city streets at night, littered and stinking with garbage; the incurable illnesses; the grinding poverty.

People enjoy watching movies of period pieces, for which the only excuse, usually, is the elaborate costumes. Spectacles like these spare one the less pleasant realities: the infrequent bathing, the reeking bodies, the lack of proper sanitation. Everything, apart from the costumes, is conceptually two-dimensional.

People idealize the distant future also, with images of scientific inventions: space ships, for example, that whisk the fortunate traveler off to some planet where Eden still exists. No Eden, of course, could offer an improvement on the life they know already, for wherever Eden is, *there will they be!* Unless they have achieved spiritual enlightenment, science will never be able to increase their happiness. Only the inner science of yoga communion can accomplish that feat. And for this, no Eden is necessary.

We must whittle away at the false images shimmering at the edges of our minds. For wherever we are, there—quite simply—are we: the same old moods, the same headaches, the same fatigue and seizures of selfish jealousy and anger. We won't change merely by transporting our bodies elsewhere, either in time or in space.

Not even suicide can take us out of our misery, if we are miserable. Death is no option. For life goes on, whether with or without a body. To flee the present in favor of some far-off paradise is to face forever that same old reality: one's self.

Many people recall their childhood nostalgically. They gloss over the fact that in those cute little bodies there lived the same egos, the same personalities—differently decked out, in some respects differently motivated, but still the same old bewildered, but still-hopeful, self.

Paramhansa Yogananda explained that there is only one way of escape: We must live in the present. "Most people," he said, "live in the past or the future. When you can be truly happy in the present, then you have God."

People often construct ivory towers in the mind, from the top of which they gaze down onto an unreal world. It would show greater discrimination if they visualized that tower as standing on a foundation of wood, with a hive of termites eating away at that foundation. Perhaps we should emulate those termites, and gnaw away at the base of our own "ivory tower" of unrealistic dreams!

Whittle away, or gnaw, at your dreams and attachments! The more non-attached you can be in yourself, the freer you will find yourself to be. The more you learn to live fully here and now, completely accepting the present, the more energy will be released for you to enjoy the present.

Numerous are the ways to God, though they lessen in number as the mind travels inward. All of those ways demand, ultimately, that one live in the eternal present. Some seekers achieve this state by the process described thus far in this chapter: that is, by gradual elimination of the consciousness of a "there" and a "then." *Neti neti,* this practice is known as in India: "Not this, not that." As in peeling an onion one finds it reduced finally to nothing, so with the gradual elimination of "there and then" one discovers the eternal present. Time and space become eliminated altogether. What remains is divine consciousness.

There is another way for achieving that timeless and spaceless state: not by shrinking one's ego-awareness to nothingness (which is what the practice of elimination—*"neti, neti"*—accomplishes), but by expanding it to infinity. In this case, one applies Paramhansa Yogananda's description of divine vision: "center everywhere, circumference nowhere."

Don't think of anything as distant from you. Place *yourself* at the edge of your consciousness. Don't discount those images of a distant, or a future, paradise; instead, place yourself clearly at the scene. From your own ego-center see the waving palm trees, the smiling natives, the long, slow-rolling waves as they advance majestically toward the shore.

Then, instead of trying to draw happiness from them, *make them a gift of your own happiness!* Bless them with wave upon wave of bliss.

Next, go still deeper into that scene: Feel yourself centered in every atom. Radiate light and bliss outward in all directions.

You will find it helpful also to take an opposite image: a hellish, gray place filled with weeping and unhappy people. Bless that place and those people with bliss. Continue this visualization until you see the place filled with light, and the sufferers happy and smiling.

Try to feel God not only near you, but in distant places. Listen to music as it comes through those places from Him. Hear music also in the inhabitants' higher aspirations. That music really exists; it varies from country to country and from culture to culture! In time, you will actually hear melodies and will be able to produce beautiful, soul-stirring songs. In the communion of music you will find that you can *give* joy rather than only receiving it. Thus, your sense of "I" will dissolve in a greater reality.

Ultimately, the music will merge into the great sound of AUM. Listen to AUM, then—or listen *for* it. Listen in your spiritually sensitive right ear. Commune there with the Holy Word, the "Amen." Absorb yourself ever more deeply in that Cosmic Sound.

The Bhagavad Gita in Chapter Four, verses 18–22, says of the yogi who has achieved oneness with God:

"He is a yogi, discriminating among men, who beholds inaction in action, and action in inaction. He has attained the goal of all action (and is free).

"The sages call that man wise whose pursuits have no selfish plan or motive, and whose activities are purified of all karmic consequences by the fire of wisdom.

"Relinquishing attachment to the fruits of action, supremely contented within himself, freed of dependence on everything outward, such a yogi is free even while engaged in activity.

"He who has renounced the sense of 'I-ness' and 'my-ness,' who has transcended all attachment to sensory enjoyment, and whose heart's feelings are guided by soul-awareness, incurs no sin even in performing outward action.

"He who contentedly accepts whatever comes of itself, who remains above duality and is untouched by envy and the pairs of opposites, and who is even-minded during success and failure, is free forever from the bonds of karma."

CHAPTER TWENTY-SIX

The Redeeming Light

"For as the lightning cometh out of the east, and shineth even unto the west: so shall also the coming of the son of man be." (Matthew 24:27)

When people use analogies, they naturally select those to which others can relate easily. Jesus used them frequently in his teaching, and made it a point, similarly, to keep them simple and recognizable. It is all the more surprising, then, that the above analogy bears no resemblance at all to the way people actually see lightning. This phenomenon behaves in many ways, but rarely, if ever, in this way. Usually, it runs somewhat vertically from earth to sky, or from sky to earth, or short distances between one cloud and another. Certainly it is not common, and may never even happen, for lightning to flash from one side of the horizon all the way to the opposite. Still less is it likely that such a flash would begin in the east, specifically, and go all the way across—again, specifically—to the west. This metaphor, in other words—unlike the norm in such cases, and not at all like the way Jesus normally taught—attempts to explain the unique by the extraordinary! It is a paradox, not an explanation.

In Chapter Twenty-Two we saw how the Bible

repeatedly describes the inner light as appearing "eastward" in the forehead. This can only be what Jesus intended by, coming "out of the east." East, in mystical writing, is situated in the forehead. Here it is that the divine light is first seen. North in the body is the top of the head; south, the base of the spine; west, the back of the head. The light of the body is the "single," or spiritual, eye, visible between the eyebrows when the mind is calm and at rest. In meditation this light enters the brain and, after a time, fills the whole body. As Jesus said, *"If thine eye be single, thy whole body shall be full of light."* (Matthew 6:22) The Second Coming of Christ describes, as we said earlier, an inner event. The above verse speaks of this coming in terms of light; it could also have done so in terms of sound: the Word of God, or AUM. Had the early writers, or their translators, been aware of these mystical truths, they might have recast the above sentence to read more like the following: "The coming of Christ will appear in the east like lightning, and will fill people's consciousness."

In other words, Jesus may not have begun this statement with an analogy at all. His description of lightning doesn't depict the way lightning strikes. Discounting this fact, the statement may be perfectly apt if, for example, Jesus was only describing the suddenness of the Christ light as it dawns upon the mind. Viewed thus, his statement is perfectly clear, and isn't even metaphorical.

In these chapters we have emphasized the *inner* nature of Christ's mission, and our need to be transformed by *inner* grace. "To all who received him, to them gave he power to become the sons of God." We have also made the further point that there must be *cooperation* with divine grace for the devotee to achieve transformation from a deluded human being, confined in egoic limitation, into a "son of God"—that is, to become, like Jesus, one with the Christ consciousness.

The inner light has power to effect this transformation. The sudden awakening suggested by the image of lightning, however, requires much preliminary work: a work not outward, in the form of service or teaching or converting others as people commonly believe, but inward. It is a process of *inner* purification. Outward service is beneficial also to those who serve God in others, for it purifies their hearts of selfish desires.

The inner light, when it comes, heralds a higher state of consciousness. The higher this state, the more complete the inner change. In time, that light blazes "as of a million suns," as it is described in the Indian scriptures. Even ordinary human beings, long before they even see the inner light, use light as a metaphor for any sort of mental awakening.

As sunlight, on entering the ocean, loses power at increasing depths, and finally becomes invisible, so with the divine light as it enters human consciousness. Many of the creatures that live at great depths produce a luminescence of their own, to compensate for the absence of outer light. Even so, the delusion-darkened ego produces its own version of spiritual awareness by the excitement it generates in its relation to matter.

People's awareness darkens as their awareness becomes denser, with matter-identification. This, indeed, is the way cosmic creation is manifested: from Spirit to divine ideation, to light and energy, to the seeming substantiality of matter; and from *sattwa guna* (the spiritually elevating quality) to *rajo guna* (the activating quality) to *tamo guna* (the spiritually darkening, dense quality). Matter, in its relative density, expresses *tamo guna*. Energy, which itself displays light, appears dark in its manifestation as matter. The more a person identifies himself with the material plane, the less he experiences of the spiritual light.

Around the bodies of saints, and especially around their heads, spiritually sensitive persons often see an astral light, or aura. Around people of lower awareness, the light becomes progressively dim. The aura, even when bright, is invisible to most people even as, to them, the light in their own foreheads is invisible. The effects of that light can easily be inferred, however, from the way it acts through the human brain. Accompanying it, ever-increasingly as the inner light develops, is a corresponding clarity of mind.

Take the example of someone who tries late at night to solve a problem—even a trivial one, like some clue in a crossword puzzle. If his brain is tired, the problem may seem to him insoluble. The following morning, however, when his brain is refreshed, the solution comes effortlessly. This phenomenon is relatively common. It is often explained as the result of subconscious activity during sleep. In fact, however, the solution is almost always produced by a renewal of energy: an increase of inner light which, when focused on the problem, simply attracts the right answers. Solutions may also come by simply taking a short break from work, energizing the body and brain through wholesome exercise, or refreshing oneself in other ways, such as by deep breathing.

407

The denser a person's consciousness, the less able the spiritual light is to penetrate that mental fog. Thus, if the person is deeply identified with matter, he finds it difficult to think clearly or even, sometimes, to think at all. People who are completely identified with their bodies consider the senses and sense pleasures the be-all and end-all of existence. Seldom, if ever, do they have an abstract thought. By nature they are reactive, not active in a creative sense. A clear mind is a sign, outwardly, that the inner light also is clear. A dull mind, on the other hand, is a "clear" sign that the inner light is dull and unfocused.

The English language is fortunate in the way it treats the word "light." It contains two meanings for light. The first is the one we've been using: the opposite of darkness. The second meaning pertains to lightness of weight. This coincidence is fortunate in that it expresses a truth everyone knows: The more light in a person's consciousness, the more light-weighted he also feels—not in pounds or kilos, but in awareness. Influences that increase this sense of lightness increase also the mind's receptivity to the visible light. Dense, heavy foods, however, especially if they form the major part of a person's diet, cloud the mind and make its consciousness heavy. Too much sleep darkens the mind and results in sluggish thinking processes, as if thought itself were so heavy it had to be pushed strenuously over a rough floor toward its solution. Alcoholic beverages and consciousness-changing drugs darken the mind. Too much sensory stimulation and sensual indulgence also darken the mind. All activity, in fact, that absorbs one in materiality, and that lessens one's spiritual awareness, obscures the mind, reducing its clarity. The spiritual reason for moral living, then, is that it lightens the consciousness, loosens the shackles of ego- and matter-consciousness, and attunes one more sensitively to the redeeming inner light.

Divine redemption, then, means withdrawing from identification with delusion, and becoming inwardly absorbed in the light of truth.

When the sky is darkened by clouds, the sunlight grows dim: not because its power is any weaker, but because the intervening vapor obscures it. The same is true of the mind. Darkness enters people's consciousness because of their attachment to material grossness. Mental clarity is affected also by clouds of doubt and restlessness, and by clouds of emotion such as fear, anger, and hatred. All these are the foes of calm feeling and intuition. Anything that prevents one from seeing life with dispassion, and therefore objectively, obscures the inner light.

A Bengali friend of the author's lived in Calcutta during the unrest that attended the partition of India and Pakistan in 1948. For some days he was forced to protect himself and his family by barricading themselves in their home. Eventually he was obliged to go out for food. He made the trip by car, and took with him a rifle, poised carefully across the steering wheel, for protection. At a certain point on the road he suddenly found himself confronted by someone with a gun aimed directly at his head. This person happened to be the chief of police, and was in fact a personal friend. So darkened was his mind, however, by the pervasive atmosphere of hatred that he failed even to recognize the man in the car as his friend. Only the fact that both of them had weapons pointed at each other averted a tragedy, creating a standoff between them. After a few seconds, the policeman lowered his gun, blinked a few times, then recognized the man before him as a friend of his. Thus, the crisis passed.

During those moments of tension, however, the policeman's face was barely recognizable. As he returned to normal consciousness, his expression changed. It was as if a cloud had settled over his countenance, then passed as he became himself again. He shook himself, then exclaimed in wonder, "I don't know what came over me. Please friend, I beg you to forgive me!"

This case was an extraordinary demonstration of how extremely dark the mind can become when it is clouded by emotion. Even in less critical situations, when the clouds of emotion aren't so dense and the inner light is able to shine through more clearly, its subtle rays cannot penetrate the fog of materialism.

Jesus likened the Christ light to lightning in the suddenness of its appearance. The real work on the spiritual path is to prepare the mind for this instantaneous transformation. Were the Christ light to come without prior preparation, the mind would be unable to contain it, and would receive a shock as if of high-voltage electricity on the wiring of a house.

A science-fiction story appeared years ago about a planet that received its illumination from several suns. Together, the suns kept it constantly bathed in daylight. Once in every thousand years, however, these suns became so disposed that the stars beyond them could be briefly seen by the inhabitants. Many people, overwhelmed by such a sudden and extraordinary event, went mad.

Their reaction was not, perhaps, wholly believable, but spiritually speaking, the point of the story is both clear and valid. The mental jolt from gross daylight to an almost mystical glimpse of infinity was, to the inhabitants, terrifying. How much greater would the shock have been had they found the daylight reduced to relative dimness before the intensity of the *inner* light, and to feel their egos dissolving in infinite bliss! That mystical light appears, at first, as a darker island in the general darkness behind closed eyelids. That island is a deep violet in color, and is surrounded by a thin ring of pale luminescence. In place of the physical light of this world, which comes from the sun, there gradually appears, and with growing intensity, the light of the spiritual eye: and what is known also in mystical tradition as "the star of the east." This is not the Christ consciousness, but it heralds the coming of that supernal event.

Human consciousness, conditioned as it is by ordinary, worldly experience, is unable to absorb itself in this light, or to accept what Yogananda called "the liberating shock of omnipresence." It is not that this light hurts the eyes; indeed, they find it soothing. But it would be too great a shock to someone who was not ready to receive it. Moreover, it isn't that omnipresence, the state that follows, is devastating. The ego, however, must be conditioned by long and deep meditation to surrender into a greater self-awareness.

In the last chapter we implied that one might theoretically by-pass time, with sufficient wisdom. In reality, however, the mind is chained, like Andromeda of Greek mythology, to the rock of time. Even wisdom would come as a great shock to one whose consciousness was not yet spiritually refined. One cannot *philosophize* one's way to the level of wisdom required for banishing time. Like Perseus, who saved Andromeda, one must have first slain the gorgon of delusion.

The scriptures counsel an accepting attitude toward everyone. Most people don't live at high stages of spiritual development. Fanaticism—to take one example—is common in religious circles. Though deplored by those who are charitable and broad-minded, fanaticism and its underlying bigotry are simply evidence of immaturity. To urge one who was spiritually ignorant to take a broader view and renounce the emotional zeal by which he defines his devotion, might do him more harm than good. Too sudden an expansion from his customary, though limited, perspective might only bewilder him with its sweeping panorama of things as they really are.

The disciple of a certain master received from another disciple, more advanced than himself, a spiritual touch—a transferral of spiritual grace—and was lifted to a high state of awareness, giving him a glimpse of infinite consciousness. This new awareness, however, was one for which he was wholly unprepared. He had been joyfully following the path of personal devotion to God. The glimpse he received now was of the impersonal vastness of God. It wasn't possible for him to fit this abstract view into the one he'd been developing.

From then on he could no longer delight in a personal relationship with God. Unfortunately, he couldn't love God either in that impersonal aspect. Thereafter, when he lectured or wrote on spiritual topics, his way of expressing himself was dry and intellectual. The other disciple received a severe scolding from the guru for his unfortunate, if well intentioned, generosity.

A young disciple of Paramhansa Yogananda's, similarly, once asked another, who was highly advanced, to give him a taste of divine ecstasy. The older one demurred, saying, "If I did so, your bliss, which you haven't yet earned, would be temporary. Later on, you would be unable to bear your life any longer. You are not yet ready for ecstasy."

As Yogananda said in *Autobiography of a Yogi,* regarding the *samadhi* state, or supreme ecstasy, it "can never [come] through one's mere intellectual willingness or open-mindedness." It comes in time, however: "with a natural inevitability to the sincere devotee. His intense craving begins to pull at God with an irresistible force."

Absorption in the light comes not by passivity. Nor can it be forcefully commandeered. It comes at last, however, by steadfast, deep devotion. Everything in these pages has been written to help you to reach enlightenment. Most important of all is an attitude of loving receptivity toward the Christ consciousness, through that one whom God has ordained as your true, or *sat,* guru. As we saw earlier in the Bible, *"As many as received him, to them gave he power to become the sons of God."* (John 1:12)

And as the Bhagavad Gita states in Chapter Ten,

Verses 10 and 11: *"On those who are ever united to me through meditation, and who worship me with love, I confer that yoga of wisdom by which they attain Me.*

"I, then, who dwell in their hearts, showering My grace upon them, dispel forever their darkness born of ignorance, and uplift them in the shining light of wisdom."

ABOUT THE AUTHOR

J. Donald Walters is widely considered one of the foremost living experts on spiritual practice.

An American born in Rumania and educated in England and America, Walters was raised as an Episcopalian. He studied at Haverford College and Brown University. Later, through his discipleship with the great Indian sage, Paramhansa Yogananda, Walters became steeped in the wisdom of India. He was eventually initiated into an Indian monastic order and took the spiritual name, Swami Kriyananda.

Walters' books and music have sold over 2.5 million copies worldwide and are translated into twenty-four languages. He has written more than 70 books and composed over 400 pieces of music. He is also the founder of Ananda, a network of spiritual communities with branches all over the world.

INDEX OF BIBLE QUOTATIONS

INDEX OF BHAGAVAD GITA QUOTATIONS

INDEX OF QUOTATIONS
BY PARAMHANSA YOGANANDA

GENERAL INDEX

SELECTIONS FROM
<u>CRYSTAL CLARITY PUBLISHERS</u>

THE HINDU WAY OF AWAKENING
ITS REVELATION, ITS SYMBOLS: AN ESSENTIAL VIEW OF RELIGION
Swami Kriyananda (J. Donald Walters)

". . . provides an understanding of Hinduism as the inner way that all souls tread, and with a genuine tolerance and appreciation of religious diversity that is so much needed in our world."—*Light of Consciousness*

This book gives hope—for each one of us, for life, for the future. It is, as the subtitle claims, an essential view of religion; it points to that essence of eternal truth which animates every great religion in the world. *The Hindu Way of Awakening* reveals the vital connections between Hindu understanding and our modern life and culture.

AUTOBIOGRAPHY OF A YOGI
Paramhansa Yogananda

One of the great spiritual classics of this century. This is a verbatim reprinting of the original, 1946, edition. Although subsequent reprintings, reflecting revisions made after the author's death in 1952, have sold over a million copies and have been translated into more than nineteen languages, the few thousand of the original have long since disappeared into the hands of collectors. Now the 1946 edition is again available, with all its inherent power, just as the great master of yoga first presented it.

THE PATH
ONE MAN'S QUEST ON THE ONLY PATH THERE IS
Swami Kriyananda (J. Donald Walters)

The Path is the moving story of Kriyananda's years with Paramhansa Yogananda, author of the spiritual classic *Autobiography of a Yogi*. *The Path* completes Yogananda's life story and includes more than 400 never-before-published stories about Yogananda, India's emissary to the West and the first yoga master to spend the greater part of his life in America.

AWAKEN TO SUPERCONSCIOUSNESS
MEDITATION FOR INNER PEACE, INTUITIVE GUIDANCE, AND GREATER AWARENESS
J. Donald Walters

Many people have experienced moments of raised consciousness and enlightenment—or superconsciousness—but do not know how to purposely enter such an exalted state. Superconsciousness is the hidden mechanism at work behind intuition, spiritual and physical healing, successful problem solving, and finding deep, lasting joy. In *Awaken to Superconsciousness*, J. Donald Walters shares his knowledge of the ancient yoga tradition, explains how to apply yoga principles to daily life, describes how to attain inner peace, and provides inspiring meditative exercises.

THE ART AND SCIENCE OF RAJA YOGA
J. Donald Walters

This book contains fourteen lessons in which the original yoga science emerges in all its glory—a proven system for realizing one's spiritual destiny. This is the most comprehensive course on yoga and meditation offered today, giving you a profound and intimate understanding of how to apply these age-old teachings on a practical as well as spiritual level in this modern age. You will receive a complete and detailed presentation of yoga postures, yoga philosophy, affirmations, meditation instruction, and breathing techniques.

Also included are numerous suggestions for daily routines and helpful information on diet and alternative healing techniques. Bonus audio CD contains a guided yoga postures session, a guided meditation, and an inspiring talk on the art of meditation.

MEDITATION FOR STARTERS
J. Donald Walters

Learn the secrets of deep, joyful meditation! J. Donald Walters, an internationally respected spiritual teacher, has practiced meditation daily for over fifty years. *Meditation for Starters* offers simple but powerful guidelines for attaining inner peace. This is a book for long-time meditators as well as for beginners. It is also "for starters" in the secondary sense that all of life's activities are enhanced if they are started with meditation.

THE RUBAIYAT OF OMAR KHAYYAM EXPLAINED
PARAMHANSA YOGANANDA
Edited by J. Donald Walters

Nearly 50 years ago, Yogananda discovered a scripture previously unknown to the world. It was hidden in the beautiful sensual imagery of the beloved poem, *The Rubaiyat of Omar Khayyam*. Yogananda's commentary reveals the spiritual mystery behind this world-famous love poem. Long considered a celebration of earthly pleasures, *The Rubaiyat* is now revealed to be a profound spiritual teaching. Also available as an audio book.

OUT OF THE LABYRINTH
FOR THOSE WHO WANT TO BELIEVE, BUT CAN'T
J. Donald Walters

The last hundred years of scientific and philosophical thought have caused dramatic upheavals in how we view our universe, our spiritual beliefs, and ourselves. This book provides fresh insight and understanding to the problem of meaninglessness and to the question of whether enduring spiritual and moral truths exist. Walters demonstrates the genuine compatibility of scientific and religious values, and how science and our most cherished moral values actually enrich and reinforce one another.

MUSIC SELECTIONS FROM CLARITY SOUND & LIGHT

Secrets of Love
MELODIES TO OPEN YOUR HEART
Donald Walters

Unlike any music you have ever heard, *Secrets of Love* will transform your life. Each musical selection captures the essence of one of the many aspects of love. Perfect as background music, "mood" music, or music for relaxation, all eighteen songs can also be actively used as dynamic tools for awakening the loving qualities within your heart. Liner notes include instruction for unlocking the transformative power of the music—how to listen receptively and with deep concentration. On CD

Music to Awaken Superconsciousness
Donald Walters

A companion to the book, *Awaken to Superconsciousness*. Each of the lush instrumental selections is designed to help the listener more easily access higher states of awareness: deep calmness, joy, radiant health, and self-transcendence. Instruction in the liner notes guides listeners to actively achieve superconsciousness; or, the album can be used simply as background music for relaxation and meditation, drawing the listener upward toward states of expansive joy. On CD

Surrender
MYSTICAL MUSIC FOR YOGA
Derek Bell and Agni / Compositions by Donald Walters

Famed harpist Derek Bell and composer Donald Walters, the team behind the best-selling albums *The Mystic Harp* and *Mystic Harp 2*, have now created a "music for yoga" album. Contoured to mirror the flow of real yoga classes, and wonderful also as background relaxation music. Features sitar player Agni, and includes tabla, keyboards, and cello. On CD

Mantra
Swami Kriyananda

For millennia, the *Gayatri Mantra* and the *Mahamrityunjaya Mantra* have echoed down the banks of the holy river Ganges. Chanted in Sanskrit by Swami Kriyananda to a rich tamboura accompaniment. On CD

Mantra of Eternity
Swami Kriyananda

Continuous vocal chanting of AUM, the cosmic vibration of spirit in creation. On CD

Wave of the Sea

Lift your heart in devotion with chants written by Paramhansa Yogananda and Swami Kriyananda, as well as traditional Indian chants and mantras. Arranged for voice, harmonium, guitar, flute, harp, kirtals, and tabla, they are performed by musicians from Ananda World Brotherhood Village. On CD

I, Omar
J. Donald Walters

If the soul could sing, here would be its voice. *I, Omar* is inspired by *The Rubaiyat of Omar Khayyam*. Its beautiful melody is taken up in turn by English horn, oboe, flute, harp, guitar, cello, violin, and strings. The reflective quality of this instrumental album makes it a perfect companion for quiet reading or other inward activities. On CD

Kriyananda Chants Yogananda

A direct disciple of Paramhansa Yogananda, Swami Kriyananda chants the spiritualized songs of his guru in a unique and deeply inward way. Throughout the ages, chanting has been a means to achieve deeper meditation. Let this music uplift your spirit. On CD

For a free Crystal Clarity catalog, or to place an order,
please call 800-424-1055 or 530-478-7600.
Or visit our website: www.crystalclarity.com